A POP REVOLUTION

The Transatlantic Music Scene, 1965 To 1969

lovingly compiled by the invisible man

with the intensive care of GW Publications

Copyright © AD 2011 by the invisible man (aka Gary Watton)
Published in Great Britain by GW Publications; 25
Gordonville; Coleraine; BT52 1EF

The right of the invisible man (aka Gary Watton) to be identified as the Author of the Work has been asserted by him in accordance with the Copyright, Designs, and Patents Act 1988.

A CIP catalogue record for this title is available from the British Library.
ISBN 978-0-9562725-3-9
The cover idea and artwork was conceived and executed by Gary Watton.
Printed and bound in Great Britain by
CPI Antony Rowe, Chippenham and Eastbourne

Suffolk County Council	
30127 07602401 2	
Askews & Holts	May-2011
781.6409	£9.99

PLEASE ALLOW ME TO INTRODUCE MYSELF
(I'm A Man Of Wealth And Taste)

For the five or six of you who are remotely interested, the invisible man (aka Gary Watton) is a highly talented, super-deluxe, hi-tech, state-of the art writer, who has constructed previous publications on popular music under a number of different guises: namely 'The Song For Today' by Jimmie Oliver; 'An Essential Guide To Music In The 1970s' by Johnny Zero; and 'A Concise Guide To Eighties' Music' by Karl Vorderman. As he gets older and grumpier, he is threatening to write a book in which he puts the world to rights. Whilst the world was getting turned on to the revolutionary new sounds showcased in this fine book, the author's own activities in this golden era were exclusively confined to having his nappy changed: "Oh but I was so much older then/I'm younger than that now." You can send the author feedback to: gw930@hotmail.co.uk

ABOUT THE PUBLISHERS

You may be harbouring hopes of attracting the interest of the high-profile publishers. However, unless you yourself are also high-profile (i.e. a 'multi-talented' contestant on X Factor), the chances are that the high-profile publishers will send you a nice, polite 'good luck elsewhere' reply when they eventually are sufficiently aroused to scan over your manuscript. You would be well advised to look in our direction. All genres are catered for, and you will be afforded a fair hearing and a quick response. Indeed if you feel that you have a book in you (and you ought to), then feel free to email details of your proposed publication to: thunderball007@hotmail.co.uk

INTRODUCTION

The latter half of the 1960s represented a revolution both in popular music and also socially. As well as being a period of unabated Cold War tension, as demonstrated by the escalating conflict in Vietnam, and aside from the tremendous social upheaval characterised by the emergence of the permissive society, not to mention the economic instability exacerbated by the perpetual cycle of boom and bust, the late 'sixties was an era that witnessed growing strife that spilled onto the streets and manifested itself in student protests and anti-war riots. There was moreover much upheaval in the world of 'pop' which found itself undergoing a number of transformations.

In the first instance, 1965 to 1969 saw the birth of the album as an art form of some substance, whereas before LPs were neither intended nor regarded to be of enduring appeal. Now, more and more performers were committing due care and attention in the pursuit of a long player which would attract positive reviews from critics and stand the test of time. Furthermore, whereas before musicians regarded themselves or were indeed viewed as merely entertainers, they now saw themselves and wished to be projected as artists and not just performers. They now felt that they had something meaningful to say and thus felt the need to commit their observations onto record as they made their very own 'state of the nation' musical statements. As well as stepping away from a previous stance of being apolitical or apathetic, the new generation of performers or artists regarded themselves as spokespersons for the youth and the standard-bearers of the developing sub-culture in which adolescents and teenagers campaigned for the need to 'make love, not war'. All of this was anathema of course to the older

INTRODUCTION (continued)

generation and in hindsight it all smacked of gross naivety, the youthful feeling that they could conquer a world of cynicism with their very own ideals of peace and love.

However, two major problems arose. First of all, when the forces of the Establishment feel threatened, they soon re-group and channel their energies to snuff out the potential insurrection. There have been many successful revolutions in world history, but what is rarely recorded is the fact there have been a great deal more that failed and were often mercilessly curtailed at their outset. Therefore, "if history has taught us anything" (to quote Michael Corleone) it is that the odds of confronting the established order and winning are rather slim, in spite of the spectaculars of 1776, 1789, or 1917. Therefore, it is easy with hindsight to see how the burgeoning youth sub-culture of the late-sixties was doomed to failure. Was it a complete failure? No, there were many liberal social reforms such as equality for women and protecting the rights of minorities which eventually found their way into law. However, although a new generation of politicians such as Bill Clinton and Tony Blair owed their formative years to the influence of the sixties' youth revolution, this same era still spawned a conservative reaction which culminated in the election and re-election of Nixon and Reagan in the USA and Mrs Thatcher in Britain. If the agents of change in the latter part of the 'sixties were urging reform, well the electorate in their respective countries clearly had other ideas.

Also ominous to the successful prosecution of the hippie campaign for love and peace was the substantial amounts of illegal and dangerous substances which many of the protagonists experimented with. It is true that the great artists

INTRODUCTION (more)

of this era owed some of their creativity to the stimulus of LSD and of marijuana, but such was the implosion of the flower power generation at the ill-fated Altamont festival in December 1969 that the naive optimism of Woodstock four months earlier was already but a pipedream. If you want to challenge the Establishment, it is best to do so with a clear head, and minds that were afflicted with all manner of substances was clearly not the way to do it.

Meanwhile back on planet pop, another transformation was taking place, alongside the emergence of the album as an art form. Now, the artists were promoting their new genre, known as rock, by means of relentless touring and festival appearances. Yes, the epoch from 1965 to the end of the decade witnessed the rise of the great outdoor festival as a new social gathering in which thousands would come into the sun (in theory) to pay homage to their new heroes. Speaking of heroes, this was the period which also gave birth to the guitar hero. No longer was a guitarist a smiling accomplice who lurked innocently in the background. Now guitarists were often viewed at least on a par with the lead vocalist. Eric Clapton, Jeff Beck, Peter Green, Jimi Hendrix, Pete Townshend, Jimmy Page, and Keith Richards were seven such axemen who were held in the kind of esteem that was previously reserved for singers only. Even drummers were not to be left behind. Ginger Baker, Keith Moon, Mitch Mitchell, and later John Bonham were celebrated drummers whose presence and histrionics on stage by itself would warrant sell-out crowds. This was clearly the age of the musician, as well as the era of the album. Rock music was clearly on a journey far from its origins. It would have been inconceivable a decade earlier that the crooners,

INTRODUCTION (still)

balladeers, and skiffle merchants were igniting the runaway train of rock. Rock itself would branch out in due course into heavy metal, punk, and grunge. Other forms of music appeared for the first time during the metamorphosis in popular music of 1965 to 1969, most notably Britain's importation of Jamaican ska and rock steady which between them paved the way for the growth of reggae in the 1970s.

Were the years from 1965 to the end of the decade a pop revolution? You bet your life, they were. Even artists and their streetwise managers belatedly started to flex their muscles after having had rings run around them by record companies and concert promoters. Rock musicians were slowly starting to wake up to the fact that music was a dog eat dog business and henceforth they were resolved to assert themselves in recording contracts too.

Robin Williams once quipped that "If you remember the 'sixties, you weren't there". This assembly of facts, assessment, and assorted observations is both intended as a companion for those who were there and those who weren't.

FOR EMILY, WHENEVER I MAY FIND HER

What, I hear you exclaim, possessed me to take leave of my few remaining senses and lovingly compile this masterpiece/monstrosity (or maybe monstrous masterpiece)? Well, all sorts of different books cater for all sorts of different tastes, and this treasure trove of charts and assorted facts appeals to the anoraks, stattos, and train-spotters who prefer to dip into a book of facts rather than subject themselves to wading their way through a piece of fiction for five hundred pages only to discover at the end, eventually, that it was indeed the butler who did it. Enjoy your browsing!

1965

UK singles chart for the week ending January the 2nd
1 **I Feel Fine** - The Beatles
2 Downtown - Petula Clark
3 Walk Tall - Val Doonican
4 I'm Gonna Be Strong - Gene Pitney
5 I Understand - Freddie And The Dreamers
6 I Could Easily Fall - Cliff Richard And The Shadows
7 Yeh Yeh - Georgie Fame
8 No Arms Could Ever Hold You - The Bachelors
9 Somewhere - PJ Proby
10 Terry - Twinkle

UK Number One album: *Beatles For Sale* - The Beatles
US Billboard Number One album: *Roustabout* - Elvis Presley
US Cashbox Number One single: *I Feel Fine* - The Beatles
Also this week: It is revealed that Stanley Matthews is to be knighted. (1st)

US Billboard singles for the week ending January the 2nd
1 **I Feel Fine** - The Beatles
2 Come See About Me - The Supremes
3 Mr Lonely - Bobby Vinton
4 She's Not There - The Zombies
5 Love Potion Number Nine - The Searchers
6 Goin' Out Of My Head - Little Anthony & The Imperials
7 She's Not There - The Zombies
8 Amen - The Impressions
9 The Jerk - The Larks
10 The Wedding - Julie Rogers

I Feel Fine became the fourth of five million-selling UK singles for the Beatles.

1965

1 **I Feel Fine** - The Beatles
2 Yeh Yeh - Georgie Fame
3 Downtown - Petula Clark
4 Terry - Twinkle
5 Walk Tall - Val Doonican
6 I'm Gonna Be Strong - Gene Pitney
7 Girl Don't Come - Sandie Shaw
8 Somewhere - PJ Proby
9 I Could Easily Fall - Cliff Richard And The Shadows
10 Go Now! - The Moody Blues

UK Number One album: *Beatles For Sale* - The Beatles
US Billboard Number One album: *Beatles VI* - The Beatles
US Cashbox Number One single: *I Feel Fine* - The Beatles
*Also this week:*Lyndon Johnson proclaims his "Great Society" in a speech. (4th)

US Billboard singles for the week ending January the 9th
1 **I Feel Fine** - The Beatles
2 Come See About Me - The Supremes
3 Mr Lonely - Bobby Vinton
4 Love Potion Number Nine - The Searchers
5 Downtown - Petula Clark
6 Goin' Out Of My Head - Little Anthony & The Imperials
7 Amen - The Impressions
8 The Jerk - The Larks
9 You've Lost That Lovin' Feelin' - The Righteous Brothers
10 The Wedding - Julie Rogers

1965

 1 **Yeh Yeh** - Georgie Fame
 2 I Feel Fine - The Beatles
 3 Go Now! - The Moody Blues
 4 Terry - Twinkle
 5 Girl Don't Come - Sandie Shaw
 6 Somewhere - PJ Proby
 7 Walk Tall - Val Doonican
 8 Downtown - Petula Clark
 9 Ferry Cross The Mersey - Gerry And The Pacemakers
10 Cast Your Fate To The Wind - Sounds Orchestral

UK Number One album: *Beatles For Sale* - The Beatles
US Billboard Number One album: *Beatles VI* - The Beatles
US Cashbox Number One single: *I Feel Fine* - The Beatles
Also this week: Sean Lemass is the first Irish Prime Minister
(or Taoiseach) to visit Belfast. (15th)

US Billboard singles for the week ending January the 16th
 1 **Come See About Me** - The Supremes
 2 I Feel Fine - The Beatles
 3 Love Potion Number Nine - The Searchers
 4 Downtown - Petula Clark
 5 You've Lost That Lovin' Feelin' - The Righteous Brothers
 6 Mr Lonely - Bobby Vinton
 7 The Jerk - The Larks
 8 Goin' Out Of My Head - Little Anthony & The Imperials
 9 How Sweet It is (To Be Loved By You) -Marvin Gaye
10 Keep Searchin' (We'll Follow The Sun) - Del Shannon

1965

UK singles chart for the week ending January the 23rd
1 **Yeh Yeh** - Georgie Fame
2 Go Now! - The Moody Blues
3 Girl Don't Come - Sandie Shaw
4 Terry - Twinkle
5 Cast Your Fate To The Wind - Sounds Orchestral
6 Somewhere - PJ Proby
7 I Feel Fine - The Beatles
8 Ferry Cross The Mersey - Gerry And The Pacemakers
9 Walk Tall - Val Doonican
10 Downtown - Petula Clark

UK Number One album: *Beatles For Sale* - The Beatles
US Billboard Number One album: *Beatles VI* - The Beatles
US Cashbox Number One single: *Downtown* - Petula Clark
Also this week: Lyndon Johnson is sworn in as United States'
President. (20th)

US Billboard singles for the week ending January the 23rd
1 **Downtown** - Petula Clark
2 You've Lost That Lovin' Feelin' - The Righteous Brothers
3 Love Potion Number Nine - The Searchers
4 I Feel Fine - The Beatles
5 Come See About Me - The Supremes
6 The Name Game - Shirley Ellis
7 Mr Lonely - Bobby Vinton
8 The Jerk - The Larks
9 How Sweet It Is (To Be Loved By You) - Marvin Gaye
10 Keep Searchin' (We'll Follow The Sun) - Del Shannon

1965

 1 **Go Now**! - The Moody Blues
 2 You've Lost That Lovin' Feelin' - Cilla Black
 3 You've Lost That Lovin' Feelin' - The Righteous Brothers
 4 Yeh Yeh - Georgie Fame
 5 Come Tomorrow - Manfred Mann
 6 Tired Of Waiting For You - The Kinks
 7 Terry - Twinkle
 8 Girl Don't Come - Sandie Shaw
 9 Ferry Cross The Mersey - Gerry And The Pacemakers
10 Cast Your Fate To The Wind - Sounds Orchestral

UK Number One album: *Beatles For Sale* - The Beatles
US Billboard Number One album: *Beatles VI* - The Beatles
US Cashbox Number One single: *Downtown* - Petula Clark
Also this week: Millions watch the television coverage of
Winston Churchill's funeral. (30th)

US Billboard singles for the week ending January the 30th
 1 **Downtown -** Petula Clark
 2 You've Lost That Lovin' Feelin' - The Righteous Brothers
 3 The Name Game - Shirley Ellis
 4 Love Potion Number Nine - The Searchers
 5 Hold What You've Got - Joe Tex
 6 How Sweet It Is (To Be Loved By You) - Marvin Gaye
 7 This Diamond Ring - Gary Lewis & The Playboys
 8 Come See About Me - The Supremes
 9 Keep Searchin' (We'll Follow The Sun) - Del Shannon
10 All Day And All Of The Night - The Kinks

1965

UK singles chart for the week ending February the 6th
1 **You've Lost That Lovin' Feelin'** - The Righteous Brothers
2 Tired Of Waiting For You - The Kinks
3 Go Now! - The Moody Blues
4 Come Tomorrow - Manfred Mann
5 You've Lost That Lovin' Feelin' - Cilla Black
6 Keep Searchin' (We'll Follow The Sun) - Del Shannon
7 Cast Your Fate To The Wind - Sounds Orchestral
8 Yeh Yeh - Georgie Fame
9 Girl Don't Come - Sandie Shaw
10 Terry - Twinkle

UK Number One album: *The Rolling Stones Number 2* - The Rolling Stones
US Billboard Number One album: *Beatles VI* - The Beatles
US Cashbox Number One single: *You've Lost That Lovin' Feelin'* - The Righteous Brothers
Also this week: Australian Ron Clarke beats his 5000 metres world record. (1st)

US Billboard singles for the week ending February the 6th
1 **You've Lost That Lovin' Feelin'** - The Righteous Brothers
2 Downtown - Petula Clark
3 The Name Game - Shirley Ellis
4 This Diamond Ring - Gary Lewis & The Playboys
5 Hold What You've Got - Joe Tex
6 Love Potion Number Nine - The Searchers
7 All Day And All Of The Night - The Kinks
8 My Girl - The Temptations
9 How Sweet It Is (To Be Loved By You) - Marvin Gaye
10 Shake - Sam Cooke

The Righteous Brothers would have to wait over 25 years until their next UK Number 1.

1965

 1 **You've Lost That Lovin' Feelin'** - The Righteous Brothers
 2 Tired Of Waiting For You - The Kinks
 3 Keep Searchin' (We'll Follow The Sun) - Del Shannon
 4 Go Now! - The Moody Blues
 5 I'll Never Find Another You - The Seekers
 6 Come Tomorrow - Manfred Mann
 7 The Special Years - Val Doonican
 8 Cast Your Fate To The Wind - Sounds Orchestral
 9 You've Lost That Lovin' Feelin' - Cilla Black
10 Baby Please Don't Go - Them

UK Number One album: *The Rolling Stones Number 2* - The Rolling Stones
US Billboard Number One album: *Beatles VI* - The Beatles
US Cashbox Number One single: *You've Lost That Lovin' Feelin'* - The Righteous Brothers
Also this week: Ringo Starr marries Liverpool hairdresser Maureen Cox. (11th)

US Billboard singles for the week ending February the 13th
 1 **You've Lost That Lovin' Feelin'** - The Righteous Brothers
 2 Downtown - Petula Clark
 3 This Diamond Ring - Gary Lewis & The Playboys
 4 The Name Game - Shirley Ellis
 5 My Girl - The Temptations
 6 Hold What You've Got - Joe Tex
 7 All Day And All Of The Night - The Kinks
 8 Shake - Sam Cooke
 9 The Jolly Green Giant - The Kingsmen
10 I Go To Pieces - Peter & Gordon

1965

 1 **Tired Of Waiting For You** - The Kinks
 2 I'll Never Find Another You - The Seekers
 3 You've Lost That Lovin' Feelin' - The Righteous Brothers
 4 Keep Searchin' (We'll Follow The Sun) - Del Shannon
 5 The Game Of Love - Wayne Fontana And The Mindbenders
 6 Don't Let Me Be Misunderstood - The Animals
 7 The Special Years - Val Doonican
 8 Come Tomorrow - Manfred Mann
 9 Funny How Love Can Be - The Ivy League
10 Go Now! - The Moody Blues

UK Number One album: *The Rolling Stones Number 2* - The Rolling Stones
US Billboard Number One album: *Beatles VI* - The Beatles
US Cashbox Number One single: *You've Lost That Lovin' Feelin'* - The Righteous Brothers
Also this week: Gambia gains its independence from Britain. (17th)

US Billboard singles for the week ending February the 20th

 1 **This Diamond Ring** - Gary Lewis & The Playboys
 2 You've Lost That Lovin' Feelin' - The Righteous Brothers
 3 Downtown - Petula Clark
 4 My Girl - The Temptations
 5 The Name Game - Shirley Ellis
 6 The Jolly Green Giant - The Kingsmen
 7 All Day And All Of The Night - The Kinks
 8 Shake - Sam Cooke
 9 I Go To Pieces - Peter & Gordon
10 The Boy From New York City - The Ad Libs

1965

UK singles chart for the week ending February the 27th

1 **I'll Never Find Another You** - The Seekers
2 The Game Of Love - Wayne Fontana And The Mindbenders
3 Don't Let Me Be Misunderstood - The Animals
4 You've Lost That Lovin' Feelin' - The Righteous Brothers
5 Tired Of Waiting For You - The Kinks
6 Keep Searchin' (We'll Follow The Sun) - Del Shannon
7 The Special Years - Val Doonican
8 It Hurts So Much (To See You Go) - Jim Reeves
9 Funny How Love Can Be - The Ivy League
10 It's Not Unusual - Tom Jones

UK Number One album: *Beatles For Sale* - The Beatles
US Billboard Number One album: *Beatles VI* - The Beatles
US Cashbox Number One single: *This Diamond Ring* - Gary
Lewis & The Playboys
Also this week: The TSR-2 flies faster than the speed of sound.
(22nd)

US Billboard singles for the week ending February the 27th

1 **This Diamond Ring** - Gary Lewis & The Playboys
2 You've Lost That Lovin' Feelin' - The Righteous Brothers
3 My Girl - The Temptations
4 Downtown - Petula Clark
5 The Jolly Green Giant - The Kingsmen
6 Tell Her No - The Zombies
7 Shake - Sam Cooke
8 The Boy From New York City - The Ad Libs
9 I Go To Pieces - Peter & Gordon
10 King Of The Road - Roger Miller

1965

1 **I'll Never Find Another You** - The Seekers
2 It's Not Unusual - Tom Jones
3 The Game Of Love - Wayne Fontana And The Mindbenders
4 Silhouettes - Herman's Hermits
5 Don't Let Me Be Misunderstood - The Animals
6 I Must Be Seeing Things - Gene Pitney
7 The Special Years - Val Doonican
8 Funny How Love Can Be - The Ivy League
9 Come And Stay With Me - Marianne Faithfull
10 Tired Of Waiting For You - The Kinks

UK Number One album: *The Rolling Stones Number 2* - The Rolling Stones
US Billboard Number One album: *Beatles VI* - The Beatles
US Cashbox Number One single: *Eight Days A Week* - The Beatles
Also this week: President Johnson has talks with Martin Luther King. (5th)

US Billboard singles for the week ending March the 6th
1 **My Girl** - The Temptations
2 This Diamond Ring - Gary Lewis & The Playboys
3 You've Lost That Lovin' Feelin' - The Righteous Brothers
4 The Jolly Green Giant - The Kingsmen
5 Eight Days A Week - The Beatles
6 Tell Her No - The Zombies
7 King Of The Road - Roger Miller
8 The Birds And The Bees - Jewel Akens
9 Ferry Cross The Mersey - Gerry & The Pacemakers
10 Downtown - Petula Clark

1965

UK singles chart for the week ending March the 13th

1 **It's Not Unusual** - Tom Jones
2 I'll Never Find Another You - The Seekers
3 Silhouettes - Herman's Hermits
4 I'll Stop At Nothing - Sandie Shaw
5 The Game Of Love - Wayne Fontana And The Mindbenders
6 The Last Time - The Rolling Stones
7 Come And Stay With Me - Marianne Faithfull
8 Don't Let Me Be Misunderstood - The Animals
9 I Must Be Seeing Things - Gene Pitney
10 Yes I Will - The Hollies

UK Number One album: *The Rolling Stones Number 2* - The Rolling Stones
US Billboard Number One album: *Mary Poppins* - Soundtrack
US Cashbox Number One single: *Eight Days A Week* - The Beatles
Also this week: Goldie the eagle is recaptured by Regent's Park Zoo. (10th)

US Billboard singles for the week ending March the 13th

1 **Eight Days A Week** - The Beatles
2 My Girl - The Temptations
3 Stop! In The Name Of Love - The Supremes
4 This Diamond Ring - Gary Lewis & The Playboys
5 The Birds And The Bees - Jewel Akens
6 King Of The Road - Roger Miller
7 Ferry Cross The Mersey - Gerry & The Pacemakers
8 Can't You Hear My Heartbeat - Herman's Hermits
9 The Jolly Green Giant - The Kingsmen
10 Hurt So Bad - Little Anthony & The Imperials

1965

 1 **The Last Time** - The Rolling Stones
 2 It's Not Unusual - Tom Jones
 3 Silhouettes - Herman's Hermits
 4 I'll Never Find Another You - The Seekers
 5 Come And Stay With Me - Marianne Faithfull
 6 Goodbye My Love - The Searchers
 7 I Must Be Seeing Things - Gene Pitney
 8 I'll Stop At Nothing - Sandie Shaw
 9 Yes I Will - The Hollies
10 The Game Of Love - Wayne Fontana And The Mindbenders

UK Number One album: *The Rolling Stones Number 2* - The Rolling Stones
US Billboard Number One album: *Goldfinger* - Soundtrack
US Cashbox Number One single: *Eight Days A Week* - The Beatles
Also this week: Colonel Leonev's spacecraft safely returns to the USSR. (19th)

US Billboard singles for the week ending March the 20th
 1 **Eight Days A Week** - The Beatles
 2 Stop! In The Name Of Love - The Supremes
 3 The Birds And The Bees - Jewel Akens
 4 King Of The Road - Roger Miller
 5 Can't You Hear My Heartbeat - Herman's Hermits
 6 Ferry Cross The Mersey - Gerry & The Pacemakers
 7 My Girl - The Temptations
 8 This Diamond Ring - Gary Lewis & The Playboys
 9 Goldfinger - Shirley Bassey
10 Shotgun - Junior Walker & The All Stars

1965

1 **The Last Time** - The Rolling Stones
2 It's Not Unusual - Tom Jones
3 Silhouettes - Herman's Hermits
4 Come And Stay With Me - Marianne Faithfull
5 Goodbye My Love - The Searchers
6 I'll Never Find Another You - The Seekers
7 I'll Stop At Nothing - Sandie Shaw
8 Concrete And Clay - Unit Four Plus Two
9 I Must Be Seeing Things - Gene Pitney
10 The Minute You're Gone - Cliff Richard

UK Number One album: *The Rolling Stones Number 2* - The Rolling Stones
US Billboard Number One album: *Goldfinger* - Soundtrack
US Cashbox Number One single: *Stop! In The Name Of Love* - The Supremes
Also this week: Ranger 9 is launched into space at Cape Kennedy. (21st)

US Billboard singles for the week ending March the 27th

1 **Stop! In The Name Of Love** - The Supremes
2 Can't You Hear My Heartbeat - Herman's Hermits
3 The Birds And The Bees - Jewel Akens
4 Eight Days A Week - The Beatles
5 King Of The Road - Roger Miller
6 Ferry Cross The Mersey - Gerry & The Pacemakers
7 Shotgun - Junior Walker & The All Stars
8 Goldfinger - Shirley Bassey
9 My Girl - The Temptations
10 This Diamond Ring - Gary Lewis & The Playboys

1965

UK singles chart for the week ending April the 3rd
  1 **The Last Time** - The Rolling Stones
  2 Concrete And Clay - Unit Four Plus Two
  3 It's Not Unusual - Tom Jones
  4 Goodbye My Love - The Searchers
  5 For Your Love - The Yardbirds
  6 The Minute You're Gone - Cliff Richard
  7 Catch The Wind - Donovan
  8 Come And Stay With Me - Marianne Faithfull
  9 Silhouettes - Herman's Hermits
10 I'll Never Find Another You - The Seekers

UK Number One album: *The Rolling Stones Number 2* - The Rolling Stones
US Billboard Number One album: *Goldfinger* - Soundtrack
US Cashbox Number One single: *Can't You Hear My Heartbeat* - Herman's Hermits
Also this week: Prime Minister Harold Wilson meets President Charles de Gaulle to discuss Vietnam. (2nd)

US Billboard singles for the week ending April the 3rd
  1 **Stop! In The Name Of Love** - The Supremes
  2 Can't You Hear My Heartbeat - Herman's Hermits
  3 I'm Telling You Now - Freddie & The Dreamers
  4 Shotgun - Junior Walker & The All Stars
  5 The Birds And The Bees - Jewel Akens
  6 King Of The Road - Roger Miller
  7 Eight Days A Week - The Beatles
  8 Goldfinger - Shirley Bassey
  9 Nowhere To Run - Martha & The Vandellas
10 Red Roses For A Blue Lady - Vic Dana

1965

1 **Concrete And Clay** - Unit Four Plus Two
2 The Last Time - The Rolling Stones
3 For Your Love - The Yardbirds
4 The Minute You're Gone - Cliff Richard
5 Catch The Wind - Donovan
6 Here Comes The Night - Them
7 It's Not Unusual - Tom Jones
8 Come And Stay With Me - Marianne Faithfull
9 Silhouettes - Herman's Hermits
10 I Can't Explain - The Who

UK Number One album: *The Rolling Stones Number 2* - The Rolling Stones
US Billboard Number One album: *Mary Poppins* - Soundtrack
US Cashbox Number One single: *I'm Telling You Now* - Freddie & The Dreamers
Also this week: Future President, Richard Nixon, pays a visit to Moscow. (10th)

US Billboard singles for the week ending April the 10th

1 **I'm Telling You Now** - Freddie & The Dreamers
2 Stop! In The Name Of Love - The Supremes
3 Can't You Hear My Heartbeat - Herman's Hermits
4 Shotgun - Junior Walker & The All Stars
5 The Birds And The Bees - Jewel Akens
6 King Of The Road - Roger Miller
7 Game Of Love - Wayne Fontana & The Mindbenders
8 Nowhere To Run - Martha & The Vandellas
9 I Know A Place - Petula Clark
10 Red Roses For A Blue Lady - Vic Dana

1965

1 **The Minute You're Gone** - Cliff Richard
2 Concrete And Clay - Unit Four Plus Two
3 For Your Love - The Yardbirds
4 Catch The Wind - Donovan
5 Here Comes The Night - Them
6 The Last Time - The Rolling Stones
7 Stop! In The Name Of Love - The Supremes
8 I Can't Explain - The Who
9 Times They Are A-Changin' - Bob Dylan
10 Pop Go The Workers - The Barron Knights

UK Number One album: *The Freewheelin' Bob Dylan* - Bob Dylan
US Billboard Number One album: *Mary Poppins* - Soundtrack
US Cashbox Number One single: *I'm Telling You Now* - Freddie & The Dreamers
Also this week: 26 people are killed in an aeroplane crash in Jersey. (14th)

US Billboard singles for the week ending April the 17th
1 **I'm Telling You Now** - Freddie & The Dreamers
2 Stop! In The Name Of Love - The Supremes
3 Game Of Love - Wayne Fontana & The Mindbenders
4 I Know A Place - Petula Clark
5 Shotgun - Junior Walker & The All Stars
6 Can't You Hear My Heartbeat - Herman's Hermits
7 Tired Of Waiting For You - The Kinks
8 Nowhere To Run - Martha & The Vandellas
9 The Clapping Song (Clap Pat Clap Slap) - Shirley Ellis
10 Go Now! - The Moody Blues

1965

1 **Ticket To Ride** - The Beatles
2 Here Comes The Night - Them
3 The Minute You're Gone - Cliff Richard
4 Concrete And Clay - Unit Four Plus Two
5 Little Things - Dave Berry
6 Catch The Wind - Donovan
7 For Your Love - The Yardbirds
8 King Of The Road - Roger Miller
9 The Last Time - The Rolling Stones
10 Pop Go The Workers - The Barron Knights

UK Number One album: *The Rolling Stones Number 2* - The Rolling Stones
US Billboard Number One album: *Mary Poppins* - Soundtrack
US Cashbox Number One single: *Game Of Love* - Wayne Fontana & The Mindbenders
Also this week: The notorious gangster Reggie Kray gets married in London. (19th)

US Billboard singles for the week ending April the 24th

1 **Game Of Love** - Wayne Fontana & The Mindbenders
2 Mrs. Brown You've Got A Lovely Daughter - Herman's Hermits
3 I'm Telling You Now - Freddie & The Dreamers
4 I Know A Place - Petula Clark
5 Stop! In The Name Of Love - The Supremes
6 Tired Of Waiting For You - The Kinks
7 I'll Never Find Another You - The Seekers
8 The Clapping Song (Clap Pat Clap Slap) - Shirley Ellis
9 Shotgun - Junior Walker & The All Stars
10 Silhouettes - Herman's Hermits

1965

1 **Ticket To Ride** - The Beatles
2 The Minute You're Gone - Cliff Richard
3 Here Comes The Night - Them
4 King Of The Road - Roger Miller
5 Pop Go The Workers - The Barron Knights
6 Little Things - Dave Berry
7 Bring It On Home To Me - The Animals
8 Concrete And Clay - Unit Four Plus Two
9 Catch The Wind - Donovan
10 Stop! In The Name Of Love - The Supremes

UK Number One album: *Beatles For Sale* - The Beatles
US Billboard Number One album: *Mary Poppins* - Soundtrack
US Cashbox Number One single: *Mrs. Brown You've Got A Lovely Daughter* - Herman's Hermits
Also this week: Prime Minister Harold Wilson visits the Pope in the Vatican. (28th)

US Billboard singles for the week ending May the 1st

1 **Mrs. Brown You've Got A Lovely Daughter** - Herman's Hermits
2 Game Of Love - Wayne Fontana & The Mindbenders
3 I Know A Place - Petula Clark
4 I'm Telling You Now - Freddie & The Dreamers
5 I'll Never Find Another You - The Seekers
6 Tired Of Waiting For You - The Kinks
7 Count Me In - Gary Lewis & The Playboys
8 Silhouettes - Herman's Hermits
9 The Last Time - The Rolling Stones
10 Stop! In The Name Of Love - The Supremes

1965

UK singles chart for the week ending May the 8th

1 **Ticket To Ride** - The Beatles
2 King Of The Road - Roger Miller
3 Here Comes The Night - Them
4 A World Of Our Own - The Seekers
5 True Love Ways - Peter And Gordon
6 Pop Go The Workers - The Barron Knights
7 The Minute You're Gone - Cliff Richard
8 Bring It On Home To Me - The Animals
9 Catch The Wind - Donovan
10 Little Things - Dave Berry

UK Number One album: *Beatles For Sale* - The Beatles
US Billboard Number One album: *Mary Poppins* - Soundtrack
US Cashbox Number One single: *Mrs. Brown You've Got A Lovely Daughter* - Herman's Hermits
Also this week: Rhodesia holds a general election. (7th)

US Billboard singles for the week ending May the 8th

1 **Mrs. Brown You've Got A Lovely Daughter** - Herman's Hermits
2 Count Me In - Gary Lewis & The Playboys
3 Ticket To Ride - The Beatles
4 Game Of Love - Wayne Fontana & The Mindbenders
5 I'll Never Find Another You - The Seekers
6 I Know A Place - Petula Clark
7 Silhouettes - Herman's Hermits
8 I'm Telling You Now - Freddie & The Dreamers
9 The Last Time - The Rolling Stones
10 Cast Your Fate To The Wind - Sounds Orchestral

1965

UK singles chart for the week ending May the 15th
1 **King Of The Road** - Roger Miller
2 Ticket To Ride - The Beatles
3 A World Of Our Own - The Seekers
4 True Love Ways - Peter And Gordon
5 Where Are You Now (My Love) - Jackie Trent
6 Here Comes The Night - Them
7 Bring It On Home To Me - The Animals
8 Pop Go The Workers - The Barron Knights
9 The Minute You're Gone - Cliff Richard
10 Subterranean Homesick Blues - Bob Dylan

UK Number One album: *Beatles For Sale* - The Beatles
US Billboard Number One album: *Mary Poppins* - Soundtrack
US Cashbox Number One single: *Mrs. Brown You've Got A Lovely Daughter* - Herman's Hermits
Also this week: The Soviets' Lunar V fails to land on the moon. (12th)

US Billboard singles for the week ending May the 15th
1 **Mrs. Brown You've Got A Lovely Daughter** - Herman's Hermits
2 Count Me In - Gary Lewis & The Playboys
3 Ticket To Ride - The Beatles
4 I'll Never Find Another You - The Seekers
5 Silhouettes - Herman's Hermits
6 Help Me, Rhonda - The Beach Boys
7 I Know A Place - Petula Clark
8 I'll Be Doggone - Marvin Gaye
9 Just Once In My Life - The Righteous Brothers
10 Wooly Bully - Sam The Sham & The Pharaohs

1965

 1 **Where Are You Now** (**My Love**) - Jackie Trent
 2 True Love Ways - Peter And Gordon
 3 Ticket To Ride - The Beatles
 4 King Of The Road - Roger Miller
 5 A World Of Our Own - The Seekers
 6 This Little Bird - Marianne Faithfull
 7 Wonderful World - Herman's Hermits
 8 Long Live Love - Sandie Shaw
 9 Subterranean Homesick Blues - Bob Dylan
10 Pop Go The Workers - The Barron Knights

UK Number One album: *The Freewheelin' Bob Dylan* - Bob Dylan
US Billboard Number One album: *Mary Poppins* - Soundtrack
US Cashbox Number One single: *Mrs. Brown You've Got A Lovely Daughter* - Herman's Hermits
Also this week: China explodes her second nuclear bomb. (16th)

US Billboard singles for the week ending May the 22nd
 1 **Ticket To Ride** - The Beatles
 2 Mrs. Brown You've Got A Lovely Daughter - Herman's Hermits
 3 Count Me In - Gary Lewis & The Playboys
 4 Help Me, Rhonda - The Beach Boys
 5 I'll Never Find Another You - The Seekers
 6 Back In My Arms Again - The Supremes
 7 Silhouettes - Herman's Hermits
 8 Wooly Bully - Sam The Sham & The Pharaohs
 9 Just Once In My Life - The Righteous Brothers
10 Crying In The Chapel - Elvis Presley

1965

 1 **Long Live Love** - Sandie Shaw
 2 Where Are You Now (My Love) - Jackie Trent
 3 True Love Ways - Peter And Gordon
 4 A World Of Our Own - The Seekers
 5 King Of The Road - Roger Miller
 6 This Little Bird - Marianne Faithfull
 7 Ticket To Ride - The Beatles
 8 Poor Man's Son - Rockin' Berries
 9 Subterranean Homesick Blues - Bob Dylan
10 The Clapping Song - Shirley Ellis

UK Number One album: *Bringing It All Back Home* - Bob Dylan
US Billboard Number One album: *Mary Poppins* - Soundtrack
US Cashbox Number One single: *Ticket To Ride* - The Beatles
Also this week: A state of emergency is declared in Rhodesia. (28th)

US Billboard singles for the week ending May the 29th
 1 **Help Me, Rhonda** - The Beach Boys
 2 Ticket To Ride - The Beatles
 3 Back In My Arms Again - The Supremes
 4 Mrs. Brown You've Got A Lovely Daughter - Herman's Hermits
 5 Wooly Bully - Sam The Sham & The Pharaohs
 6 Crying In The Chapel - Elvis Presley
 7 Count Me In - Gary Lewis & The Playboys
 8 I'll Never Find Another You - The Seekers
 9 Just A Little - The Beau Brummels
10 It's Not Unusual - Tom Jones

1965

 1 **Long Live Love** - Sandie Shaw
 2 Where Are You Now (My Love) - Jackie Trent
 3 A World Of Our Own - The Seekers
 4 True Love Ways - Peter And Gordon
 5 Poor Man's Son - Rockin' Berries
 6 This Little Bird - Marianne Faithfull
 7 The Clapping Song - Shirley Ellis
 8 Trains And Boats And Planes - Burt Bacharach
 9 King Of The Road - Roger Miller
10 Ticket To Ride - The Beatles

UK Number One album: *The Sound Of Music* - Soundtrack
US Billboard Number One album: *Mary Poppins* - Soundtrack
US Cashbox Number One single: *Back In My Arms Again* - The Supremes
Also this week: Edward White becomes the first American to walk in space. (3rd)

US Billboard singles for the week ending June the 5th

 1 **Help Me**, **Rhonda** - The Beach Boys
 2 Wooly Bully - Sam The Sham & The Pharaohs
 3 Back In My Arms Again - The Supremes
 4 Crying In The Chapel - Elvis Presley
 5 Ticket To Ride - The Beatles
 6 Mrs. Brown You've Got A Lovely Daughter - Herman's Hermits
 7 I Can't Help Myself - The Four Tops
 8 Just A Little - The Beau Brummels
 9 Engine Engine #9 - Roger Miller
10 It's Not Unusual - Tom Jones

1965

 1 **Long Live Love** - Sandie Shaw
 2 Crying In The Chapel - Elvis Presley
 3 A World Of Our Own - The Seekers
 4 The Price Of Love - The Everly Brothers
 5 Poor Man's Son - Rockin' Berries
 6 Trains And Boats And Planes - Burt Bacharach
 7 The Clapping Song - Shirley Ellis
 8 This Little Bird - Marianne Faithfull
 9 Where Are You Now (My Love) - Jackie Trent
10 I'm Alive - The Hollies

UK Number One album: *The Sound Of Music* - Soundtrack
US Billboard Number One album: *Mary Poppins* - Soundtrack
US Cashbox Number One single: *Help Me, Rhonda* - The Beach Boys
Also this week: It is announced that The Beatles are to receive MBEs. (11th)

US Billboard singles for the week ending June the 12th
 1 **Back In My Arms Again** - The Supremes
 2 Wooly Bully - Sam The Sham & The Pharaohs
 3 Crying In The Chapel - Elvis Presley
 4 I Can't Help Myself - The Four Tops
 5 Help Me, Rhonda - The Beach Boys
 6 Mr. Tambourine Man - The Byrds
 7 Engine Engine #9 - Roger Miller
 8 Wonderful World - Herman's Hermits
 9 Ticket To Ride - The Beatles
10 Just A Little - The Beau Brummels

1965

1 **Crying In The Chapel** - Elvis Presley
2 The Price Of Love - The Everly Brothers
3 Long Live Love - Sandie Shaw
4 I'm Alive - The Hollies
5 Trains And Boats And Planes - Burt Bacharach
6 Poor Man's Son - Rockin' Berries
7 The Clapping Song - Shirley Ellis
8 A World Of Our Own - The Seekers
9 Marie - The Bachelors
10 Colours - Donovan

UK Number One album: *The Sound Of Music* - Soundtrack
US Billboard Number One album: *Mary Poppins* - Soundtrack
US Cashbox Number One single: *I Can't Help Myself* - The Four Tops
Also this week: President Charles de Gaulle condemns the US involvement in the Vietnam conflict. (16th)

US Billboard singles for the week ending June the 19th
1 **I Can't Help Myself** - The Four Tops
2 Mr. Tambourine Man - The Byrds
3 Wooly Bully - Sam The Sham & The Pharaohs
4 Crying In The Chapel - Elvis Presley
5 Back In My Arms Again - The Supremes
6 Wonderful World - Herman's Hermits
7 Help Me, Rhonda - The Beach Boys
8 Engine Engine #9 - Roger Miller
9 For Your Love - The Yardbirds
10 Hush, Hush, Sweet Charlotte - Patti Page

Crying In The Chapel was Elvis's 15th UK No.1. He would have to wait 5 years for the 16th.

1965

UK singles chart for the week ending June the 26th
1 **I'm Alive** - The Hollies
2 Crying In The Chapel - Elvis Presley
3 The Price Of Love - The Everly Brothers
4 Trains And Boats And Planes - Burt Bacharach
5 Colours - Donovan
6 The Clapping Song - Shirley Ellis
7 Long Live Love - Sandie Shaw
8 Poor Man's Son - Rockin' Berries
9 Set Me Free - The Kinks
10 Looking Thru The Eyes Of Love - Gene Pitney

UK Number One album: *The Sound Of Music* - Soundtrack
US Billboard Number One album: *Mary Poppins* - Soundtrack
US Cashbox Number One single: *I Can't Help Myself* - The Four Tops
Also this week: Bobby Kennedy proposes a nuclear arms limitation treaty. (23rd)

US Billboard singles for the week ending June the 26th
1 **Mr**. **Tambourine Man** - The Byrds
2 I Can't Help Myself - The Four Tops
3 Wooly Bully - Sam The Sham & The Pharaohs
4 (I Can't Get No) Satisfaction - The Rolling Stones
5 Wonderful World - Herman's Hermits
6 Crying In The Chapel - Elvis Presley
7 For Your Love - The Yardbirds
8 Hush, Hush, Sweet Charlotte - Patti Page
9 Help Me, Rhonda - The Beach Boys
10 Seventh Son - Johnny Rivers

The Hollies would have to wait a whopping 23 years until their next UK Number 1 single.

1965

  1 **Crying In The Chapel** - Elvis Presley
  2 I'm Alive - The Hollies
  3 The Price Of Love - The Everly Brothers
  4 Colours - Donovan
  5 Looking Thru The Eyes Of Love - Gene Pitney
  6 Trains And Boats And Planes - Burt Bacharach
  7 Long Live Love - Sandie Shaw
  8 The Clapping Song - Shirley Ellis
  9 Set Me Free - The Kinks
10 Anyway Anyhow Anywhere - The Who

UK Number One album: *The Sound Of Music* - Soundtrack
US Billboard Number One album: *Mary Poppins* - Soundtrack
US Cashbox Number One single: *Mr. Tambourine Man* - The Byrds
Also this week: Jim Clark wins the French Grand Prix in his Lotus. (27th)

US Billboard singles for the week ending July the 3rd
  1 **I Can't Help Myself** - The Four Tops
  2 (I Can't Get No) Satisfaction - The Rolling Stones
  3 Mr. Tambourine Man - The Byrds
  4 Wooly Bully - Sam The Sham & The Pharaohs
  5 Wonderful World - Herman's Hermits
  6 For Your Love - The Yardbirds
  7 Seventh Son - Johnny Rivers
  8 Crying In The Chapel - Elvis Presley
  9 Yes, I'm Ready - Barbara Mason
10 What The World Needs Now Is Love - Jackie DeShannon

1965

UK singles chart for the week ending July the 10th
1 **I'm Alive** - The Hollies
2 Crying In The Chapel - Elvis Presley
3 Looking Thru The Eyes Of Love - Gene Pitney
4 Heart Full Of Soul - The Yardbirds
5 To Know You Is To Love You - Peter And Gordon
6 The Price Of Love - The Everly Brothers
7 Colours - Donovan
8 Mr. Tambourine Man - The Byrds
9 Leave A Little Love - Lulu
10 Tossing And Turning - The Ivy League

UK Number One album: *The Sound Of Music* - Soundtrack
US Billboard Number One album: *Beatles VI* - The Beatles
US Cashbox Number One single: *(I Can't Get No) Satisfaction* - The Rolling Stones
Also this week: Martin Luther King demands an end to the Vietnam War. (4th)

US Billboard singles for the week ending July the 10th
1 (**I Can't Get No**) **Satisfaction** - The Rolling Stones
2 I Can't Help Myself - The Four Tops
3 Mr. Tambourine Man - The Byrds
4 Wonderful World - Herman's Hermits
5 Wooly Bully - Sam The Sham & The Pharaohs
6 Yes, I'm Ready - Barbara Mason
7 Seventh Son - Johnny Rivers
8 Cara, Mia - Jay & The Americans
9 You Turn Me On (Turn On Song) - Ian Whitcomb
10 What The World Needs Now Is Love - Jackie DeShannon

1965

 1 **I'm Alive** - The Hollies
 2 Heart Full Of Soul - The Yardbirds
 3 Mr. Tambourine Man - The Byrds
 4 Looking Thru The Eyes Of Love - Gene Pitney
 5 Crying In The Chapel - Elvis Presley
 6 To Know You Is To Love You - Peter And Gordon
 7 Tossing And Turning - The Ivy League
 8 Leave A Little Love - Lulu
 9 The Price Of Love - The Everly Brothers
10 In The Middle Of Nowhere - Dusty Springfield

UK Number One album: *The Sound Of Music* - Soundtrack
US Billboard Number One album: *Beatles VI* - The Beatles
US Cashbox Number One single: *(I Can't Get No) Satisfaction*
- The Rolling Stones
Also this week: President Johnson orders more troops to be sent
to Vietnam. (13th)

US Billboard singles for the week ending July the 17th

 1 **(I Can't Get No) Satisfaction** - The Rolling Stones
 2 I Can't Help Myself - The Four Tops
 3 I'm Henry VIII, I Am - Herman's Hermits
 4 Mr. Tambourine Man - The Byrds
 5 Cara, Mia - Jay & The Americans
 6 Yes, I'm Ready - Barbara Mason
 7 Seventh Son - Johnny Rivers
 8 You Turn Me On (Turn On Song) - Ian Whitcomb
 9 What The World Needs Now Is Love - Jackie DeShannon
10 What's New Pussycat? - Tom Jones

1965

1 **Mr**. **Tambourine Man** - The Byrds
2 Heart Full Of Soul - The Yardbirds
3 Tossing And Turning - The Ivy League
4 I'm Alive - The Hollies
5 To Know You Is To Love You - Peter And Gordon
6 Crying In The Chapel - Elvis Presley
7 Looking Thru The Eyes Of Love - Gene Pitney
8 Leave A Little Love - Lulu
9 In The Middle Of Nowhere - Dusty Springfield
10 You've Got Your Troubles - The Fortunes

UK Number One album: *The Sound Of Music* - Soundtrack
US Billboard Number One album: *Beatles VI* - The Beatles
US Cashbox Number One single: *(I Can't Get No) Satisfaction*
- The Rolling Stones
Also this week: The House of Lords votes to abolish capital
punishment. (20th)

US Billboard singles for the week ending July the 24th

1 (**I Can't Get No**) **Satisfaction** - The Rolling Stones
2 I'm Henry VIII, I Am - Herman's Hermits
3 I Can't Help Myself - The Four Tops
4 What's New Pussycat? - Tom Jones
5 Cara, Mia - Jay & The Americans
6 Yes, I'm Ready - Barbara Mason
7 What The World Needs Now Is Love - Jackie DeShannon
8 Seventh Son - Johnny Rivers
9 Mr. Tambourine Man - The Byrds
10 You Turn Me On (Turn On Song) - Ian Whitcomb

1965

UK singles chart for the week ending July the 31st

1 **Mr. Tambourine Man** - The Byrds
2 Heart Full Of Soul - The Yardbirds
3 You've Got Your Troubles - The Fortunes
4 Tossing And Turning - The Ivy League
5 Help! - The Beatles
6 We Gotta Get Out Of This Place - The Animals
7 I'm Alive - The Hollies
8 In The Middle Of Nowhere - Dusty Springfield
9 To Know You Is To Love You - Peter And Gordon
10 There But For Fortune - Joan Baez

UK Number One album: *The Sound Of Music* - Soundtrack
US Billboard Number One album: *Beatles VI* - The Beatles
US Cashbox Number One single: *(I Can't Get No) Satisfaction* - The Rolling Stones
Also this week: Edward Heath is elected leader of the Conservative Party, replacing Sir Alec Douglas-Home. (27th)

US Billboard singles for the week ending July the 31st

1 **(I Can't Get No) Satisfaction** - The Rolling Stones
2 I'm Henry VIII, I Am - Herman's Hermits
3 What's New Pussycat? - Tom Jones
4 Cara, Mia - Jay & The Americans
5 Yes, I'm Ready - Barbara Mason
6 I Can't Help Myself - The Four Tops
7 What The World Needs Now Is Love - Jackie DeShannon
8 Save Your Heart For Me - Gary Lewis & The Playboys
9 I Like It Like That - The Dave Clark Five
10 Seventh Son - Johnny Rivers

1965

1 **Help**! - The Beatles
2 Mr. Tambourine Man - The Byrds
3 You've Got Your Troubles - The Fortunes
4 We Gotta Get Out Of This Place - The Animals
5 Tossing And Turning - The Ivy League
6 Heart Full Of Soul - The Yardbirds
7 Catch Us If You Can - The Dave Clark Five
8 There But For Fortune - Joan Baez
9 In The Middle Of Nowhere - Dusty Springfield
10 I'm Alive - The Hollies

UK Number One album: *The Sound Of Music* - Soundtrack
US Billboard Number One album: *Beatles VI* - The Beatles
US Cashbox Number One single: *I'm Henry VIII, I Am* - Herman's Hermits
Also this week: Forest fires sweep across the French Riviera. (2nd)

US Billboard singles for the week ending August the 7th

1 **I'm Henry VIII, I Am** - Herman's Hermits
2 (I Can't Get No) Satisfaction - The Rolling Stones
3 What's New Pussycat? - Tom Jones
4 Save Your Heart For Me - Gary Lewis & The Playboys
5 I Got You Babe - Sonny & Cher
6 Yes, I'm Ready - Barbara Mason
7 I Like It Like That - The Dave Clark Five
8 Cara, Mia - Jay & The Americans
9 I Can't Help Myself - The Four Tops
10 Don't Just Stand There - Patty Duke

1965

1 **Help**! - The Beatles
2 We Gotta Get Out Of This Place - The Animals
3 You've Got Your Troubles - The Fortunes
4 Mr. Tambourine Man - The Byrds
5 Catch Us If You Can - The Dave Clark Five
6 Tossing And Turning - The Ivy League
7 Everyone's Gone To The Moon - Jonathan King
8 There But For Fortune - Joan Baez
9 In Thoughts Of You - Billy Fury
10 Summer Nights - Marianne Faithfull

UK Number One album: *Help!* - The Beatles
US Billboard Number One album: *Beatles VI* - The Beatles
US Cashbox Number One single: *I Got You Babe* - Sonny & Cher
Also this week: The Queen withdraws the OBE from the disgraced spy Kim Philby. (13th)

US Billboard singles for the week ending August the 14th
1 **I Got You Babe** - Sonny & Cher
2 (I Can't Get No) Satisfaction - The Rolling Stones
3 Save Your Heart For Me - Gary Lewis & The Playboys
4 I'm Henry VIII, I Am - Herman's Hermits
5 What's New Pussycat? - Tom Jones
6 Unchained Melody - The Righteous Brothers
7 It's The Same Old Song - The Four Tops
8 Don't Just Stand There - Patty Duke
9 California Girls - The Beach Boys
10 Down In The Boondocks - Billy Joe Royal

1965

UK singles chart for the week ending August the 21st
1 **Help**! - The Beatles
2 You've Got Your Troubles - The Fortunes
3 We Gotta Get Out Of This Place - The Animals
4 I Got You Babe - Sonny & Cher
5 Walk In The Black Forest (Eine Schwarzwaldfahrt) - Horst Jankowski
6 Everyone's Gone To The Moon - Jonathan King
7 Catch Us If You Can - The Dave Clark Five
8 Mr. Tambourine Man - The Byrds
9 Zorba's Dance - Marcello Minerbi
10 In Thoughts Of You - Billy Fury

UK Number One album: *Help!* - The Beatles
US Billboard Number One album: *Out Of Our Heads* - The Rolling Stones
US Cashbox Number One single: *I Got You Babe* - Sonny & Cher
Also this week: The photographer David Bailey marries Catherine Deneuve. (18th)

US Billboard singles for the week ending August the 21st
1 **I Got You Babe** - Sonny & Cher
2 Save Your Heart For Me - Gary Lewis & The Playboys
3 Help! - The Beatles
4 California Girls - The Beach Boys
5 Unchained Melody - The Righteous Brothers
6 (I Can't Get No) Satisfaction - The Rolling Stones
7 It's The Same Old Song - The Four Tops
8 Don't Just Stand There - Patty Duke
9 I'm Henry VIII, I Am - Herman's Hermits
10 Down In The Boondocks - Billy Joe Royal

1965

 1 **I Got You Babe** - Sonny & Cher
 2 Help! - The Beatles
 3 Walk In The Black Forest (Eine Schwarzwaldfahrt) - Horst Jankowski
 4 Everyone's Gone To The Moon - Jonathan King
 5 All I Really Want To Do - The Byrds
 6 We Gotta Get Out Of This Place - The Animals
 7 Zorba's Dance - Marcello Minerbi
 8 You've Got Your Troubles - The Fortunes
 9 Catch Us If You Can - The Dave Clark Five
10 Don't Make My Baby Blue - The Shadows

UK Number One album: *Help!* - The Beatles
US Billboard Number One album: *Out Of Our Heads* - The Rolling Stones
US Cashbox Number One single: *Help!* - The Beatles
Also this week: Indian troops cross the Kashmir cease-fire line. (25th)

US Billboard singles for the week ending August the 28th

 1 **I Got You Babe** - Sonny & Cher
 2 Help! - The Beatles
 3 California Girls - The Beach Boys
 4 Unchained Melody - The Righteous Brothers
 5 It's The Same Old Song - The Four Tops
 6 Like A Rolling Stone - Bob Dylan
 7 Save Your Heart For Me - Gary Lewis & The Playboys
 8 Hold Me, Thrill Me, Kiss Me - Mel Carter
 9 Down In The Boondocks - Billy Joe Royal
10 Papa's Got A Brand New Bag - James Brown

1965

 1 **I Got You Babe** - Sonny & Cher
 2 Help! - The Beatles
 3 (I Can't Get No) Satisfaction - The Rolling Stones
 4 All I Really Want To Do - The Byrds
 5 Walk In The Black Forest (Eine Schwarzwaldfahrt) - Horst Jankowski
 6 Zorba's Dance - Marcello Minerbi
 7 Everyone's Gone To The Moon - Jonathan King
 8 Make It Easy On Yourself - The Walker Brothers
 9 Like A Rolling Stone - Bob Dylan
10 See My Friend - The Kinks

UK Number One album: *Help!* - The Beatles
US Billboard Number One album: *Out Of Our Heads* - The Rolling Stones
US Cashbox Number One single: *Help!* - The Beatles
Also this week: The space capsule Gemini V returns safely to earth. (29th)

US Billboard singles for the week ending September the 4th
 1 **Help**! - The Beatles
 2 Like A Rolling Stone - Bob Dylan
 3 California Girls - The Beach Boys
 4 Unchained Melody - The Righteous Brothers
 5 It's The Same Old Song - The Four Tops
 6 I Got You Babe - Sonny & Cher
 7 You Were On My Mind - We Five
 8 Papa's Got A Brand New Bag - James Brown
 9 Eve Of Destruction - Barry McGuire
10 Hold Me, Thrill Me, Kiss Me - Mel Carter

1965

UK singles chart for the week ending September the 11th
1 (**I Can't Get No**) **Satisfaction** - The Rolling Stones
2 I Got You Babe - Sonny & Cher
3 Make It Easy On Yourself - The Walker Brothers
4 Walk In The Black Forest (Eine Schwarzwaldfahrt) - Horst Jankowski
5 Help! - The Beatles
6 Like A Rolling Stone - Bob Dylan
7 All I Really Want To Do - The Byrds
8 Zorba's Dance - Marcello Minerbi
9 All I Really Want To Do - Cher
10 Laugh At Me - Sonny

UK Number One album: *Help!* - The Beatles
US Billboard Number One album: *Help!* - The Beatles
US Cashbox Number One single: *Help!* - The Beatles
Also this week: Indian troops launch a full-scale invasion of Pakistan. (8th)

US Billboard singles for the week ending September the 11th
1 **Help**! - The Beatles
2 Like A Rolling Stone - Bob Dylan
3 Eve Of Destruction - Barry McGuire
4 You Were On My Mind - We Five
5 California Girls - The Beach Boys
6 Unchained Melody - The Righteous Brothers
7 I Got You Babe - Sonny & Cher
8 Papa's Got A Brand New Bag - James Brown
9 It Ain't Me Babe - The Turtles
10 The "In" Crowd - Ramsey Lewis

1965

1 (**I Can't Get No**) **Satisfaction** - The Rolling Stones
2 I Got You Babe - Sonny & Cher
3 Make It Easy On Yourself - The Walker Brothers
4 Like A Rolling Stone - Bob Dylan
5 Look Through Any Window - The Hollies
6 Walk In The Black Forest (Eine Schwarzwaldfahrt) - Horst Jankowski
7 Tears - Ken Dodd
8 Help! - The Beatles
9 Laugh At Me - Sonny
10 Zorba's Dance - Marcello Minerbi

UK Number One album: *Help!* - The Beatles
US Billboard Number One album: *Help!* - The Beatles
US Cashbox Number One single: *Like A Rolling Stone* - Bob Dylan
Also this week: Harold Wilson declares his liking for the television programme Coronation Street. (16th)

US Billboard singles for the week ending September the 18th
1 **Help**! - The Beatles
2 Eve Of Destruction - Barry McGuire
3 Like A Rolling Stone - Bob Dylan
4 You Were On My Mind - We Five
5 Catch Us If You Can - The Dave Clark Five
6 The "In" Crowd - Ramsey Lewis
7 Hang On Sloopy - The McCoys
8 It Ain't Me Babe - The Turtles
9 I Got You Babe - Sonny & Cher
10 Heart Full Of Soul - The Yardbirds

1965

1 **Make It Easy On Yourself** - The Walker Brothers
2 (I Can't Get No) Satisfaction - The Rolling Stones
3 Tears - Ken Dodd
4 I Got You Babe - Sonny & Cher
5 Look Through Any Window - The Hollies
6 Like A Rolling Stone - Bob Dylan
7 Walk In The Black Forest (Eine Schwarzwaldfahrt) - Horst Jankowski
8 Zorba's Dance - Marcello Minerbi
9 Eve Of Destruction - Barry McGuire
10 Laugh At Me - Sonny

UK Number One album: *Help!* - The Beatles
US Billboard Number One album: *Help!* - The Beatles
US Cashbox Number One single: *Eve Of Destruction* - Barry McGuire
Also this week: Pakistan war planes raid the holy Sikh city of Amritsar. (22nd)

US Billboard singles for the week ending September the 25th

1 **Eve Of Destruction** - Barry McGuire
2 Hang On Sloopy - The McCoys
3 You Were On My Mind - We Five
4 Catch Us If You Can - The Dave Clark Five
5 Help! - The Beatles
6 The "In" Crowd - Ramsey Lewis
7 Like A Rolling Stone - Bob Dylan
8 It Ain't Me Babe - The Turtles
9 Heart Full Of Soul - The Yardbirds
10 Laugh At Me - Sonny & Cher

1965

UK singles chart for the week ending October the 2nd
1 **Tears** - Ken Dodd
2 Make It Easy On Yourself - The Walker Brothers
3 (I Can't Get No) Satisfaction - The Rolling Stones
4 Look Through Any Window - The Hollies
5 If You Gotta Go, Go Now - Manfred Mann
6 Eve Of Destruction - Barry McGuire
7 I Got You Babe - Sonny & Cher
8 Like A Rolling Stone - Bob Dylan
9 Walk In The Black Forest (Eine Schwarzwaldfahrt) - Horst Jankowski
10 Il Silenzio - Nini Rosso

UK Number One album: *Help!* - The Beatles
US Billboard Number One album: *Help!* - The Beatles
US Cashbox Number One single: *Hang On Sloopy* - The McCoys
Also this week: Aston Martin reveals its first four-seater, the DB6. (29th)

US Billboard singles for the week ending October the 2nd
1 **Hang On Sloopy** - The McCoys
2 Eve Of Destruction - Barry McGuire
3 Yesterday - The Beatles
4 Catch Us If You Can - The Dave Clark Five
5 You Were On My Mind - We Five
6 The "In" Crowd - Ramsey Lewis
7 Treat Her Right - Roy Head
8 You've Got Your Troubles - The Fortunes
9 Baby Don't Go - Sonny & Cher
10 Laugh At Me - Sonny & Cher

1965

1 **Tears** - Ken Dodd
2 If You Gotta Go, Go Now - Manfred Mann
3 Make It Easy On Yourself - The Walker Brothers
4 Eve Of Destruction - Barry McGuire
5 Almost There - Andy Williams
6 Hang On Sloopy - The McCoys
7 Look Through Any Window - The Hollies
8 (I Can't Get No) Satisfaction - The Rolling Stones
9 Il Silenzio - Nini Rosso
10 Like A Rolling Stone - Bob Dylan

UK Number One album: *Help!* - The Beatles
US Billboard Number One album: *Help!* - The Beatles
US Cashbox Number One single: *Yesterday* - The Beatles
Also this week: The new 620-foot Post Office Tower is opened in London. (7th)

US Billboard singles for the week ending October the 9th

1 **Yesterday** - The Beatles
2 Hang On Sloopy - The McCoys
3 Treat Her Right - Roy Head
4 Eve Of Destruction - Barry McGuire
5 The "In" Crowd - Ramsey Lewis
6 Catch Us If You Can - The Dave Clark Five
7 You've Got Your Troubles - The Fortunes
8 Baby Don't Go - Sonny & Cher
9 You Were On My Mind - We Five
10 Do You Believe In Magic - The Lovin' Spoonful

1965

1 **Tears** - Ken Dodd
2 Almost There - Andy Williams
3 If You Gotta Go, Go Now - Manfred Mann
4 Eve Of Destruction - Barry McGuire
5 Hang On Sloopy - The McCoys
6 Make It Easy On Yourself - The Walker Brothers
7 Look Through Any Window - The Hollies
8 Il Silenzio - Nini Rosso
9 Message Understood - Sandie Shaw
10 (I Can't Get No) Satisfaction - The Rolling Stones

UK Number One album: *The Sound Of Music* - Soundtrack
US Billboard Number One album: *Help!* - The Beatles
US Cashbox Number One single: *Yesterday* - The Beatles
Also this week: Bertrand Russell rips up his Labour Party
membership card. (14th)

US Billboard singles for the week ending October the 16th
1 **Yesterday** - The Beatles
2 Treat Her Right - Roy Head
3 Hang On Sloopy - The McCoys
4 A Lover's Concerto - The Toys
5 Keep On Dancing - The Gentrys
6 The "In" Crowd - Ramsey Lewis
7 Just A Little Bit Better - Herman's Hermits
8 Baby Don't Go - Sonny & Cher
9 Do You Believe In Magic - The Lovin' Spoonful
10 Eve Of Destruction - Barry McGuire

1965

1 **Tears** - Ken Dodd
2 Almost There - Andy Williams
3 If You Gotta Go, Go Now - Manfred Mann
4 Eve Of Destruction - Barry McGuire
5 Hang On Sloopy - The McCoys
6 Message Understood - Sandie Shaw
7 Make It Easy On Yourself - The Walker Brothers
8 Some Of Your Lovin' - Dusty Springfield
9 Evil Hearted You/Still I'm Sad - The Yardbirds
10 It's Good News Week - Hedgehoppers Anonymous

UK Number One album: *The Sound Of Music* - Soundtrack
US Billboard Number One album: *Help!* - The Beatles
US Cashbox Number One single: *A Lover's Concerto* - The Toys
Also this week: Police discover a boy's body on the Pennine Moors. (21st)

US Billboard singles for the week ending October the 23rd

1 **Yesterday** - The Beatles
2 Treat Her Right - Roy Head
3 A Lover's Concerto - The Toys
4 Get Off Of My Cloud - The Rolling Stones
5 Keep On Dancing - The Gentrys
6 Hang On Sloopy - The McCoys
7 Just A Little Bit Better - Herman's Hermits
8 Everybody Loves A Clown - Gary Lewis & The Playboys
9 Positively 4th Street - Bob Dylan
10 You're The One - The Vogues

1965

UK singles chart for the week ending October the 30th
1 **Tears** - Ken Dodd
2 Almost There - Andy Williams
3 Eve Of Destruction - Barry McGuire
4 Evil Hearted You/Still I'm Sad - The Yardbirds
5 Yesterday Man - Chris Andrews
6 It's Good News Week - Hedgehoppers Anonymous
7 If You Gotta Go, Go Now - Manfred Mann
8 Hang On Sloopy - The McCoys
9 Here It Comes Again - The Fortunes
10 Yesterday - Matt Monro

UK Number One album: *The Sound Of Music* - Soundtrack
US Billboard Number One album: *Help!* - The Beatles
US Cashbox Number One single: *Yesterday* - The Beatles
Also this week: 36 people are killed when an aeroplane crashes
at Heathrow Airport. (27th)

US Billboard singles for the week ending October the 30th
1 **Yesterday** - The Beatles
2 A Lover's Concerto - The Toys
3 Get Off Of My Cloud - The Rolling Stones
4 Keep On Dancing - The Gentrys
5 Everybody Loves A Clown - Gary Lewis & The Playboys
6 Treat Her Right - Roy Head
7 You're The One - The Vogues
8 Positively 4th Street - Bob Dylan
9 Hang On Sloopy - The McCoys
10 1-2-3 - Len Barry

1965

1 **Get Off Of My Cloud** - The Rolling Stones
2 Tears - Ken Dodd
3 Evil Hearted You/Still I'm Sad - The Yardbirds
4 Yesterday Man - Chris Andrews
5 It's Good News Week - Hedgehoppers Anonymous
6 Here It Comes Again - The Fortunes
7 Almost There - Andy Williams
8 Yesterday - Matt Monro
9 Eve Of Destruction - Barry McGuire
10 It's My Life - The Animals

UK Number One album: *The Sound Of Music* - Soundtrack
US Billboard Number One album: *Help!* - The Beatles
US Cashbox Number One single: *Get Off Of My Cloud* - The Rolling Stones
Also this week: Ian Smith declares a state of emergency in Rhodesia. (5th)

US Billboard singles for the week ending November the 6th

1 **Get Off Of My Cloud** - The Rolling Stones
2 A Lover's Concerto - The Toys
3 Yesterday - The Beatles
4 Everybody Loves A Clown - Gary Lewis & The Playboys
5 Keep On Dancing - The Gentrys
6 You're The One - The Vogues
7 Positively 4th Street - Bob Dylan
8 1-2-3 - Len Barry
9 Rescue Me - Fontella Bass
10 Taste Of Honey - Herb Alpert

Get Off Of My Cloud became the fifth successive UK Number One for the Rolling Stones.

1965

UK singles chart for the week ending November the 13th
1 **Get Off Of My Cloud** - The Rolling Stones
2 Tears - Ken Dodd
3 Yesterday Man - Chris Andrews
4 Here It Comes Again - The Fortunes
5 Evil Hearted You/Still I'm Sad - The Yardbirds
6 It's Good News Week - Hedgehoppers Anonymous
7 It's My Life - The Animals
8 Yesterday - Matt Monro
9 Almost There - Andy Williams
10 The Carnival Is Over - The Seekers

UK Number One album: *The Sound Of Music* - Soundtrack
US Billboard Number One album: *The Sound Of Music* - Soundtrack
US Cashbox Number One single: *Get Off Of My Cloud* - The Rolling Stones
Also this week: Rhodesia makes a Unilateral Declaration of Independence. (11th)

US Billboard singles for the week ending November the 13th
1 **Get Off Of My Cloud** - The Rolling Stones
2 A Lover's Concerto - The Toys
3 1-2-3 - Len Barry
4 You're The One - The Vogues
5 I Hear A Symphony - The Supremes
6 Rescue Me - Fontella Bass
7 Everybody Loves A Clown - Gary Lewis & The Playboys
8 Let's Hang On! - The Four Seasons
9 Taste Of Honey - Herb Alpert
10 Ain't That Peculiar - Marvin Gaye

1965

1 **Get Off Of My Cloud** - The Rolling Stones
2 The Carnival Is Over - The Seekers
3 Yesterday Man - Chris Andrews
4 Tears - Ken Dodd
5 My Generation - The Who
6 1-2-3 - Len Barry
7 It's My Life - The Animals
8 Here It Comes Again - The Fortunes
9 Evil Hearted You/Still I'm Sad - The Yardbirds
10 Positively 4th Street - Bob Dylan

UK Number One album: *The Sound Of Music* - Soundtrack
US Billboard Number One album: *The Sound Of Music* - Soundtrack
US Cashbox Number One single: *I Hear A Symphony* - The Supremes
Also this week: Britain's Labour government opts to impose sanctions on Rhodesia. (16th)

US Billboard singles for the week ending November the 20th
1 **I Hear A Symphony** - The Supremes
2 1-2-3 - Len Barry
3 Get Off Of My Cloud - The Rolling Stones
4 Rescue Me - Fontella Bass
5 Let's Hang On! - The Four Seasons
6 Turn! Turn! Turn! (To Everything There Is A Season) - The Byrds
7 A Lover's Concerto - The Toys
8 Ain't That Peculiar - Marvin Gaye
9 Taste Of Honey - Herb Alpert
10 You're The One - The Vogues

1965

1 **The Carnival Is Over** - The Seekers
2 My Generation - The Who
3 Get Off Of My Cloud - The Rolling Stones
4 1-2-3 - Len Barry
5 Tears - Ken Dodd
6 Yesterday Man - Chris Andrews
7 It's My Life - The Animals
8 Wind Me Up (Let Me Go) - Cliff Richard
9 Here It Comes Again - The Fortunes
10 Positively 4th Street - Bob Dylan

UK Number One album: *The Sound Of Music* - Soundtrack
US Billboard Number One album: *Whipped Cream And Other Delights* - Herb Alpert's Tijuana Brass
US Cashbox Number One single: *1-2-3* - Len Barry
Also this week: The inquiry into Timothy John Evans' conviction begins. (22nd)

US Billboard singles for the week ending November the 27th

1 **I Hear A Symphony** - The Supremes
2 Turn! Turn! Turn! (To Everything There Is A Season) - The Byrds
3 1-2-3 - Len Barry
4 Let's Hang On! - The Four Seasons
5 Get Off Of My Cloud - The Rolling Stones
6 Rescue Me - Fontella Bass
7 Taste Of Honey - Herb Alpert
8 Ain't That Peculiar - Marvin Gaye
9 I Got You (I Feel Good) - James Brown
10 You've Got To Hide Your Love Away - The Silkie

1965

1 **The Carnival Is Over** - The Seekers
2 My Generation - The Who
3 1-2-3 - Len Barry
4 Get Off Of My Cloud - The Rolling Stones
5 A Lover's Concerto - The Toys
6 Tears - Ken Dodd
7 Wind Me Up (Let Me Go) - Cliff Richard
8 Positively 4th Street - Bob Dylan
9 Princess In Rags - Gene Pitney
10 Yesterday Man - Chris Andrews

UK Number One album: *The Sound Of Music* - Soundtrack
US Billboard Number One album: *Whipped Cream And Other Delights* - Herb Alpert's Tijuana Brass
US Cashbox Number One single: *Turn! Turn! Turn! (To Everything There Is A Season)* - The Byrds
Also this week: Prime Minister Harold Wilson proposes tougher sanctions for Rhodesia. (1st)

1 **Turn! Turn! Turn! (To Everything There Is A Season**) - The Byrds
2 I Hear A Symphony - The Supremes
3 1-2-3 - Len Barry
4 Let's Hang On! - The Four Seasons
5 I Got You (I Feel Good) - James Brown
6 Rescue Me - Fontella Bass
7 Taste Of Honey - Herb Alpert
8 Ain't That Peculiar - Marvin Gaye
9 I Can Never Go Home Anymore - The Shangri-Las
10 Over And Over - The Dave Clark Five

1965

UK singles chart for the week ending December the 11th
1 **The Carnival Is Over** - The Seekers
2 Day Tripper/We Can Work It Out - The Beatles
3 My Generation - The Who
4 Wind Me Up (Let Me Go) - Cliff Richard
5 A Lover's Concerto - The Toys
6 1-2-3 - Len Barry
7 The River - Ken Dodd
8 Tears - Ken Dodd
9 Get Off Of My Cloud - The Rolling Stones
10 Princess In Rags - Gene Pitney

UK Number One album: *The Sound Of Music* - Soundtrack
US Billboard Number One album: *Whipped Cream And Other Delights* - Herb Alpert's Tijuana Brass
US Cashbox Number One single: *Let's Hang On* - The Four Seasons
Also this week: UNICEF is awarded the Nobel Prize for Peace. (10th)

US Billboard singles for the week ending December the 11th
1 **Turn**! **Turn**! **Turn**! (**To Everything There Is A Season**) - The Byrds
2 I Hear A Symphony - The Supremes
3 Let's Hang On! - The Four Seasons
4 I Got You (I Feel Good) - James Brown
5 Over And Over - The Dave Clark Five
6 I Can Never Go Home Anymore - The Shangri-Las
7 1-2-3 - Len Barry
8 Taste Of Honey - Herb Alpert
9 Rescue Me - Fontella Bass
10 I Will - Dean Martin

1965

1 **Day Tripper/We Can Work It Out** - The Beatles
2 The Carnival Is Over - The Seekers
3 Wind Me Up (Let Me Go) - Cliff Richard
4 1-2-3 - Len Barry
5 My Generation - The Who
6 The River - Ken Dodd
7 Tears - Ken Dodd
8 Maria - PJ Proby
9 A Lover's Concerto - The Toys
10 My Ship Is Coming In - The Walker Brothers

UK Number One album: *The Sound Of Music* - Soundtrack
US Billboard Number One album: *Whipped Cream And Other Delights* - Herb Alpert's Tijuana Brass
US Cashbox Number One single: *Taste Of Honey* - Herb Alpert & Tijuana Brass
Also this week: Goldie the golden eagle escapes again from Regent's Park zoo. (15th)

US Billboard singles for the week ending December the 18th
1 **Turn! Turn! Turn! (To Everything There Is A Season**) - The Byrds
2 Over And Over - The Dave Clark Five
3 I Got You (I Feel Good) - James Brown
4 Let's Hang On! - The Four Seasons
5 I Hear A Symphony - The Supremes
6 I Can Never Go Home Anymore - The Shangri-Las
7 Make The World Go Away - Eddy Arnold
8 England Swings - Roger Miller
9 Fever - The McCoys
10 I Will - Dean Martin

1965

UK singles chart for the week ending December the 25th

1 **Day Tripper/We Can Work It Out** - The Beatles
2 Wind Me Up (Let Me Go) - Cliff Richard
3 The River - Ken Dodd
4 The Carnival Is Over - The Seekers
5 Tears - Ken Dodd
6 My Ship Is Coming In - The Walker Brothers
7 My Generation - The Who
8 1-2-3 - Len Barry
9 A Lover's Concerto - The Toys
10 Let's Hang On! - The Four Seasons

UK Number One album: *Rubber Soul* - The Beatles
US Billboard Number One album: *Whipped Cream And Other Delights* - Herb Alpert's Tijuana Brass
US Cashbox Number One single: *Over And Over* - The Dave Clark Five
Also this week: Charles De Gaulle is re-elected as France's President. (19th)

US Billboard singles for the week ending December the 25th

1 **Over And Over** - The Dave Clark Five
2 Turn! Turn! Turn! (To Everything There Is A Season) - The Byrds
3 I Got You (I Feel Good) - James Brown
4 Let's Hang On! - The Four Seasons
5 The Sounds Of Silence - Simon And Garfunkel
6 Make The World Go Away - Eddy Arnold
7 Fever - The McCoys
8 England Swings - Roger Miller
9 Ebb Tide - The Righteous Brothers
10 I Can Never Go Home Anymore - The Shangri-Las

THE BEST 10 SONGS OF 1965?

Goldfinger by Shirley Bassey

The welsh songbird had previously reached the UK pop summit with the double-A side 'I Reach For The Stars' and 'Climb Ev'ry Mountain'. However, her singing career is best remembered for her association with the James Bond movie themes. The prime example is 'Goldfinger' which briefly invaded the US Top 10. This film is frequently cited as arguably the best 007 movie, and one could easily presume that Bassey's outstanding vocals were the ideal curtain-raiser for the subsequent action.

In My Life by The Beatles

As the Beatles started to mature into performers of a more sophisticated pop, as exemplified on their 'Rubber Soul' album, so John Lennon himself penned a love song which was a far cry from the jolly, up-tempo material of the Mersey sound. 'In My Life' is presumably a tribute to his first wife, Cynthia, but it is also a gentle, sentimental look back at the people and places who had shaped Lennon's upbringing.

Make It Easy On Yourself by The Walker Brothers

They weren't brothers, and none of them was actually called Walker, but this trio stepped forth to deliver vocal performances which found favour with the British record-buying public. Here, the guys were reminding a jilted lover that breaking up is so very hard to do. This wasn't exactly a happy-go-lucky 45, but this melodrama nevertheless deservedly climbed to the top of the tree in the UK singles chart.

Mr. Tambourine Man by The Byrds

Session musicians were drafted in for this recording and only Jim McGuinn actually played his guitar on this memorable track. Even though the Byrds were merely relegated to harmonies on this smash hit, they were greatly encouraged by its favourable reception. Bob Dylan couldn't complain either, as here was the first prominent occasion when others dipped into his repertoire and reaped the benefits. The Byrds would continue to do justice to a number of Dylan tunes.

My Generation by The Who

This became one of the great anthems for the emerging mods' movement, as young folk turned onto Pete Townshend's lyrics which correctly observed that there was a yawning generation gap between the mod upstarts and their war-hardened parents. This song is notable for Roger Daltrey's deliberate stuttering and Keith Moon's characteristically energetic drum sound. The disenfranchised youth may have been largely inarticulate, but here Townshend was acting as their spokesperson.

THE BEST 10 SONGS OF 1965? (Continued)

Stop! In The Name Of Love by The Supremes

The Supremes had a hugely successful 1965 as they cemented their position as the world's best girl group. 'Stop! In The Name Of Love' ranks among their very best recordings and was one of five successive Number One singles on the Billboard Hot 100. Diana, Florence, and Mary had come a long way since their inner-city origins, and now they were the flagship act for Detroit's highly influential Tamla Motown record company.

Tears by Ken Dodd

Ken Dodd was an unlikely chart-topper, but his tearjerker was actually one of the biggest-selling singles in the UK in 1965. This year witnessed a number of sad songs which proved surprisingly popular with record-buyers, such as 'Go Now', 'The Minute You're Gone', and 'The Carnival Is Over'. However it was the toothy comedian Dodd who emerged with the most successful of them all. He was sufficiently tickled pink by 'Tears' to issue a follow-up entitled 'The River'.

Unchained Melody by The Righteous Brothers

Bobby Hatfield and Bill Medley built upon the foundations of the outstanding 'You've Lost That Lovin' Feeling' with an impressive attempt at the 'fifties ballad 'Unchained Melody'. The musical accompaniment was suitably tremendous as the 'brothers' found themselves back in the US Top 10. It took the UK a further quarter of a century to appreciate this item when it was belatedly rewarded with a British Number One.

Where Are You Now My Love by Jackie Trent

Cilla Black, Petula Clark, Sandie Shaw, and Dusty Springfield were all reminders that the hit parade was not just a playground for young males. However, perhaps the best British-made single in 1965 from a female artist was this offering. Jackie Trent is ably assisted by a piano as she pines for a lost love. More big-selling singles should have followed.

You're So Good To Me by The Beach Boys

In the previous year, Brian Wilson quit touring to concentrate on composing and recording new material. This peculiar decision paid dividends as the Beach Boys' leading songwriter started to branch out with tunes that were on a superior level to most of the other stuff floating on planet pop. 'You're So Good To Me', a prime cut from the 'Summer Days (And Summer Nights)' album is one such shining example. Here again, the group's harmonies excel themselves, inspired by the Four Freshmen. The Beach Boys were in some respects the prototype boy band.

THE BEST ALBUM OF 1965?
Highway 61 Revisited
by **Bob Dylan**;
peaked in the UK charts at No.4
peaked in the US charts at No.3
produced by Bob Johnston
released in August

This new offering from Mr Zimmerman was something of a watershed in a number of respects. Not only was Dylan incurring the wrath of Luddite folk music devotees by plugging his new tunes into electric sockets, but here arguably for the first time was an album of substance, carefully constructed, and thus historically it represented a new departure from the previous formula of artists hastily compiling a dozen filler material to complement the one or two 'quality' singles that featured on any given long player. 'Highway 61 Revisited', it can be claimed, heralds the dawning of a new genre: folk rock. No longer was Dylan and other folksters merely strumming protest songs on acoustic guitar, accompanied possibly by harmonica. Now folk music was, horror of horrors, selling its soul (in the eyes of some zealots) and embracing modern technology. Electric guitars, bass guitar, drums, and keyboards were all drafted in to complement the bard of the folk scene. A defiant Dylan merely responded to being called a "Judas" in mid-concert in Manchester by exhorting his group to "play f***ing louder" on their rendition of 'Like A Rolling Stone'. Seminal track is an often over-used description in popular music tomes, but scarcely a soul anywhere questions its suitability in relation to Dylan's six-minute album opener which, unlike the other ten songs, was actually produced by

THE BEST ALBUM OF 1965? (Continued)

Tom Wilson. Such indeed is the enduring appeal of 'Like A Rolling Stone' that music critic Greil Marcus was sufficiently moved to compose a whole publication on this one song.

'Ballad Of A Thin Man' follows a similar theme as the sixties' leading songwriter sings once more of alienation and of being the outsider on the periphery, looking inside at the American dream. This was Generation X material, twenty years ahead of its time. Brian Jones, himself an increasingly peripheral figure in the Rolling Stones, was convinced that these two tracks in particular were a commentary on his state of mind. "How's your paranoia meter?", Dylan once famously asked Mr Jones. Was it pure coincidence that 'Ballad Of A Thin Man' contains the lyric "Something is happening here and you don't know what it is/Do you, Mr Jones?" A credible case can be made that the subsequent 'Blonde On Blonde' project contains better songs, but Highway 61 Revisited is less patchy, in spite of the presence of the lengthy 'Desolation Row'. For the uninitiated, 'From A Buick 6', 'It Takes A Lot To Laugh, It Takes A Train To Cry', and 'Queen Jane Approximately' are gems waiting to be unearthed. Bob Dylan was emphatically laying down a marker that he was the leading spokesperson for the new generation that viewed the Establishment with disdain and suspicion. Dylan remained an enigma thereafter, allowing his constant flow of product to speak on his behalf. The quality of his output may have varied through time, but Dylan's status as the main man of the 1960s' music scene was cemented by this LP.

The album's best song? - *Like A Rolling Stone*

SPORT IN 1965

English Division One soccer champions: Manchester United
English FA Cup final: Liverpool 2 Leeds United 1
English League Cup winners: Chelsea
Scottish Division One soccer champions: Kilmarnock
Scottish FA Cup final: Glasgow Celtic 3 Dunfermline Athletic 2
Scottish League Cup winners: Glasgow Celtic
Irish League soccer champions: Derry City; Irish Cup winners: Coleraine
League Of Ireland soccer champions: Drumcondra; cup winners: Shamrock Rovers
European Cup final: Inter Milan 1 Benfica 0
European Cup-Winners' Cup final: West Ham United 2 Munich 1860 0
European Fairs' Cup final: Ferencvaros 1 Juventus 0
English county cricket champions: Worcestershire
Five Nations' rugby union champions: Wales (triple crown)
Formula One world drivers' champion: Jim Clark
Gaelic football All-Ireland champions: Galway; hurling champions: Tipperary
British Open golf champion: Peter Thomson
US Masters golf champion: Jack Nicklaus
US Open golf champion: Gary Player
USPGA golf champion: Dave Marr
Rugby league Challenge Cup final: Wigan 20 Hunslet 16
Wimbledon men's singles tennis champion: Roy Emerson
Wimbledon ladies' singles tennis champion: Margaret Smith
The Aintree Grand National steeplechase winner: Jay Trump
The Epsom Derby winner: Sea Bird II
The Ryder Cup: Great Britain & Ireland 12.5 USA 19.5

DEATHS IN 1965

January 4th: Thomas Stearns Eliot (US poet), aged 76
January 20th: Alan Freed (US disc jockey), aged 43
January 24th: Winston Leonard Spencer Churchill (British statesman), aged 90
February 15th: Nat King Cole (US singer), aged 45
February 21st: Malcolm X, born Malcolm Little (US agitator), aged 39
February 23rd: Arthur Stanley Jefferson (US comedian, aka Stan Laurel), aged 74
March 6th: Herbert Stanley Morrison (British politician), aged 77
March 17th: King Farouk (ex-Egyptian monarch), aged 45
April 21st: Edward Appleton (British physicist), aged 72
April 27th: Edward R. Murrow (US broadcaster), aged 57
May 21st: Geoffrey de Havilland (British aircraft pioneer), aged 82
July 14th: Adlai Stevenson (US statesman), aged 65
July 19th: Syngman Rhee (ex-South Korean President), aged 90
July 25th: Freddie Mills (British boxer), aged 46
August 27th: Charles Edouard Jeanneret (French architect), aged 77
September 4th: Dr Albert Schweitzer (French 1952 Nobel Prize winner), aged 90
November 6th: Edgar Varese (US composer), aged 81
November 16th: William Thomas Cosgrave (ex-Irish President), aged 85
December 16th: William Somerset Maugham (British author), aged 91
December 22nd: Richard Frederick Dimbleby (British broadcaster), aged 52

COMMERCIAL BREAK:
An Essential Guide To Music In The 1970s
by Johnny Zero

This 360-page well of information contains the following:
Every Top 10 UK singles chart in the 1970s
The Number 1 UK album for each week
The Number 1 US album for each week
The Number 1 US single for each week
A top news story for each week
The concert highlights of each year
The sporting highlights of each year
The deaths of each year
The Oscar winners of the 1970s
Plus extra coverage of 120 notable recordings
Featured albums from Led Zeppelin, the Rolling Stones, Neil
Young, Elton John, Bob Marley And The Wailers, Pink Floyd,
the Eagles, Fleetwood Mac, Kate Bush, and Blondie
You can order a copy online or in-store for £9.99.

1966

1 **Day Tripper/We Can Work It Out** - The Beatles
2 Wind Me Up (Let Me Go) - Cliff Richard
3 The River - Ken Dodd
4 The Carnival Is Over - The Seekers
5 Tears - Ken Dodd
6 My Ship Is Coming In - The Walker Brothers
7 My Generation - The Who
8 1-2-3 - Len Barry
9 A Lover's Concerto - The Toys
10 Let's Hang On! - The Four Seasons

UK Number One album: *Rubber Soul* - The Beatles
US Billboard Number One album: *Whipped Cream And Other Delights* - Herb Alpert's Tijuana Brass
US Cashbox Number One single: *We Can Work It Out* - The Beatles
Also this week: The rebel regime of Rhodesia is obliged to introduce petrol rationing, in the wake of sanctions. (27th)

US Billboard singles for the week ending January the 1st

1 **The Sounds Of Silence** - Simon And Garfunkel
2 We Can Work It Out - The Beatles
3 I Got You (I Feel Good) - James Brown
4 Turn! Turn! Turn! (To Everything There Is A Season) - The Byrds
5 Over And Over - The Dave Clark Five
6 Let's Hang On! - The Four Seasons
7 Fever - The McCoys
8 Ebb Tide - The Righteous Brothers
9 England Swings - Roger Miller
10 Make The World Go Away - Eddy Arnold

1966

1 **Day Tripper/We Can Work It Out** - The Beatles
2 Wind Me Up (Let Me Go) - Cliff Richard
3 The Carnival Is Over - The Seekers
4 The River - Ken Dodd
5 Keep On Running - The Spencer Davis Group
6 My Ship Is Coming In - The Walker Brothers
7 Tears - Ken Dodd
8 Let's Hang On! - The Four Seasons
9 Merry Gentle Pops - The Barron Knights
10 Till The End Of The Day - The Kinks

UK Number One album: *Rubber Soul* - The Beatles
US Billboard Number One album: *Rubber Soul* - The Beatles
US Cashbox Number One single: *We Can Work It Out* - The Beatles
Also this week: Barber and Boycott amass 200 runs together in an Ashes test match. (7th)

US Billboard singles for the week ending January the 8th
1 **We Can Work It Out** - The Beatles
2 The Sounds Of Silence - Simon And Garfunkel
3 She's Just My Style - Gary Lewis & The Playboys
4 Flowers On The Wall - The Statler Brothers
5 Ebb Tide - The Righteous Brothers
6 Over And Over - The Dave Clark Five
7 I Got You (I Feel Good) - James Brown
8 Five O'Clock World - The Vogues
9 Turn! Turn! Turn! (To Everything There Is A Season) - The Byrds
10 Day Tripper - The Beatles

1966

UK singles chart for the week ending January the 15th
1 **Day Tripper/We Can Work It Out** - The Beatles
2 Keep On Running - The Spencer Davis Group
3 Wind Me Up (Let Me Go) - Cliff Richard
4 The Carnival Is Over - The Seekers
5 My Ship Is Coming In - The Walker Brothers
6 The River - Ken Dodd
7 Let's Hang On! - The Four Seasons
8 Till The End Of The Day - The Kinks
9 A Must To Avoid - Herman's Hermits
10 Merry Gentle Pops - The Barron Knights

UK Number One album: *Rubber Soul* - The Beatles
US Billboard Number One album: *Rubber Soul* - The Beatles
US Cashbox Number One single: *We Can Work It Out* - The Beatles
Also this week: Rhodesia expels three visiting Labour Members of Parliament. (13th)

US Billboard singles for the week ending January the 15th
1 **We Can Work It Out** - The Beatles
2 The Sounds Of Silence - Simon And Garfunkel
3 She's Just My Style - Gary Lewis & The Playboys
4 Five O'Clock World - The Vogues
5 Ebb Tide - The Righteous Brothers
6 Day Tripper - The Beatles
7 Flowers On The Wall - The Statler Brothers
8 The Men In My Little Girl's Life - Mike Douglas
9 As Tears Go By - The Rolling Stones
10 No Matter What Shape (Your Stomach's In) - The T-Bones

1966

 1 **Keep On Running** - The Spencer Davis Group
 2 Day Tripper/We Can Work It Out - The Beatles
 3 My Ship Is Coming In - The Walker Brothers
 4 Let's Hang On! - The Four Seasons
 5 Wind Me Up (Let Me Go) - Cliff Richard
 6 Spanish Flea - Herb Alpert And The Tijuana Brass
 7 The Carnival Is Over - The Seekers
 8 A Must To Avoid - Herman's Hermits
 9 The River - Ken Dodd
10 Till The End Of The Day - The Kinks

UK Number One album: *Rubber Soul* - The Beatles
US Billboard Number One album: *Rubber Soul* - The Beatles
US Cashbox Number One single: *We Can Work It Out* - The Beatles
Also this week: Indira Gandhi is elected Prime Minister of India. (19th)

US Billboard singles for the week ending January the 22nd

 1 **The Sounds Of Silence** - Simon And Garfunkel
 2 We Can Work It Out - The Beatles
 3 She's Just My Style - Gary Lewis & The Playboys
 4 Five O'Clock World - The Vogues
 5 Day Tripper - The Beatles
 6 No Matter What Shape (Your Stomach's In) - The T-Bones
 7 The Men In My Little Girl's Life - Mike Douglas
 8 A Must To Avoid - Herman's Hermits
 9 As Tears Go By - The Rolling Stones
10 You Didn't Have To Be So Nice - The Lovin' Spoonful

1966

1 **Michelle** - The Overlanders
2 Keep On Running - The Spencer Davis Group
3 Spanish Flea - Herb Alpert And The Tijuana Brass
4 Day Tripper/We Can Work It Out - The Beatles
5 Let's Hang On! - The Four Seasons
6 A Must To Avoid - Herman's Hermits
7 My Ship Is Coming In - The Walker Brothers
8 Till The End Of The Day - The Kinks
9 The River - Ken Dodd
10 You Were On My Mind - Crispian St. Peters

UK Number One album: *Rubber Soul* - The Beatles
US Billboard Number One album: *Rubber Soul* - The Beatles
US Cashbox Number One single: *The Sounds Of Silence* -
Simon And Garfunkel
Also this week: 117 are killed when an aeroplane crashes into
Mont Blanc. (24th)

US Billboard singles for the week ending January the 29th
1 **We Can Work It Out** - The Beatles
2 Barbara Ann - The Beach Boys
3 She's Just My Style - Gary Lewis & The Playboys
4 No Matter What Shape (Your Stomach's In) - The T-Bones
5 Five O'Clock World - The Vogues
6 As Tears Go By - The Rolling Stones
7 The Men In My Little Girl's Life - Mike Douglas
8 A Must To Avoid - Herman's Hermits
9 My Love - Petula Clark
10 Jenny Take A Ride! - Mitch Ryder & The Detroit Wheels

1966

1 **Michelle** - The Overlanders
2 Keep On Running - The Spencer Davis Group
3 Spanish Flea - Herb Alpert And The Tijuana Brass
4 You Were On My Mind - Crispian St. Peters
5 Love's Just A Broken Heart - Cilla Black
6 A Must To Avoid - Herman's Hermits
7 Day Tripper/We Can Work It Out - The Beatles
8 Let's Hang On! - The Four Seasons
9 My Ship Is Coming In - The Walker Brothers
10 Till The End Of The Day - The Kinks

UK Number One album: *Rubber Soul* - The Beatles
US Billboard Number One album: *Rubber Soul* - The Beatles
US Cashbox Number One single: *Barbara Ann* - The Beach Boys
Also this week: 133 are killed when an aeroplane crashes in Tokyo Bay. (4th)

US Billboard singles for the week ending February the 5th

1 **My Love** - Petula Clark
2 Barbara Ann - The Beach Boys
3 No Matter What Shape (Your Stomach's In) - The T-Bones
4 We Can Work It Out - The Beatles
5 Lightnin' Strikes - Lou Christie
6 The Men In My Little Girl's Life - Mike Douglas
7 She's Just My Style - Gary Lewis & The Playboys
8 Five O'Clock World - The Vogues
9 A Must To Avoid - Herman's Hermits
10 Crying Time - Ray Charles

1966

 1 **Michelle** - The Overlanders
 2 You Were On My Mind - Crispian St. Peters
 3 Spanish Flea - Herb Alpert And The Tijuana Brass
 4 These Boots Are Made For Walkin' - Nancy Sinatra
 5 Love's Just A Broken Heart - Cilla Black
 6 Keep On Running - The Spencer Davis Group
 7 A Groovy Kind Of Love - The Mindbenders
 8 A Must To Avoid - Herman's Hermits
 9 Mirror, Mirror - Pinkerton's Assorted Colours
10 Like A Baby - Len Barry

UK Number One album: *Rubber Soul* - The Beatles
US Billboard Number One album: *Rubber Soul* - The Beatles
US Cashbox Number One single: *Lightnin' Strikes* - Lou Christie
Also this week: Freddie Laker announces the formation of his new airline. (8th)

US Billboard singles for the week ending February the 12th
 1 **My Love** - Petula Clark
 2 Lightnin' Strikes - Lou Christie
 3 Uptight (Everything's Alright) - Stevie Wonder
 4 Barbara Ann - The Beach Boys
 5 We Can Work It Out - The Beatles
 6 No Matter What Shape (Your Stomach's In) - The T-Bones
 7 Crying Time - Ray Charles
 8 My World Is Empty Without You - The Supremes
 9 Five O'Clock World - The Vogues
10 Don't Mess With Bill - The Marvelettes

1966

1 **These Boots Are Made For Walkin**' - Nancy Sinatra
2 19th Nervous Breakdown - The Rolling Stones
3 You Were On My Mind - Crispian St. Peters
4 Spanish Flea - Herb Alpert And The Tijuana Brass
5 Michelle - The Overlanders
6 A Groovy Kind Of Love - The Mindbenders
7 Love's Just A Broken Heart - Cilla Black
8 Keep On Running - The Spencer Davis Group
9 Tomorrow - Sandie Shaw
10 Mirror, Mirror - Pinkerton's Assorted Colours

UK Number One album: *The Sound Of Music* - Soundtrack
US Billboard Number One album: *Whipped Cream And Other Delights* - Herb Alpert's Tijuana Brass
US Cashbox Number One single: *Lightnin' Strikes* - Lou Christie
Also this week: Australia retain the cricket Ashes after Cowper hits 307 runs against England. (16th)

US Billboard singles for the week ending February the 19th
1 **Lightnin**' **Strikes** - Lou Christie
2 These Boots Are Made For Walkin' - Nancy Sinatra
3 Uptight (Everything's Alright) - Stevie Wonder
4 My Love - Petula Clark
5 My World Is Empty Without You - The Supremes
6 Crying Time - Ray Charles
7 Barbara Ann - The Beach Boys
8 Don't Mess With Bill - The Marvelettes
9 No Matter What Shape (Your Stomach's In) - The T-Bones
10 The Ballad Of The Green Berets - Staff Sergeant Barry Sadler

1966

1 **These Boots Are Made For Walkin**' - Nancy Sinatra
2 19th Nervous Breakdown - The Rolling Stones
3 A Groovy Kind Of Love - The Mindbenders
4 You Were On My Mind - Crispian St. Peters
5 My Love - Petula Clark
6 Spanish Flea - Herb Alpert And The Tijuana Brass
7 Sha La La La Lee - The Small Faces
8 Barbara Ann - The Beach Boys
9 Tomorrow - Sandie Shaw
10 Love's Just A Broken Heart - Cilla Black

UK Number One album: *The Sound Of Music* - Soundtrack
US Billboard Number One album: *Whipped Cream And Other Delights* - Herb Alpert's Tijuana Brass
US Cashbox Number One single: *These Boots Are Made For Walkin'* - Nancy Sinatra
Also this week: Nobby Stiles scores as England beat West Germany 1-0 in a pre-World Cup friendly soccer match. (23rd)

US Billboard singles for the week ending February the 26th

1 **These Boots Are Made For Walkin**' - Nancy Sinatra
2 Lightnin' Strikes - Lou Christie
3 The Ballad Of The Green Berets - Staff Sergeant Barry Sadler
4 Uptight (Everything's Alright) - Stevie Wonder
5 My World Is Empty Without You - The Supremes
6 My Love - Petula Clark
7 Don't Mess With Bill - The Marvelettes
8 California Dreamin' - The Mamas & The Papas
9 Elusive Butterfly - Bob Lind
10 Working My Way Back To You - The Four Seasons

1966

 1 **These Boots Are Made For Walkin**' - Nancy Sinatra
 2 19th Nervous Breakdown - The Rolling Stones
 3 A Groovy Kind Of Love - The Mindbenders
 4 My Love - Petula Clark
 5 Sha La La La Lee - The Small Faces
 6 Barbara Ann - The Beach Boys
 7 Backstage - Gene Pitney
 8 Spanish Flea - Herb Alpert And The Tijuana Brass
 9 You Were On My Mind - Crispian St. Peters
10 Make The World Go Away - Eddy Arnold

UK Number One album: *The Sound Of Music* - Soundtrack
US Billboard Number One album: *Going Places* - Herb Alpert And His Tijuana Brass
US Cashbox Number One single: *The Ballad Of The Green Berets* - Staff Sergeant Barry Sadler
Also this week: 130 people are killed when a Boeing 707 aeroplane crashes into Mount Fuji. (5th)

US Billboard singles for the week ending March the 5th
 1 **The Ballad Of The Green Berets** - Staff Sergeant Barry Sadler
 2 These Boots Are Made For Walkin' - Nancy Sinatra
 3 Lightnin' Strikes - Lou Christie
 4 Listen People - Herman's Hermits
 5 California Dreamin' - The Mamas & The Papas
 6 Elusive Butterfly - Bob Lind
 7 My Love - Petula Clark
 8 Uptight (Everything's Alright) - Stevie Wonder
 9 Working My Way Back To You - The Four Seasons
10 My World Is Empty Without You - The Supremes

1966

1 **These Boots Are Made For Walkin'** - Nancy Sinatra
2 A Groovy Kind Of Love - The Mindbenders
3 Barbara Ann - The Beach Boys
4 Backstage - Gene Pitney
5 Spanish Flea - Herb Alpert And The Tijuana Brass
6 Sha La La La Lee - The Small Faces
7 I Can't Let Go - The Hollies
8 19th Nervous Breakdown - The Rolling Stones
9 My Love - Petula Clark
10 The Sun Ain't Gonna Shine Anymore - The Walker Brothers

UK Number One album: *The Sound Of Music* - Soundtrack
US Billboard Number One album: *Ballads Of The Green Berets* - Staff Sergeant Barry Sadler
US Cashbox Number One single: *The Ballad Of The Green Berets* - Staff Sergeant Barry Sadler
Also this week: Holland's Princess Beatrix marries Claus von Amsberg. (10th)

US Billboard singles for the week ending March the 12th

1 **The Ballad Of The Green Berets** - Staff Sergeant Barry Sadler
2 These Boots Are Made For Walkin' - Nancy Sinatra
3 Listen People - Herman's Hermits
4 California Dreamin' - The Mamas & The Papas
5 Elusive Butterfly - Bob Lind
6 19th Nervous Breakdown - The Rolling Stones
7 Nowhere Man - The Beatles
8 Lightnin' Strikes - Lou Christie
9 I Fought The Law - The Bobby Fuller Four
10 Homeward Bound - Simon And Garfunkel

1966

1 **The Sun Ain't Gonna Shine Anymore** - The Walker Brothers
2 I Can't Let Go - The Hollies
3 Sha La La La Lee - The Small Faces
4 A Groovy Kind Of Love - The Mindbenders
5 Barbara Ann - The Beach Boys
6 Shapes Of Things - The Yardbirds
7 Backstage - Gene Pitney
8 Dedicated Follower Of Fashion - The Kinks
9 These Boots Are Made For Walkin' - Nancy Sinatra
10 Make The World Go Away - Eddy Arnold

UK Number One album: *The Sound Of Music* - Soundtrack
US Billboard Number One album: *Ballads Of The Green Berets* - Staff Sergeant Barry Sadler
US Cashbox Number One single: *The Ballad Of The Green Berets* - Staff Sergeant Barry Sadler
Also this week: Arkle wins the Cheltenham Gold Cup. (17th)

US Billboard singles for the week ending March the 19th
1 **The Ballad Of The Green Berets** - Staff Sergeant Barry Sadler
2 19th Nervous Breakdown - The Rolling Stones
3 These Boots Are Made For Walkin' - Nancy Sinatra
4 Nowhere Man - The Beatles
5 Elusive Butterfly - Bob Lind
6 Listen People - Herman's Hermits
7 California Dreamin' - The Mamas & The Papas
8 Homeward Bound - Simon And Garfunkel
9 I Fought The Law - The Bobby Fuller Four
10 Daydream - The Lovin' Spoonful

1966
UK singles chart for the week ending March the 26th
1 **The Sun Ain't Gonna Shine Anymore** - The Walker
Brothers
2 I Can't Let Go - The Hollies
3 Shapes Of Things - The Yardbirds
4 Sha La La La Lee - The Small Faces
5 Barbara Ann - The Beach Boys
6 Dedicated Follower Of Fashion - The Kinks
7 A Groovy Kind Of Love - The Mindbenders
8 Elusive Butterfly - Bob Lind
9 Backstage - Gene Pitney
10 Make The World Go Away - Eddy Arnold

UK Number One album: *The Sound Of Music* - Soundtrack
US Billboard Number One album: *Ballads Of The Green
Berets* - Staff Sergeant Barry Sadler
US Cashbox Number One single: *The Ballad Of The Green
Berets* - Staff Sergeant Barry Sadler
Also this week: Soccer's Jules Rimet Trophy vanishes. (20th)

US Billboard singles for the week ending March the 26th
1 **The Ballad Of The Green Berets** - Staff Sergeant Barry
Sadler
2 19th Nervous Breakdown - The Rolling Stones
3 Nowhere Man - The Beatles
4 These Boots Are Made For Walkin' - Nancy Sinatra
5 Homeward Bound - Simon And Garfunkel
6 Daydream - The Lovin' Spoonful
7 California Dreamin' - The Mamas & The Papas
8 Soul And Inspiration - The Righteous Brothers
9 Elusive Butterfly - Bob Lind
10 Listen People - Herman's Hermits

1966

UK singles chart for the week ending April the 2nd
1 **The Sun Ain't Gonna Shine Anymore** - The Walker Brothers
2 I Can't Let Go - The Hollies
3 Shapes Of Things - The Yardbirds
4 Dedicated Follower Of Fashion - The Kinks
5 Elusive Butterfly - Bob Lind
6 Elusive Butterfly - Val Doonican
7 Sha La La La Lee - The Small Faces
8 Make The World Go Away - Eddy Arnold
9 Barbara Ann - The Beach Boys
10 Somebody Help Me - The Spencer Davis Group

UK Number One album: *The Sound Of Music* - Soundtrack
US Billboard Number One album: *Ballads Of The Green Berets* - Staff Sergeant Barry Sadler
US Cashbox Number One single: *19th Nervous Breakdown* - The Rolling Stones
Also this week: British people vote in a general election. (31st)

US Billboard singles for the week ending April the 2nd
1 **The Ballad Of The Green Berets** - Staff Sergeant Barry Sadler
2 19th Nervous Breakdown - The Rolling Stones
3 Soul And Inspiration - The Righteous Brothers
4 Daydream - The Lovin' Spoonful
5 Homeward Bound - Simon And Garfunkel
6 Nowhere Man - The Beatles
7 California Dreamin' - The Mamas & The Papas
8 These Boots Are Made For Walkin' - Nancy Sinatra
9 Bang Bang (My Baby Shot Me Down) - Cher
10 Sure Gonna Miss Her - Gary Lewis & The Playboys

1966

UK singles chart for the week ending April the 9th

1 **The Sun Ain't Gonna Shine Anymore** - The Walker Brothers

2 Somebody Help Me - The Spencer Davis Group

3 I Can't Let Go - The Hollies

4 Dedicated Follower Of Fashion - The Kinks

5 Elusive Butterfly - Bob Lind

6 Hold Tight - Dave Dee, Dozy, Beaky, Mick, and Tich

7 Elusive Butterfly - Val Doonican

8 Shapes Of Things - The Yardbirds

9 Sound Of Silence - The Bachelors

10 Make The World Go Away - Eddy Arnold

UK Number One album: *The Sound Of Music* - Soundtrack
US Billboard Number One album: *Ballads Of The Green Berets* - Staff Sergeant Barry Sadler
US Cashbox Number One single: *Daydream* - The Lovin' Spoonful
Also this week: Sophia Loren marries Carlo Ponti. (9th)

US Billboard singles for the week ending April the 9th

1 **Soul And Inspiration** - The Righteous Brothers

2 Daydream - The Lovin' Spoonful

3 19th Nervous Breakdown - The Rolling Stones

4 Bang Bang (My Baby Shot Me Down) - Cher

5 The Ballad Of The Green Berets - Staff Sergeant Barry Sadler

6 Nowhere Man - The Beatles

7 Secret Agent Man - Johnny Rivers

8 I'm So Lonesome I Could Cry - B.J. Thomas

9 Sure Gonna Miss Her - Gary Lewis & The Playboys

10 California Dreamin' - The Mamas & The Papas

1966

  1 **Somebody Help Me** - The Spencer Davis Group
  2 The Sun Ain't Gonna Shine Anymore - The Walker Brothers
  3 Sound Of Silence - The Bachelors
  4 Hold Tight - Dave Dee, Dozy, Beaky, Mick, and Tich
  5 Substitute - The Who
  6 Elusive Butterfly - Val Doonican
  7 Elusive Butterfly - Bob Lind
  8 Make The World Go Away - Eddy Arnold
  9 Dedicated Follower Of Fashion - The Kinks
  10 You Don't Have To Say You Love Me - Dusty Springfield

UK Number One album: *The Sound Of Music* - Soundtrack
US Billboard Number One album: *Going Places* - Herb Alpert And His Tijuana Brass
US Cashbox Number One single: *Soul And Inspiration* - The Righteous Brothers
Also this week: Dean Rusk states that France is not vital to NATO. (12th)

US Billboard singles for the week ending April the 16th
  1 **Soul And Inspiration** - The Righteous Brothers
  2 Daydream - The Lovin' Spoonful
  3 Bang Bang (My Baby Shot Me Down) - Cher
  4 Secret Agent Man - Johnny Rivers
  5 Time Won't Let Me - The Outsiders
  6 19th Nervous Breakdown - The Rolling Stones
  7 The Ballad Of The Green Berets - Staff Sergeant Barry Sadler
  8 I'm So Lonesome I Could Cry - B.J. Thomas
  9 Good Lovin' - The Young Rascals
  10 Kicks - Paul Revere & The Raiders

1966

 1 **Somebody Help Me** - The Spencer Davis Group
 2 You Don't Have To Say You Love Me - Dusty Springfield
 3 Sound Of Silence - The Bachelors
 4 Hold Tight - Dave Dee, Dozy, Beaky, Mick, and Tich
 5 Elusive Butterfly - Val Doonican
 6 Bang Bang (My Baby Shot Me Down) - Cher
 7 The Sun Ain't Gonna Shine Anymore - The Walker Brothers
 8 Substitute - The Who
 9 I Put A Spell On You - Alan Price
10 The Pied Piper - Crispian St. Peters

UK Number One album: *The Sound Of Music* - Soundtrack
US Billboard Number One album: *Going Places* - Herb Alpert
And His Tijuana Brass
US Cashbox Number One single: *Soul And Inspiration* - The
Righteous Brothers
Also this week: Murder suspects Ian Brady and Myra Hindley
go on trial in London. (19th)

US Billboard singles for the week ending April the 23rd
 1 **Soul And Inspiration** - The Righteous Brothers
 2 Bang Bang (My Baby Shot Me Down) - Cher
 3 Secret Agent Man - Johnny Rivers
 4 Daydream - The Lovin' Spoonful
 5 Time Won't Let Me - The Outsiders
 6 Good Lovin' - The Young Rascals
 7 Kicks - Paul Revere & The Raiders
 8 Sloop John B - The Beach Boys
 9 I'm So Lonesome I Could Cry - B.J. Thomas
10 Monday, Monday - The Mamas & The Papas

1966

1 **You Don't Have To Say You Love Me** - Dusty Springfield
2 Pretty Flamingo - Manfred Mann
3 Somebody Help Me - The Spencer Davis Group
4 Bang Bang (My Baby Shot Me Down) - Cher
5 Hold Tight - Dave Dee, Dozy, Beaky, Mick, and Tich
6 Daydream - The Lovin' Spoonful
7 Sound Of Silence - The Bachelors
8 The Pied Piper - Crispian St. Peters
9 I Put A Spell On You - Alan Price
10 Alfie - Cilla Black

UK Number One album: *Aftermath* - The Rolling Stones
US Billboard Number One album: *Going Places* - Herb Alpert And His Tijuana Brass
US Cashbox Number One single: *Good Lovin'* - The Young Rascals
Also this week: Hoverlloyd begins its cross-Channel hovercraft service. (30th)

US Billboard singles for the week ending April the 30th

1 **Good Lovin**' - The Young Rascals
2 Soul And Inspiration - The Righteous Brothers
3 Monday, Monday - The Mamas & The Papas
4 Sloop John B - The Beach Boys
5 Secret Agent Man - Johnny Rivers
6 Kicks - Paul Revere & The Raiders
7 Time Won't Let Me - The Outsiders
8 Bang Bang (My Baby Shot Me Down) - Cher
9 Daydream - The Lovin' Spoonful
10 Leaning On The Lamp Post - Herman's Hermits

1966

1 **Pretty Flamingo** - Manfred Mann
2 Daydream - The Lovin' Spoonful
3 Bang Bang (My Baby Shot Me Down) - Cher
4 You Don't Have To Say You Love Me - Dusty Springfield
5 Sloop John B - The Beach Boys
6 The Pied Piper - Crispian St. Peters
7 Hold Tight - Dave Dee, Dozy, Beaky, Mick, and Tich
8 Sound Of Silence - The Bachelors
9 Alfie - Cilla Black
10 Homeward Bound - Simon And Garfunkel

UK Number One album: *Aftermath* - The Rolling Stones
US Billboard Number One album: *Going Places* - Herb Alpert
And His Tijuana Brass
US Cashbox Number One single: *Monday, Monday* - The
Mamas & The Papas
Also this week: The two Moors murderers, Ian Brady and Myra
Hindley, are sentenced to life imprisonment. (6th)

US Billboard singles for the week ending May the 7th

1 **Monday**, **Monday** - The Mamas & The Papas
2 Good Lovin' - The Young Rascals
3 Sloop John B - The Beach Boys
4 Soul And Inspiration - The Righteous Brothers
5 Kicks - Paul Revere & The Raiders
6 Secret Agent Man - Johnny Rivers
7 Rainy Day Women Nos. 12 & 35 - Bob Dylan
8 Bang Bang (My Baby Shot Me Down) - Cher
9 Leaning On The Lamp Post - Herman's Hermits
10 Gloria - The Shadows Of Knight

1966

UK singles chart for the week ending May the 14th
 1 **Pretty Flamingo** - Manfred Mann
 2 Daydream - The Lovin' Spoonful
 3 Sloop John B - The Beach Boys
 4 Bang Bang (My Baby Shot Me Down) - Cher
 5 The Pied Piper - Crispian St. Peters
 6 You Don't Have To Say You Love Me - Dusty Springfield
 7 Hold Tight - Dave Dee, Dozy, Beaky, Mick, and Tich
 8 Sound Of Silence - The Bachelors
 9 Homeward Bound - Simon And Garfunkel
10 Shotgun Wedding - Roy C

UK Number One album: *Aftermath* - The Rolling Stones
US Billboard Number One album: *Going Places* - Herb Alpert
And His Tijuana Brass
US Cashbox Number One single: *Monday, Monday* - The
Mamas & The Papas
Also this week: Police beat up 100 protesting priests in
Barcelona. (11th)

US Billboard singles for the week ending May the 14th
 1 **Monday**, Monday - The Mamas & The Papas
 2 Good Lovin' - The Young Rascals
 3 Rainy Day Women Nos. 12 & 35 - Bob Dylan
 4 Kicks - Paul Revere & The Raiders
 5 Sloop John B - The Beach Boys
 6 Soul And Inspiration - The Righteous Brothers
 7 How Does That Grab You, Darlin' - Nancy Sinatra
 8 Message To Michael - Dionne Warwick
 9 When A Man Loves A Woman - Percy Sledge
10 Gloria - The Shadows Of Knight

1966

UK singles chart for the week ending May the 21st
1 **Pretty Flamingo** - Manfred Mann
2 Sloop John B - The Beach Boys
3 Daydream - The Lovin' Spoonful
4 Wild Thing - The Troggs
5 Paint It Black - The Rolling Stones
6 Shotgun Wedding - Roy C
7 You Don't Have To Say You Love Me - Dusty Springfield
8 The Pied Piper - Crispian St. Peters
9 Sorrow - The Merseys
10 Rainy Day Women Nos.12 & 35 - Bob Dylan

UK Number One album: *Aftermath* - The Rolling Stones
US Billboard Number One album: *If You Can Believe Your Eyes And Ears* - The Mamas & The Papas
US Cashbox Number One single: *Monday, Monday* - The Mamas & The Papas
Also this week: 8,000 Vietnam protesters encircle the White House. (15th)

US Billboard singles for the week ending May the 21st
1 **Monday, Monday** - The Mamas & The Papas
2 Rainy Day Women Nos.12 & 35 - Bob Dylan
3 Good Lovin' - The Young Rascals
4 When A Man Loves A Woman - Percy Sledge
5 A Groovy Kind Of Love - The Mindbenders
6 Kicks - Paul Revere & The Raiders
7 How Does That Grab You, Darlin' - Nancy Sinatra
8 Message To Michael - Dionne Warwick
9 Sloop John B - The Beach Boys
10 Love Is Like An Itching In My Heart - The Supremes

1966

1 **Paint It Black** - The Rolling Stones
2 Wild Thing - The Troggs
3 Strangers In The Night - Frank Sinatra
4 Pretty Flamingo - Manfred Mann
5 Sorrow - The Merseys
6 Sloop John B - The Beach Boys
7 Shotgun Wedding - Roy C
8 Monday, Monday - The Mamas & The Papas
9 Rainy Day Women Nos.12 & 35 - Bob Dylan
10 Hey Girl - The Small Faces

UK Number One album: *Aftermath* - The Rolling Stones
US Billboard Number One album: *What Now My Love* - Herb Alpert And The Tijuana Brass
US Cashbox Number One single: *When A Man Loves A Woman* - Percy Sledge
Also this week: A British seamen's strike prompts a state of emergency. (23rd)

US Billboard singles for the week ending May the 28th

1 **When A Man Loves A Woman** - Percy Sledge
2 A Groovy Kind Of Love - The Mindbenders
3 Monday, Monday - The Mamas & The Papas
4 Paint It Black - The Rolling Stones
5 Rainy Day Women Nos.12 & 35 - Bob Dylan
6 I Am A Rock - Simon And Garfunkel
7 Did You Ever Have To Make Up Your Mind - The Lovin' Spoonful
8 Good Lovin' - The Young Rascals
9 Love Is Like An Itching In My Heart - The Supremes
10 It's A Man's Man's Man's World - James Brown

1966

1 **Strangers In The Night** - Frank Sinatra
2 Paint It Black - The Rolling Stones
3 Wild Thing - The Troggs
4 Sorrow - The Merseys
5 Monday, Monday - The Mamas & The Papas
6 Sloop John B - The Beach Boys
7 Rainy Day Women Nos.12 & 35 - Bob Dylan
8 Promises - Ken Dodd
9 When A Man Loves A Woman - Percy Sledge
10 Hey Girl - The Small Faces

UK Number One album: *Aftermath* - The Rolling Stones
US Billboard Number One album: *What Now My Love* - Herb
Alpert And The Tijuana Brass
US Cashbox Number One single: *A Groovy Kind Of Love* - The
Mindbenders
Also this week: Philips Petroleum confirms a rich North Sea
gas strike. (2nd)

US Billboard singles for the week ending June the 4th
1 **When A Man Loves A Woman** - Percy Sledge
2 A Groovy Kind Of Love - The Mindbenders
3 Paint It Black - The Rolling Stones
4 Did You Ever Have To Make Up Your Mind - The Lovin'
Spoonful
5 I Am A Rock - Simon And Garfunkel
6 Monday, Monday - The Mamas & The Papas
7 Rainy Day Women Nos.12 & 35 - Bob Dylan
8 It's A Man's Man's Man's World - James Brown
9 Green Grass - Gary Lewis & The Playboys
10 Strangers In The Night - Frank Sinatra

1966

UK singles chart for the week ending June the 11th
1 **Strangers In The Night** - Frank Sinatra
2 Paint It Black - The Rolling Stones
3 Wild Thing - The Troggs
4 Sorrow - The Merseys
5 Monday, Monday - The Mamas & The Papas
6 Promises - Ken Dodd
7 When A Man Loves A Woman - Percy Sledge
8 Don't Bring Me Down - The Animals
9 Sloop John B - The Beach Boys
10 Rainy Day Women Nos.12 & 35 - Bob Dylan

UK Number One album: *Aftermath* - The Rolling Stones
US Billboard Number One album: *What Now My Love* - Herb Alpert And The Tijuana Brass
US Cashbox Number One single: *Paint It Black* - The Rolling Stones
Also this week: The television comedy 'Till Death Us Do Part', starring Warren Mitchell, is first broadcast. (6th)

US Billboard singles for the week ending June the 11th
1 **Paint It Black** - The Rolling Stones
2 Did You Ever Have To Make Up Your Mind - The Lovin' Spoonful
3 I Am A Rock - Simon And Garfunkel
4 When A Man Loves A Woman - Percy Sledge
5 A Groovy Kind Of Love - The Mindbenders
6 Strangers In The Night - Frank Sinatra
7 Monday, Monday - The Mamas & The Papas
8 It's A Man's Man's Man's World - James Brown
9 Green Grass - Gary Lewis & The Playboys
10 Barefootin' - Robert Parker

1966

UK singles chart for the week ending June the 18th
1 **Strangers In The Night** - Frank Sinatra
2 Paperback Writer - The Beatles
3 Monday, Monday - The Mamas & The Papas
4 Sorrow - The Merseys
5 When A Man Loves A Woman - Percy Sledge
6 Paint It Black - The Rolling Stones
7 Don't Bring Me Down - The Animals
8 Promises - Ken Dodd
9 Wild Thing - The Troggs
10 Under Over Sideways Down - The Yardbirds

UK Number One album: *Aftermath* - The Rolling Stones
US Billboard Number One album: *What Now My Love* - Herb Alpert And The Tijuana Brass
US Cashbox Number One single: *Strangers In The Night* - Frank Sinatra
Also this week: Scotland's Walter McGowan becomes world boxing champion. (14th)

US Billboard singles for the week ending June the 18th
1 **Paint It Black** - The Rolling Stones
2 Did You Ever Have To Make Up Your Mind - The Lovin' Spoonful
3 I Am A Rock - Simon And Garfunkel
4 When A Man Loves A Woman - Percy Sledge
5 Strangers In The Night - Frank Sinatra
6 A Groovy Kind Of Love - The Mindbenders
7 Barefootin' - Robert Parker
8 Green Grass - Gary Lewis & The Playboys
9 Cool Jerk - The Capitols
10 Red Rubber Ball - The Cyrkle

1966

UK singles chart for the week ending June the 25th

1 **Paperback Writer** - The Beatles
2 Strangers In The Night - Frank Sinatra
3 Monday, Monday - The Mamas & The Papas
4 When A Man Loves A Woman - Percy Sledge
5 Sunny Afternoon - The Kinks
6 Don't Bring Me Down - The Animals
7 Don't Answer Me - Cilla Black
8 River Deep - Mountain High - Ike And Tina Turner
9 Sorrow - The Merseys
10 Under Over Sideways Down - The Yardbirds

UK Number One album: *The Sound Of Music* - Soundtrack
US Billboard Number One album: *What Now My Love* - Herb Alpert And The Tijuana Brass
US Cashbox Number One single: *Paperback Writer* - The Beatles
Also this week: Fugitive train robber, James White, is sentenced to eighteen years' imprisonment. (20th)

US Billboard singles for the week ending June the 25th

1 **Paperback Writer** - The Beatles
2 Strangers In The Night - Frank Sinatra
3 Paint It Black - The Rolling Stones
4 Did You Ever Have To Make Up Your Mind - The Lovin' Spoonful
5 I Am A Rock - Simon And Garfunkel
6 Red Rubber Ball - The Cyrkle
7 Barefootin' - Robert Parker
8 Cool Jerk - The Capitols
9 You Don't Have To Say You Love Me - Dusty Springfield
10 Sweet Talkin' Guy - The Chiffons

1966

 1 **Paperback Writer** - The Beatles
 2 Strangers In The Night - Frank Sinatra
 3 Sunny Afternoon - The Kinks
 4 River Deep - Mountain High - Ike And Tina Turner
 5 Nobody Needs Your Love - Gene Pitney
 6 Don't Answer Me - Cilla Black
 7 When A Man Loves A Woman - Percy Sledge
 8 Monday, Monday - The Mamas & The Papas
 9 Bus Stop - The Hollies
10 Hideaway - Dave Dee, Dozy, Beaky, Mick, and Tich

UK Number One album: *The Sound Of Music* - Soundtrack
US Billboard Number One album: *What Now My Love* - Herb
Alpert And The Tijuana Brass
US Cashbox Number One single: *Paperback Writer* - The
Beatles
Also this week: USA 'planes bomb Hanoi and Haiphong for the
first time. (30th)

US Billboard singles for the week ending July the 2nd
 1 **Strangers In The Night** - Frank Sinatra
 2 Paperback Writer - The Beatles
 3 Red Rubber Ball - The Cyrkle
 4 Paint It Black - The Rolling Stones
 5 You Don't Have To Say You Love Me - Dusty Springfield
 6 Hanky Panky - Tommy James And The Shondells
 7 Cool Jerk - The Capitols
 8 I Am A Rock - Simon And Garfunkel
 9 Did You Ever Have To Make Up Your Mind - The Lovin'
Spoonful
10 Barefootin' - Robert Parker

1966

1 **Sunny Afternoon** - The Kinks
2 Paperback Writer - The Beatles
3 River Deep - Mountain High - Ike And Tina Turner
4 Nobody Needs Your Love - Gene Pitney
5 Strangers In The Night - Frank Sinatra
6 Bus Stop - The Hollies
7 Get Away - Georgie Fame & The Blue Flames
8 Don't Answer Me - Cilla Black
9 When A Man Loves A Woman - Percy Sledge
10 Hideaway - Dave Dee, Dozy, Beaky, Mick, and Tich

UK Number One album: *The Sound Of Music* - Soundtrack
US Billboard Number One album: *What Now My Love* - Herb Alpert And The Tijuana Brass
US Cashbox Number One single: *Hanky Panky* - Tommy James And The Shondells
Also this week: Anti-Vietnam War protests occur in Grosvenor Square. (3rd)

US Billboard singles for the week ending July the 9th

1 **Paperback Writer** - The Beatles
2 Red Rubber Ball - The Cyrkle
3 Strangers In The Night - Frank Sinatra
4 Hanky Panky - Tommy James And The Shondells
5 You Don't Have To Say You Love Me - Dusty Springfield
6 Wild Thing - The Troggs
7 Cool Jerk - The Capitols
8 Little Girl - The Syndicate Of Sound
9 Paint It Black - The Rolling Stones
10 Along Comes Mary - The Association

1966

UK singles chart for the week ending July the 16th
1 **Sunny Afternoon** - The Kinks
2 Nobody Needs Your Love - Gene Pitney
3 River Deep - Mountain High - Ike And Tina Turner
4 Get Away - Georgie Fame & The Blue Flames
5 Bus Stop - The Hollies
6 Strangers In The Night - Frank Sinatra
7 Paperback Writer - The Beatles
8 I Couldn't Live Without Your Love - Petula Clark
9 Out Of Time - Chris Farlowe & The Thunderbirds
10 Hideaway - Dave Dee, Dozy, Beaky, Mick, and Tich

UK Number One album: *The Sound Of Music* - Soundtrack
US Billboard Number One album: *What Now My Love* - Herb
Alpert And The Tijuana Brass
US Cashbox Number One single: *Hanky Panky* - Tommy James
And The Shondells
Also this week: French actress Brigitte Bardot marries
Guenther Sachs. (14th)

US Billboard singles for the week ending July the 16th
1 **Hanky Panky** - Tommy James And The Shondells
2 Wild Thing - The Troggs
3 Red Rubber Ball - The Cyrkle
4 You Don't Have To Say You Love Me - Dusty Springfield
5 Paperback Writer - The Beatles
6 Strangers In The Night - Frank Sinatra
7 Along Comes Mary - The Association
8 Little Girl - The Syndicate Of Sound
9 Lil' Red Riding Hood - Sam The Sham & The Pharaohs
10 Hungry - Paul Revere & The Raiders

1966

1 **Get Away** - Georgie Fame & The Blue Flames
2 Sunny Afternoon - The Kinks
3 Out Of Time - Chris Farlowe & The Thunderbirds
4 River Deep - Mountain High - Ike And Tina Turner
5 Nobody Needs Your Love - Gene Pitney
6 Black Is Black - Los Bravos
7 I Couldn't Live Without Your Love - Petula Clark
8 Bus Stop - The Hollies
9 Love Letters - Elvis Presley
10 With A Girl Like You - The Troggs

UK Number One album: *The Sound Of Music* - Soundtrack
US Billboard Number One album: *Strangers In The Night* - Frank Sinatra
US Cashbox Number One single: *Wild Thing* - The Troggs
Also this week: Frank Sinatra marries Mia Farrow in Las Vegas. (19th)

US Billboard singles for the week ending July the 23rd
1 **Hanky Panky** - Tommy James And The Shondells
2 Wild Thing - The Troggs
3 Lil' Red Riding Hood - Sam The Sham & The Pharaohs
4 The Pied Piper - Crispian St. Peters
5 You Don't Have To Say You Love Me - Dusty Springfield
6 Paperback Writer - The Beatles
7 Hungry - Paul Revere & The Raiders
8 Red Rubber Ball - The Cyrkle
9 I Saw Her Again - The Mamas & The Papas
10 Sweet Pea - Tommy Roe

1966

  1 **Out Of Time** - Chris Farlowe & The Thunderbirds
  2 Black Is Black - Los Bravos
  3 With A Girl Like You - The Troggs
  4 Get Away - Georgie Fame & The Blue Flames
  5 Sunny Afternoon - The Kinks
  6 I Couldn't Live Without Your Love - Petula Clark
  7 The More I See You - Chris Montez
  8 Love Letters - Elvis Presley
  9 River Deep - Mountain High - Ike And Tina Turner
10 Goin' Back - Dusty Springfield

UK Number One album: *The Sound Of Music* - Soundtrack
US Billboard Number One album: *Yesterday And Today* - The Beatles
US Cashbox Number One single: *They're Coming To Take Me Away Ha-Haaa!* - Napoleon XIV
Also this week: The Trades Union Congress votes to support the Labour government's planned wage freeze. (27th)

US Billboard singles for the week ending July the 30th
  1 **Wild Thing** - The Troggs
  2 Hanky Panky - Tommy James And The Shondells
  3 Lil' Red Riding Hood - Sam The Sham & The Pharaohs
  4 The Pied Piper - Crispian St. Peters
  5 I Saw Her Again - The Mamas & The Papas
  6 Hungry - Paul Revere & The Raiders
  7 Summer In The City - The Lovin' Spoonful
  8 Sweet Pea - Tommy Roe
  9 Mothers Little Helper - The Rolling Stones
10 Somewhere, My Love - Ray Conniff

1966

 1 **With A Girl Like You** - The Troggs
 2 Out Of Time - Chris Farlowe & The Thunderbirds
 3 Black Is Black - Los Bravos
 4 The More I See You - Chris Montez
 5 Get Away - Georgie Fame & The Blue Flames
 6 Love Letters - Elvis Presley
 7 Mama - Dave Berry
 8 I Couldn't Live Without Your Love - Petula Clark
 9 Sunny Afternoon - The Kinks
10 Goin' Back - Dusty Springfield

UK Number One album: *The Sound Of Music* - Soundtrack
US Billboard Number One album: *Yesterday And Today* - The Beatles
US Cashbox Number One single: *Lil' Red Riding Hood* - Sam The Sham & The Pharaohs
Also this week: Yakubu Gowon seizes power in Nigeria. (1st)

US Billboard singles for the week ending August the 6th
 1 **Wild Thing** - The Troggs
 2 Lil' Red Riding Hood - Sam The Sham & The Pharaohs
 3 Summer In The City - The Lovin' Spoonful
 4 The Pied Piper - Crispian St. Peters
 5 They're Coming To Take Me Away Ha-Haaa! - Napoleon XIV
 6 I Saw Her Again - The Mamas & The Papas
 7 Hanky Panky - Tommy James And The Shondells
 8 Sweet Pea - Tommy Roe
 9 Mothers Little Helper - The Rolling Stones
10 Somewhere, My Love - Ray Conniff

The Troggs were enjoying a Number 1 in the UK and in the USA with 2 different songs!

1966

1 **With A Girl Like You** - The Troggs
2 Out Of Time - Chris Farlowe & The Thunderbirds
3 The More I See You - Chris Montez
4 Black Is Black - Los Bravos
5 God Only Knows - The Beach Boys
6 Mama - Dave Berry
7 Love Letters - Elvis Presley
8 Yellow Submarine/Eleanor Rigby - The Beatles
9 Summer In The City - The Lovin' Spoonful
10 I Couldn't Live Without Your Love - Petula Clark

UK Number One album: *Revolver* - The Beatles
US Billboard Number One album: *Yesterday And Today* - The Beatles
US Cashbox Number One single: *Summer In The City* - The Lovin' Spoonful
Also this week: George Brown is appointed as Labour's new Foreign Secretary. (10th)

US Billboard singles for the week ending August the 13th

1 **Summer In The City** - The Lovin' Spoonful
2 Lil' Red Riding Hood - Sam The Sham & The Pharaohs
3 They're Coming To Take Me Away Ha-Haaa! - Napoleon XIV
4 Wild Thing - The Troggs
5 The Pied Piper - Crispian St. Peters
6 I Saw Her Again - The Mamas & The Papas
7 Sunny - Bobby Hebb
8 Mothers Little Helper - The Rolling Stones
9 Somewhere, My Love - Ray Conniff
10 Sweet Pea - Tommy Roe

1966

1 **Yellow Submarine/Eleanor Rigby** - The Beatles
2 With A Girl Like You - The Troggs
3 God Only Knows - The Beach Boys
4 Black Is Black - Los Bravos
5 Mama - Dave Berry
6 The More I See You - Chris Montez
7 Visions - Cliff Richard
8 Summer In The City - The Lovin' Spoonful
9 Out Of Time - Chris Farlowe & The Thunderbirds
10 They're Coming To Take Me Away Ha-Haaa! - Napoleon
XIV

UK Number One album: *Revolver* - The Beatles
US Billboard Number One album: *Yesterday And Today* - The
Beatles
US Cashbox Number One single: *Summer In The City* - The
Lovin' Spoonful
Also this week: Orbiter I is in orbit around the moon. (14th)

US Billboard singles for the week ending August the 20th
1 **Summer In The City** - The Lovin' Spoonful
2 Sunny - Bobby Hebb
3 Lil' Red Riding Hood - Sam The Sham & The Pharaohs
4 Wild Thing - The Troggs
5 They're Coming To Take Me Away Ha-Haaa! - Napoleon
XIV
6 See You In September - The Happenings
7 The Pied Piper - Crispian St. Peters
8 Mothers Little Helper - The Rolling Stones
9 I Couldn't Live Without Your Love - Petula Clark
10 Sunshine Superman - Donovan

1966

 1 **Yellow Submarine/Eleanor Rigby** - The Beatles
 2 God Only Knows - The Beach Boys
 3 With A Girl Like You - The Troggs
 4 They're Coming To Take Me Away Ha-Haaa! - Napoleon XIV
 5 Mama - Dave Berry
 6 Black Is Black - Los Bravos
 7 Visions - Cliff Richard
 8 The More I See You - Chris Montez
 9 All Or Nothing - The Small Faces
10 Lovers Of The World - David And Jonathan

UK Number One album: *Revolver* - The Beatles
US Billboard Number One album: *Yesterday And Today* - The Beatles
US Cashbox Number One single: *Sunny* - Bobby Hebb
Also this week: Francis Chichester begins his voyage around the world. (27th)

US Billboard singles for the week ending August the 27th
 1 **Summer In The City** - The Lovin' Spoonful
 2 Sunny - Bobby Hebb
 3 See You In September - The Happenings
 4 Lil' Red Riding Hood - Sam The Sham & The Pharaohs
 5 Sunshine Superman - Donovan
 6 Wild Thing - The Troggs
 7 You Can't Hurry Love - The Supremes
 8 Yellow Submarine - The Beatles
 9 I Couldn't Live Without Your Love - Petula Clark
10 Summertime - Billy Stewart

1966

UK singles chart for the week ending September the 3rd
 1 **Yellow Submarine/Eleanor Rigby** - The Beatles
 2 God Only Knows - The Beach Boys
 3 All Or Nothing - The Small Faces
 4 They're Coming To Take Me Away Ha-Haaa! - Napoleon XIV
 5 With A Girl Like You - The Troggs
 6 Mama - Dave Berry
 7 Visions - Cliff Richard
 8 Too Soon To Know - Roy Orbison
 9 Lovers Of The World - David And Jonathan
10 Summer In The City - The Lovin' Spoonful

UK Number One album: *Revolver* - The Beatles
US Billboard Number One album: *What Now My Love* - Herb Alpert And The Tijuana Brass
US Cashbox Number One single: *Sunshine Superman* - Donovan
Also this week: China pledges more aid to North Vietnam. (30th)

US Billboard singles for the week ending September the 3rd
 1 **Sunshine Superman** - Donovan
 2 Summer In The City - The Lovin' Spoonful
 3 See You In September - The Happenings
 4 You Can't Hurry Love - The Supremes
 5 Yellow Submarine - The Beatles
 6 Sunny - Bobby Hebb
 7 Land Of 1000 Dances - Wilson Pickett
 8 Working In The Coalmine - Lee Dorsey
 9 Blowin' In The Wind - Stevie Wonder
10 Summertime - Billy Stewart

1966

UK singles chart for the week ending September the 10th
1 **Yellow Submarine/Eleanor Rigby** - The Beatles
2 All Or Nothing - The Small Faces
3 God Only Knows - The Beach Boys
4 They're Coming To Take Me Away Ha-Haaa! - Napoleon XIV
5 Too Soon To Know - Roy Orbison
6 Distant Drums - Jim Reeves
7 Lovers Of The World - David And Jonathan
8 Mama - Dave Berry
9 With A Girl Like You - The Troggs
10 Working In The Coalmine - Lee Dorsey

UK Number One album: *Revolver* - The Beatles
US Billboard Number One album: *Revolver* - The Beatles
US Cashbox Number One single: *Yellow Submarine* - The Beatles
Also this week: The musical 'Oliver!' ends its six-year West End run. (10th)

US Billboard singles for the week ending September the 10th
1 **You Can't Hurry Love** - The Supremes
2 Sunshine Superman - Donovan
3 Yellow Submarine - The Beatles
4 See You In September - The Happenings
5 Summer In The City - The Lovin' Spoonful
6 Land Of 1000 Dances - Wilson Pickett
7 Sunny - Bobby Hebb
8 Working In The Coalmine - Lee Dorsey
9 Bus Stop - The Hollies
10 Guantanamera - The Sandpipers

1966

1 **All Or Nothing** - The Small Faces
2 Distant Drums - Jim Reeves
3 Yellow Submarine/Eleanor Rigby - The Beatles
4 Too Soon To Know - Roy Orbison
5 God Only Knows - The Beach Boys
6 Got To Get You Into My Life - Cliff Bennett
7 They're Coming To Take Me Away Ha-Haaa! - Napoleon XIV
8 Working In The Coalmine - Lee Dorsey
9 Lovers Of The World - David And Jonathan
10 Just Like A Woman - Manfred Mann

UK Number One album: *Revolver* - The Beatles
US Billboard Number One album: *Revolver* - The Beatles
US Cashbox Number One single: *You Can't Hurry Love* - The Supremes
Also this week: Balthazar Vorster becomes South Africa's new Prime Minister. (13th)

US Billboard singles for the week ending September the 17th

1 **You Can't Hurry Love** - The Supremes
2 Yellow Submarine - The Beatles
3 Sunshine Superman - Donovan
4 Cherish - The Association
5 Bus Stop - The Hollies
6 See You In September - The Happenings
7 Land Of 1000 Dances - Wilson Pickett
8 Wouldn't It Be Nice - The Beach Boys
9 Guantanamera - The Sandpipers
10 Sunny - Bobby Hebb

1966

1 **Distant Drums** - Jim Reeves
2 All Or Nothing - The Small Faces
3 Too Soon To Know - Roy Orbison
4 I'm A Boy - The Who
5 Yellow Submarine/Eleanor Rigby - The Beatles
6 Little Man - Sonny And Cher
7 You Can't Hurry Love - The Supremes
8 God Only Knows - The Beach Boys
9 Got To Get You Into My Life - Cliff Bennett
10 Working In The Coalmine - Lee Dorsey

UK Number One album: *Revolver* - The Beatles
US Billboard Number One album: *Revolver* - The Beatles
US Cashbox Number One single: *Cherish* - The Association
Also this week: U Thant declines to send a UN force to
Vietnam. (18th)

US Billboard singles for the week ending September the 24th
1 **Cherish** - The Association
2 You Can't Hurry Love - The Supremes
3 Sunshine Superman - Donovan
4 Yellow Submarine - The Beatles
5 Bus Stop - The Hollies
6 Beauty Is Only Skin Deep - The Temptations
7 Black Is Black - Los Bravos
8 96 Tears - ? (Question Mark) & The Mysterians
9 Wouldn't It Be Nice - The Beach Boys
10 Reach Out, I'll Be There - The Four Tops

1966

1 **Distant Drums** - Jim Reeves
2 I'm A Boy - The Who
3 You Can't Hurry Love - The Supremes
4 Little Man - Sonny And Cher
5 Too Soon To Know - Roy Orbison
6 Bend It - Dave Dee, Dozy, Beaky, Mick, And Tich
7 Winchester Cathedral - The New Vaudeville Band
8 All Or Nothing - The Small Faces
9 Yellow Submarine/Eleanor Rigby - The Beatles
10 Walk With Me - The Seekers

UK Number One album: *The Sound Of Music* - Soundtrack
US Billboard Number One album: *Revolver* - The Beatles
US Cashbox Number One single: *Cherish* - The Association
Also this week: Twenty Argentinian nationalists invade the
Falkland Islands. (29th)

US Billboard singles for the week ending October the 1st
1 **Cherish** - The Association
2 You Can't Hurry Love - The Supremes
3 Beauty Is Only Skin Deep - The Temptations
4 Black Is Black - Los Bravos
5 Bus Stop - The Hollies
6 96 Tears - ? (Question Mark) & The Mysterians
7 Reach Out, I'll Be There - The Four Tops
8 Yellow Submarine - The Beatles
9 Sunshine Superman - Donovan
10 Cherry, Cherry - Neil Diamond

1966

  1 **Distant Drums** - Jim Reeves
  2 Bend It - Dave Dee, Dozy, Beaky, Mick, And Tich
  3 I'm A Boy - The Who
  4 You Can't Hurry Love - The Supremes
  5 Little Man - Sonny And Cher
  6 Winchester Cathedral - The New Vaudeville Band
  7 Have You Seen Your Mother, Baby Standing In The Shadow
- The   Rolling Stones
  8 Too Soon To Know - Roy Orbison
  9 All I See Is You - Dusty Springfield
10 Guantanamera - The Sandpipers

UK Number One album: *The Sound Of Music* - Soundtrack
US Billboard Number One album: *Revolver* - The Beatles
US Cashbox Number One single: *Cherish* - The Association
Also this week: General Franco bans all traffic to and from a
besieged Gibraltar. (5th)

US Billboard singles for the week ending October the 8th
  1 **Cherish** - The Association
  2 Reach Out, I'll Be There - The Four Tops
  3 96 Tears - ? (Question Mark) & The Mysterians
  4 Black Is Black - Los Bravos
  5 Beauty Is Only Skin Deep - The Temptations
  6 Last Train To Clarksville - The Monkees
  7 Cherry, Cherry - Neil Diamond
  8 You Can't Hurry Love - The Supremes
  9 Psychotic Reaction - Count Five
10 I've Got You Under My Skin - The Four Seasons

1966

UK singles chart for the week ending October the 15th
1 **Distant Drums** - Jim Reeves
2 Bend It - Dave Dee, Dozy, Beaky, Mick, And Tich
3 I'm A Boy - The Who
4 Winchester Cathedral - The New Vaudeville Band
5 Have You Seen Your Mother, Baby Standing In The Shadow
- The Rolling Stones
6 You Can't Hurry Love - The Supremes
7 Guantanamera - The Sandpipers
8 Little Man - Sonny And Cher
9 I Can't Control Myself - The Troggs
10 All I See Is You - Dusty Springfield

UK Number One album: _The Sound Of Music_ - Soundtrack
US Billboard Number One album: _Revolver_ - The Beatles
US Cashbox Number One single: _Reach Out, I'll Be There_ -
The Four Tops
Also this week: The Post Office announces the creation of
postcodes. (11th)

US Billboard singles for the week ending October the 15th
1 **Reach Out**, **I'll Be There** - The Four Tops
2 Cherish - The Association
3 96 Tears - ? (Question Mark) & The Mysterians
4 Last Train To Clarksville - The Monkees
5 Psychotic Reaction - Count Five
6 Cherry, Cherry - Neil Diamond
7 Walk Away Renee - The Left Banke
8 What Becomes Of The Brokenhearted - Jimmy Ruffin
9 I've Got You Under My Skin - The Four Seasons
10 You Can't Hurry Love - The Supremes

1966

  1 **Distant Drums** - Jim Reeves
  2 Reach Out, I'll Be There - The Four Tops
  3 Bend It - Dave Dee, Dozy, Beaky, Mick, And Tich
  4 I Can't Control Myself - The Troggs
  5 I'm A Boy - The Who
  6 Winchester Cathedral - The New Vaudeville Band
  7 Guantanamera - The Sandpipers
  8 Have You Seen Your Mother, Baby Standing In The Shadow
- The Rolling Stones
  9 You Can't Hurry Love - The Supremes
10 Stop Stop Stop - The Hollies

UK Number One album: *The Sound Of Music* - Soundtrack
US Billboard Number One album: *Supremes A' Go-Go* - The
Supremes
US Cashbox Number One single: *96 Tears* - ? (Question Mark)
& The Mysterians
Also this week: A slag heap falls on the welsh village of
Aberfan, killing 116 children in the school below. (21st)

US Billboard singles for the week ending October the 22nd
  1 **Reach Out, I'll Be There** - The Four Tops
  2 96 Tears - ? (Question Mark) & The Mysterians
  3 Last Train To Clarksville - The Monkees
  4 Cherish - The Association
  5 Psychotic Reaction - Count Five
  6 Walk Away Renee - The Left Banke
  7 Poor Side Of Town - Johnny Rivers
  8 What Becomes Of The Brokenhearted - Jimmy Ruffin
  9 Dandy - Herman's Hermits
10 See See Rider - The Animals

1966

UK singles chart for the week ending October the 29th
 1 **Reach Out**, **I'll Be There** - The Four Tops
 2 I Can't Control Myself - The Troggs
 3 Distant Drums - Jim Reeves
 4 Stop Stop Stop - The Hollies
 5 Winchester Cathedral - The New Vaudeville Band
 6 Bend It - Dave Dee, Dozy, Beaky, Mick, And Tich
 7 Guantanamera - The Sandpipers
 8 I'm A Boy - The Who
 9 No Milk Today - Herman's Hermits
10 Have You Seen Your Mother, Baby Standing In The Shadow
- The Rolling Stones

UK Number One album: *The Sound Of Music* - Soundtrack
US Billboard Number One album: *Supremes A' Go-Go* - The
Supremes
US Cashbox Number One single: *Last Train To Clarksville* -
The Monkees
Also this week: George Blake escapes from prison. (22nd)

US Billboard singles for the week ending October the 29th
 1 **96 Tears** - ? (Question Mark) & The Mysterians
 2 Last Train To Clarksville - The Monkees
 3 Reach Out, I'll Be There - The Four Tops
 4 Poor Side Of Town - Johnny Rivers
 5 Walk Away Renee - The Left Banke
 6 Dandy - Herman's Hermits
 7 What Becomes Of The Brokenhearted - Jimmy Ruffin
 8 Hooray For Hazel - Tommy Roe
 9 Have You Seen Your Mother, Baby Standing In The Shadow
- The Rolling Stones
10 See See Rider - The Animals

1966

 1 **Reach Out, I'll Be There** - The Four Tops
 2 Stop Stop Stop - The Hollies
 3 I Can't Control Myself - The Troggs
 4 Distant Drums - Jim Reeves
 5 Winchester Cathedral - The New Vaudeville Band
 6 High Time - Paul Jones
 7 No Milk Today - Herman's Hermits
 8 Guantanamera - The Sandpipers
 9 Bend It - Dave Dee, Dozy, Beaky, Mick, And Tich
10 Time Drags By - Cliff Richard

UK Number One album: *The Sound Of Music* - Soundtrack
US Billboard Number One album: *Dr. Zhivago* - Soundtrack
US Cashbox Number One single: *Last Train To Clarksville* -
The Monkees
Also this week: The Viet Cong bombards Saigon with rocket-
fired shells. (1st)

US Billboard singles for the week ending November the 5th
 1 **Last Train To Clarksville** - The Monkees
 2 96 Tears - ? (Question Mark) & The Mysterians
 3 Poor Side Of Town - Johnny Rivers
 4 Reach Out, I'll Be There - The Four Tops
 5 Dandy - Herman's Hermits
 6 Hooray For Hazel - Tommy Roe
 7 What Becomes Of The Brokenhearted - Jimmy Ruffin
 8 If I Were A Carpenter - Bobby Darin
 9 Have You Seen Your Mother, Baby Standing In The Shadow
- The Rolling Stones
10 Walk Away Renee - The Left Banke

1966

1 **Reach Out**, **I'll Be There** - The Four Tops
2 Stop Stop Stop - The Hollies
3 Semi Detached Suburban Mr James - Manfred Mann
4 High Time - Paul Jones
5 Good Vibrations - The Beach Boys
6 I Can't Control Myself - The Troggs
7 Distant Drums - Jim Reeves
8 Gimme Some Lovin' - The Spencer Davis Group
9 No Milk Today - Herman's Hermits
10 Winchester Cathedral - The New Vaudeville Band

UK Number One album: *The Sound Of Music* - Soundtrack
US Billboard Number One album: *The Monkees* - The Monkees
US Cashbox Number One single: *Poor Side Of Town* - Johnny Rivers
Also this week: Fianna Fail's Jack Lynch becomes the Republic of Ireland's new Taoiseach. (9th)

US Billboard singles for the week ending November the 12th

1 **Poor Side Of Town** - Johnny Rivers
2 Last Train To Clarksville - The Monkees
3 96 Tears - ? (Question Mark) & The Mysterians
4 Good Vibrations - The Beach Boys
5 Dandy - Herman's Hermits
6 Winchester Cathedral - The New Vaudeville Band
7 You Keep Me Hangin' On - The Supremes
8 If I Were A Carpenter - Bobby Darin
9 Devil With A Blue Dress On... - Mitch Ryder & The Detroit Wheels
10 I'm Your Puppet - James & Bobby Purify

1966

1 **Good Vibrations** - The Beach Boys
2 Semi Detached Suburban Mr James - Manfred Mann
3 Reach Out, I'll Be There - The Four Tops
4 Gimme Some Lovin' - The Spencer Davis Group
5 High Time - Paul Jones
6 Holy Cow - Lee Dorsey
7 Stop Stop Stop - The Hollies
8 I Can't Control Myself - The Troggs
9 If I Were A Carpenter - Bobby Darin
10 Green Green Grass Of Home - Tom Jones

UK Number One album: *The Sound Of Music* - Soundtrack
US Billboard Number One album: *The Monkees* - The
Monkees
US Cashbox Number One single: *Good Vibrations* - The Beach
Boys
Also this week: Gemini 12, with Buzz Aldrin on board, returns
to earth. (15th)

US Billboard singles for the week ending November the 19th

1 **You Keep Me Hangin' On** - The Supremes
2 Good Vibrations - The Beach Boys
3 Winchester Cathedral - The New Vaudeville Band
4 Last Train To Clarksville - The Monkees
5 Poor Side Of Town - Johnny Rivers
6 Devil With A Blue Dress On... - Mitch Ryder & The Detroit
Wheels
7 I'm Your Puppet - James & Bobby Purify
8 96 Tears - ? (Question Mark) & The Mysterians
9 If I Were A Carpenter - Bobby Darin
10 Rain On The Roof - The Lovin' Spoonful

1966

 1 **Good Vibrations** - The Beach Boys
 2 Gimme Some Lovin' - The Spencer Davis Group
 3 Green Green Grass Of Home - Tom Jones
 4 Reach Out, I'll Be There - The Four Tops
 5 Semi Detached Suburban Mr James - Manfred Mann
 6 High Time - Paul Jones
 7 Holy Cow - Lee Dorsey
 8 Stop Stop Stop - The Hollies
 9 What Would I Be? - Val Doonican
10 If I Were A Carpenter - Bobby Darin

UK Number One album: *The Sound Of Music* - Soundtrack
US Billboard Number One album: *The Monkees* - The Monkees
US Cashbox Number One single: *Winchester Cathedral* - The New Vaudeville Band
Also this week: It is revealed that unemployment in the UK has now exceeded 500,000. (24th)

US Billboard singles for the week ending November the 26th
 1 **You Keep Me Hangin' On** - The Supremes
 2 Good Vibrations - The Beach Boys
 3 Winchester Cathedral - The New Vaudeville Band
 4 Devil With A Blue Dress On... - Mitch Ryder & The Detroit Wheels
 5 Poor Side Of Town - Johnny Rivers
 6 I'm Your Puppet - James & Bobby Purify
 7 Last Train To Clarksville - The Monkees
 8 Lady Godiva - Peter & Gordon
 9 Mellow Yellow - Donovan
10 Born Free - Roger Williams

1966

 1 **Green Green Grass Of Home** - Tom Jones
 2 Good Vibrations - The Beach Boys
 3 Gimme Some Lovin' - The Spencer Davis Group
 4 What Would I Be? - Val Doonican
 5 Semi Detached Suburban Mr James - Manfred Mann
 6 Holy Cow - Lee Dorsey
 7 Reach Out, I'll Be There - The Four Tops
 8 My Mind's Eye - The Small Faces
 9 Just One Smile - Gene Pitney
10 High Time - Paul Jones

UK Number One album: *The Sound Of Music* - Soundtrack
US Billboard Number One album: *The Monkees* - The Monkees
US Cashbox Number One single: *You Keep Me Hangin' On* - The Supremes
Also this week: Harold Wilson meets Rhodesian Prime Minister Ian Smith for crisis talks aboard HMS Tiger. (2nd)

US Billboard singles for the week ending December the 3rd

 1 **Winchester Cathedral** - The New Vaudeville Band
 2 Good Vibrations - The Beach Boys
 3 You Keep Me Hangin' On - The Supremes
 4 Devil With A Blue Dress On... - Mitch Ryder & The Detroit Wheels
 5 Mellow Yellow - Donovan
 6 I'm Your Puppet - James & Bobby Purify
 7 Lady Godiva - Peter & Gordon
 8 Born Free - Roger Williams
 9 Poor Side Of Town - Johnny Rivers
10 Last Train To Clarksville - The Monkees

1966

1 **Green Green Grass Of Home** - Tom Jones
2 Good Vibrations - The Beach Boys
3 What Would I Be? - Val Doonican
4 My Mind's Eye - The Small Faces
5 Gimme Some Lovin' - The Spencer Davis Group
6 Morningtown Ride - The Seekers
7 Semi Detached Suburban Mr James - Manfred Mann
8 Just One Smile - Gene Pitney
9 Friday On My Mind - The Easybeats
10 Holy Cow - Lee Dorsey

UK Number One album: *The Sound Of Music* - Soundtrack
US Billboard Number One album: *The Monkees* - The Monkees
US Cashbox Number One single: *Winchester Cathedral* - The New Vaudeville Band
Also this week: Ian Smith's cabinet rejects Britain's latest proposals. (6th)

US Billboard singles for the week ending December the 10th
1 **Good Vibrations** - The Beach Boys
2 Mellow Yellow - Donovan
3 Winchester Cathedral - The New Vaudeville Band
4 Devil With A Blue Dress On... - Mitch Ryder & The Detroit Wheels
5 You Keep Me Hangin' On - The Supremes
6 Lady Godiva - Peter & Gordon
7 Stop Stop Stop - The Hollies
8 Born Free - Roger Williams
9 I'm Ready For Love - Martha & The Vandellas
10 That's Life - Frank Sinatra

1966

 1 **Green Green Grass Of Home** - Tom Jones
 2 What Would I Be? - Val Doonican
 3 Morningtown Ride - The Seekers
 4 My Mind's Eye - The Small Faces
 5 Good Vibrations - The Beach Boys
 6 Friday On My Mind - The Easybeats
 7 Dead End Street - The Kinks
 8 Gimme Some Lovin' - The Spencer Davis Group
 9 You Keep Me Hangin' On - The Supremes
10 What Becomes Of The Brokenhearted - Jimmy Ruffin

UK Number One album: *The Sound Of Music* - Soundtrack
US Billboard Number One album: *The Monkees* - The Monkees
US Cashbox Number One single: *Winchester Cathedral* - The New Vaudeville Band
Also this week: The United Nations urges a worldwide oil embargo on Rhodesia. (16th)

US Billboard singles for the week ending December the 17th
 1 **Winchester Cathedral** - The New Vaudeville Band
 2 Mellow Yellow - Donovan
 3 Good Vibrations - The Beach Boys
 4 Devil With A Blue Dress On... - Mitch Ryder & The Detroit Wheels
 5 You Keep Me Hangin' On - The Supremes
 6 That's Life - Frank Sinatra
 7 Born Free - Roger Williams
 8 I'm A Believer - The Monkees
 9 Sugar Town - Nancy Sinatra
10 A Place In The Sun - Stevie Wonder

1966

1 **Green Green Grass Of Home** - Tom Jones
2 Morningtown Ride - The Seekers
3 What Would I Be? - Val Doonican
4 Sunshine Superman - Donovan
5 Dead End Street - The Kinks
6 Save Me - Dave Dee, Dozy, Beaky, Mick, And Tich
7 Friday On My Mind - The Easybeats
8 You Keep Me Hangin' On - The Supremes
9 Good Vibrations - The Beach Boys
10 My Mind's Eye - The Small Faces

UK Number One album: *The Sound Of Music* - Soundtrack
US Billboard Number One album: *The Monkees* - The Monkees
US Cashbox Number One single: *I'm A Believer* - The Monkees
Also this week: Rhodesia leaves the Commonwealth. (22nd)

US Billboard singles for the week ending December the 24th
1 **Winchester Cathedral** - The New Vaudeville Band
2 Mellow Yellow - Donovan
3 I'm A Believer - The Monkees
4 That's Life - Frank Sinatra
5 Devil With A Blue Dress On... - Mitch Ryder & The Detroit Wheels
6 Sugar Town - Nancy Sinatra
7 Snoopy Vs. The Red Baron - The Royal Guardsmen
8 Good Vibrations - The Beach Boys
9 A Place In The Sun - Stevie Wonder
10 (I Know) I'm Losing You - The Temptations

This was the only year between 1963 and 1967, the Beatles didn't obtain a Christmas No.1.

1966

1 **Green Green Grass Of Home** - Tom Jones
2 Sunshine Superman - Donovan
3 Save Me - Dave Dee, Dozy, Beaky, Mick, And Tich
4 Morningtown Ride - The Seekers
5 Dead End Street - The Kinks
6 What Would I Be? - Val Doonican
7 Friday On My Mind - The Easybeats
8 What Becomes Of The Brokenhearted - Jimmy Ruffin
9 If Every Day Was Like Christmas - Elvis Presley
10 You Keep Me Hangin' On - The Supremes

UK Number One album: *The Sound Of Music* - Soundtrack
US Billboard Number One album: *The Monkees* - The Monkees
US Cashbox Number One single: *I'm A Believer* - The Monkees
Also this week: Australia defeat India in tennis's Davis Cup final. (28th)

US Billboard singles for the week ending December the 31st
1 **I'm A Believer** - The Monkees
2 Snoopy Vs. The Red Baron - The Royal Guardsmen
3 Winchester Cathedral - The New Vaudeville Band
4 That's Life - Frank Sinatra
5 Sugar Town - Nancy Sinatra
6 Mellow Yellow - Donovan
7 Tell It Like It Is - Aaron Neville
8 (I Know) I'm Losing You - The Temptations
9 A Place In The Sun - Stevie Wonder
10 Good Thing - Paul Revere & The Raiders

THE BEST 10 SONGS OF 1966?

Dedicated Follower Of Fashion by The Kinks

Ray Davies emerged as one of the most respected songwriters of his generation as his compositions were an observation of the state of the UK, from the down-at-heel 'Dead End Street' to the nouveau riche lamenting a 'Sunny Afternoon'. Then of course there was this satirical swipe at the dandies and fashionistas who were making pilgrimage to London's Carnaby Street. Like many of their contemporaries, the Kinks were travelling away from frantic origins towards something more thoughtful.

Distant Drums by Jim Reeves

Once upon a time, air travel was the tragic undoing of many a talented globetrotter. Jim Reeves succumbed to an early grave, courtesy of an aeroplane crash on July the 31st 1964. His wife still ensured that Jim's esteemed repertoire would continue to surface beyond his untimely demise. 'Distant Drums' was his most successful posthumous smash hit, as it conquered the UK singles chart in the late summer of 1966.

Gimme Some Lovin' by The Spencer Davis Group

The teenage Stevie Winwood raised the roof with an engaging up-tempo number which stands favourable comparison with any dance song that emanated from the swinging 'sixties. This track was notable for its intro and the fabulous organ sound. Remarkably, it failed narrowly to reach the UK singles summit, though it perhaps was more deserving of this lofty position than the group's two recent chart-toppers, 'Keep On Running' and 'Somebody Help Me'.

Go Where You Wanna Go by The Mamas And The Papas

Vocal harmonies rarely sounded better than they did when this mixed gender quartet combined so well in the recording studio. Whilst Michelle was sacked and then re-instated on account of her infidelity, the group still thrived in spite of the disharmony. Along with the hit single 'I Saw Her Again', this album track was amongst the very best pop songs of 1966.

Last Train To Clarksville by The Monkees

After the Beatles had conquered the United States with both their breezy pop music and their cheeky charm, imitators were sought. In the event, four Beatles clones were found in the guise of the Monkees. Critics may have scoffed at their lack of musical prowess and the fact that they had to rely on other songwriters, nevertheless this new fab four thrilled their teenage followers with such catchy tunes as the guitar-decorated 'Last Train To Clarksville'. Here began the latest stars.

THE BEST 10 SONGS OF 1966? (continued)

Rainy Day Women Nos. 12 & 35 by Bob Dylan

Many Dylan aficionados take his music a bit too seriously, which is surprising, given that the great man was himself prone to a bit of humour. The album opener for the excellent 'Blonde On Blonde' project was one such case, in which Mr Zimmerman suggests "everybody must get stoned." What, like the early Christian martyr Stephen? No, not exactly, one can safely deduce that this was a call to indulge in some marijuana. This likeable, but rather oddball tune narrowly fell short of the US pop summit.

Reach Out, I'll Be There by The Four Tops

Nobody can put a date on the origin of disco music, but I would venture that this fine product from Tamla Motown is one of the pioneering dance-floor classics of the 1960s. The Four Tops were one of the great North American singing groups of their era, alongside the Miracles and the Temptations. This danceable delight is undoubtedly the highlight of their career.

When A Man Loves A Woman by Percy Sledge

This release hit the top of the Billboard Hot 100, whilst in the UK, it journeyed into the Top 10 in 1966 and again in 1987 when another retro item, Ben E King's 'Stand By Me' kept it away from the Number One spot. Sledge's singing is a wonder, assisted by good contributions from the organ and the backing vocalists. Regrettably, he failed to build upon this triumph.

Wild Thing by The Troggs

The Troggs not surprisingly found favour on both sides of the Atlantic with this tune which was something of a rock and pop crossover hit. There may have been only one Elvis, but there were two Presleys, including the group's lead singer Reg. Jimi Hendrix was sufficiently impressed to cover this song at the Monterey Pop Festival just prior to setting fire to his guitar. The Troggs had a few big hits, including 'Love Is All Around' in the USA in 1968, though song-writing royalties from that record weren't boosted until it was successfully covered in 1994 by Wet Wet Wet.

Wrapping Paper by Cream

They were well-named because the power trio of Ginger Baker, Jack Bruce, and Eric Clapton were the cream of the British blues scene. Their first single, 'Wrapping Paper', is by no means their best recording, but it is rather quaint and considerably better than Baker has suggested. The drummer scathingly regarded it as the worst song he had heard in his entire life, which may be attributed to his concern that it was the start of the Jack Bruce-Pete Brown song-writing axis.

THE BEST ALBUM OF 1966?
Pet Sounds
by The Beach Boys
peaked in the UK charts at No.2
peaked in the US charts at No.10
produced by Brian Wilson
released in May

Beach Boy chief composer Brian Wilson and Paul
McCartney were not only born two days apart in 1942, but they
were a mutual appreciation society. Wilson cites the Beatles'
ground-breaking 'Rubber Soul' (born in December 1965) as a
huge influence upon the development of 'Pet Sounds'.
McCartney, by the same token, attributes 'Pet Sounds' as
equally important upon the recording of Sergeant Pepper.
Wilson, it has to be remembered, was in the contradictory
position of being within a group but at the same time he had to
go it alone in terms of finding material that would challenge
the British invasion of 1964 and 1965. This was a large burden
for the fragile Wilson to shoulder but for a couple of years
anyway, he was more than equal to the task at providing
America's belated response to the Beatles, Stones, and Kinks,
amongst others. In the event, Wilson took the risky step of
forsaking the Beach Boys' tried and trusted formula of surfing
songs and pop songs about cars which largely appealed to an
alpha male psyche. Instead, he hired the finest session
musicians and a lyricist called Tony Asher and decided to build
a cycle of songs which effectively amounted to a teenage soap
opera, exploring emotions such as hope and despair which all
adolescents could relate to. Whilst the boys were on the road,
Wilson retreated to the safe haven of his home (and eventually

THE BEST ALBUM OF 1966? (continued)

his bedroom) and in the mean time knocked out a dozen tracks which took the rest of the group by surprise when they returned from touring. Reception was generally favourable though a nonplussed Mike Love (Wilson's erstwhile co-writer) urged Wilson to jettison this 'ego music' and stick to the winning formula. Wilson was not to be deterred, even if Capitol Records also raised their eyebrows at an album that in their commercial minds strayed too far away from mass appeal. With Capitol Records not providing the marketing muscle that Wilson had hoped for and indeed undermining the album's sales potential by hastening to issue a Best Of compilation which deflected attention and sales away, 'Pet Sounds' found a more sympathetic audience in the UK, no doubt helped by lavish praise from media mouthpiece Andrew Loog Oldham and PR guru Derek Taylor who each pushed the line that Brian was a genius and that 'Pet Sounds' was the greatest album imaginable. Buoyed by this partial success, Wilson scaled new heights with 'Good Vibrations' but then got dizzy in more ways than one as his 'Smile' project threatened to achieve world domination, only for an increasingly unhinged Wilson to pull the plug on that remarkable enterprise. 'Pet Sounds' features beautiful harmonies from the boys, beautiful strings and musicianship, but it was effectively a Brian Wilson solo album and showcased his own production expertise. It still sits deservedly in lofty positions in 'Greatest Album Ever' polls.

The album's best song? - *Don't Talk (Put Your Head On My Shoulder)*

SPORT IN 1966

English Division One soccer champions: Liverpool
English FA Cup final: Everton 3 Sheffield Wednesday 2
English League Cup winners: West Bromwich Albion
Scottish Division One soccer champions: Glasgow Celtic
Scottish FA Cup final: Glasgow Rangers 1 Glasgow Celtic 0
Scottish League Cup winners: Glasgow Celtic
Irish League soccer champions: Linfield; Irish Cup winners:
Glentoran
League Of Ireland soccer champions: Waterford; cup winners:
Shamrock Rovers
European Cup final: Real Madrid 2 Partizan Belgrade 1
European Cup-Winners' Cup final: Borussia Dortmund 2
Liverpool 1
European Fairs' Cup final: Barcelona beat Real Zaragoza 4-3
on aggregate
English county cricket champions: Yorkshire
Five Nations' rugby union champions: Wales
Formula One world drivers' champion: Jack Brabham
Gaelic football All-Ireland champions: Galway; hurling
champions: Cork
British Open golf champion: Jack Nicklaus
US Masters golf champion: Jack Nicklaus
US Open golf champion: Billy Casper Junior
USPGA golf champion: Al Geiberger
Rugby league Challenge Cup final: St Helens 21 Wigan 2
Wimbledon men's singles tennis champion: Manuel Santana
Wimbledon ladies' singles tennis champion: Billie Jean King
The Aintree Grand National steeplechase winner: Anglo
The Epsom Derby winner:Charlottown
World Cup soccer final: England 4 West Germany 2

DEATHS IN 1966

January 1st: Vincent Auriol (ex-French President), aged 81
January 11th: Lal Bahadur Shastri (Indian Prime Minister), aged 61
January 11th: Alberto Giacometti (Swiss sculptor), aged 64
January 16th: Sir Abubakar Tafawa Balewa (Nigerian Prime Minister), aged 53
February 1st: Buster Keaton (US actor), aged 70
February 20th: Admiral Chester William Nimitz (US commander), aged 81
April 2nd: Cecil Scott Forester (British author), aged 66
April 10th: Evelyn Arthur St.John Waugh (British author), aged 62
May 17th: Randolph Turpin (British boxer), aged 37
July 23rd: Montgomery Clift (US actor), aged 45
August 3rd: Lenny Bruce (US comedian), aged 39
September 6th: Dr Hendrik Frensch Verwoerd (South African statesman), aged 64
September 6th: Margaret Sanger (US birth control pioneer), aged 82
September 25th: William George 'Billy' Smart (British circus owner), aged 73
September 28th: Andre Breton (French poet), aged 70
October 18th: Elizabeth Arden (French cosmetics expert), aged 81
October 22nd: Dr Hewlett Johnson (British churchman), aged 92
December 15th: Walt Disney (US animator), aged 65

COMMERCIAL BREAK:
A Concise Guide To Eighties' Music
by Karl Vorderman

This fact-filled well of information features songs from such acts as Madonna, The Smiths, Michael Jackson, UB40, Madness, The Pet Shop Boys, Queen, The Specials, George Michael, David Bowie, Debbie Harry, Duran Duran, The Housemartins, Cyndi Lauper, Bob Marley and The Wailers, New Order, The Pogues, The Pretenders, Public Image Limited, Roxy Music, The Stone Roses, The Stranglers, Paul Young, and lots more! You can order a copy online or in-store for £9.99.

1967

1 **Green Green Grass Of Home** - Tom Jones
2 Morningtown Ride - The Seekers
3 Sunshine Superman - Donovan
4 Save Me - Dave Dee, Dozy, Beaky, Mick, And Tich
5 Happy Jack - The Who
6 Dead End Street - The Kinks
7 What Would I Be? - Val Doonican
8 You Keep Me Hangin' On - The Supremes
9 In The Country - Cliff Richard And The Shadows
10 My Mind's Eye - The Small Faces

UK Number One album: *The Sound Of Music* - Soundtrack
US Billboard Number One album: *The Monkees* - The Monkees
US Cashbox Number One single: *I'm A Believer* - The Monkees
Also this week: Ronald Reagan, the former movie actor, is sworn in as the new Governor of California. (1st)

US Billboard singles for the week ending January the 7th

1 **I'm A Believer** - The Monkees
2 Snoopy Vs. The Red Baron - The Royal Guardsmen
3 Tell It Like It Is - Aaron Neville
4 Winchester Cathedral - The New Vaudeville Band
5 Sugar Town - Nancy Sinatra
6 That's Life - Frank Sinatra
7 Good Thing - Paul Revere & The Raiders
8 Words Of Love - The Mamas & The Papas
9 Standing In The Shadows Of Love - The Four Tops
10 Mellow Yellow - Donovan

1967

UK singles chart for the week ending January the 14th
1 **Green Green Grass Of Home** - Tom Jones
2 Morningtown Ride - The Seekers
3 Sunshine Superman - Donovan
4 I'm A Believer - The Monkees
5 Save Me - Dave Dee, Dozy, Beaky, Mick, And Tich
6 Happy Jack - The Who
7 In The Country - Cliff Richard And The Shadows
8 Anyway That You Want Me - The Troggs
9 Dead End Street - The Kinks
10 What Would I Be? - Val Doonican

UK Number One album: *The Sound Of Music* - Soundtrack
US Billboard Number One album: *The Monkees* - The Monkees
US Cashbox Number One single: *I'm A Believer* - The Monkees
Also this week: William Rees-Mogg becomes Editor of The Times. (12th)

US Billboard singles for the week ending January the 14th
1 **I'm A Believer** - The Monkees
2 Snoopy Vs. The Red Baron - The Royal Guardsmen
3 Tell It Like It Is - Aaron Neville
4 Good Thing - Paul Revere & The Raiders
5 Sugar Town - Nancy Sinatra
6 Words Of Love - The Mamas & The Papas
7 Standing In The Shadows Of Love - The Four Tops
8 Winchester Cathedral - The New Vaudeville Band
9 That's Life - Frank Sinatra
10 Georgy Girl - The Seekers

1967

 1 **I'm A Believer** - The Monkees
 2 Green Green Grass Of Home - Tom Jones
 3 Happy Jack - The Who
 4 Morningtown Ride - The Seekers
 5 Sunshine Superman - Donovan
 6 In The Country - Cliff Richard And The Shadows
 7 Night Of Fear - The Move
 8 Save Me - Dave Dee, Dozy, Beaky, Mick, And Tich
 9 Anyway That You Want Me - The Troggs
10 Standing In The Shadows Of Love - The Four Tops

UK Number One album: *The Sound Of Music* - Soundtrack
US Billboard Number One album: *The Monkees* - The Monkees
US Cashbox Number One single: *I'm A Believer* - The Monkees
Also this week: An old Etonian, Jeremy Thorpe, is elected leader of the Liberal Party, replacing Jo Grimond. (18th)

US Billboard singles for the week ending January the 21st
 1 **I'm A Believer** - The Monkees
 2 Snoopy Vs. The Red Baron - The Royal Guardsmen
 3 Tell It Like It Is - Aaron Neville
 4 Good Thing - Paul Revere & The Raiders
 5 Words Of Love - The Mamas & The Papas
 6 Standing In The Shadows Of Love - The Four Tops
 7 Georgy Girl - The Seekers
 8 Sugar Town - Nancy Sinatra
 9 Nashville Cats - The Lovin' Spoonful
10 Tell It To The Rain - The Four Seasons

1967

1 **I'm A Believer** - The Monkees
2 Night Of Fear - The Move
3 Matthew And Son - Cat Stevens
4 Green Green Grass Of Home - Tom Jones
5 Happy Jack - The Who
6 Standing In The Shadows Of Love - The Four Tops
7 Let's Spend The Night Together/Ruby Tuesday - The Rolling Stones
8 Morningtown Ride - The Seekers
9 Hey Joe - The Jimi Hendrix Experience
10 In The Country - Cliff Richard And The Shadows

UK Number One album: *The Sound Of Music* - Soundtrack
US Billboard Number One album: *The Monkees* - The Monkees
US Cashbox Number One single: *I'm A Believer* - The Monkees
Also this week: Three US astronauts die during a launchpad rehearsal. (28th)

US Billboard singles for the week ending January the 28th
1 **I'm A Believer** - The Monkees
2 Tell It Like It Is - Aaron Neville
3 Snoopy Vs. The Red Baron - The Royal Guardsmen
4 Georgy Girl - The Seekers
5 Words Of Love - The Mamas & The Papas
6 Standing In The Shadows Of Love - The Four Tops
7 Good Thing - Paul Revere & The Raiders
8 Nashville Cats - The Lovin' Spoonful
9 Kind Of A Drag - The Buckinghams
10 (We Ain't Got) Nothin' Yet - The Blues Magoos

1967

  1 **I'm A Believer** - The Monkees
  2 Matthew And Son - Cat Stevens
  3 Night Of Fear - The Move
  4 Let's Spend The Night Together/Ruby Tuesday - The Rolling
Stones
  5 Green Green Grass Of Home - Tom Jones
  6 Hey Joe - The Jimi Hendrix Experience
  7 I've Been A Bad Bad Boy - Paul Jones
  8 Standing In The Shadows Of Love - The Four Tops
  9 Happy Jack - The Who
10 Morningtown Ride - The Seekers

UK Number One album: *The Monkees* - The Monkees
US Billboard Number One album: *The Monkees* - The
Monkees
US Cashbox Number One single: *I'm A Believer* - The
Monkees
Also this week: A porter dies during student unrest at the
London School of Economics. (31st)

US Billboard singles for the week ending February the 4th
  1 **I'm A Believer** - The Monkees
  2 Georgy Girl - The Seekers
  3 Snoopy Vs. The Red Baron - The Royal Guardsmen
  4 Tell It Like It Is - Aaron Neville
  5 Kind Of A Drag - The Buckinghams
  6 Words Of Love - The Mamas & The Papas
  7 (We Ain't Got) Nothin' Yet - The Blues Magoos
  8 98.6 - Keith
  9 Good Thing - Paul Revere & The Raiders
10 Standing In The Shadows Of Love - The Four Tops

1967

1 **I'm A Believer** - The Monkees
2 Matthew And Son - Cat Stevens
3 Let's Spend The Night Together/Ruby Tuesday - The Rolling Stones
4 Night Of Fear - The Move
5 I've Been A Bad Bad Boy - Paul Jones
6 Hey Joe - The Jimi Hendrix Experience
7 Green Green Grass Of Home - Tom Jones
8 This Is My Song - Petula Clark
9 I'm A Man - The Spencer Davis Group
10 Sugar Town - Nancy Sinatra

UK Number One album: *The Monkees* - The Monkees
US Billboard Number One album: *More Of The Monkees* - The Monkees
US Cashbox Number One single: *I'm A Believer* - The Monkees
Also this week: David Frost confronts insurance fraudster Dr Emil Savundra on television. (5th)

US Billboard singles for the week ending February the 11th

1 **I'm A Believer** - The Monkees
2 Georgy Girl - The Seekers
3 Kind Of A Drag - The Buckinghams
4 Ruby Tuesday - The Rolling Stones
5 (We Ain't Got) Nothin' Yet - The Blues Magoos
6 Tell It Like It Is - Aaron Neville
7 98.6 - Keith
8 Snoopy Vs. The Red Baron - The Royal Guardsmen
9 Love Is Here And Now You're Gone - The Supremes
10 The Beat Goes On - Sonny & Cher

1967

UK singles chart for the week ending February the 18th

 1 **This Is My Song** - Petula Clark
 2 I'm A Believer - The Monkees
 3 Let's Spend The Night Together/Ruby Tuesday - The Rolling Stones
 4 Release Me (And Let Me Love Again) - Engelbert Humperdinck
 5 Matthew And Son - Cat Stevens
 6 I've Been A Bad Bad Boy - Paul Jones
 7 Night Of Fear - The Move
 8 Sugar Town - Nancy Sinatra
 9 Snoopy Vs. The Red Baron - The Royal Guardsmen
10 Here Comes My Baby - The Tremeloes

UK Number One album: *The Monkees* - The Monkees
US Billboard Number One album: *More Of The Monkees* - The Monkees
US Cashbox Number One single: *Georgy Girl* - The Seekers
Also this week: A drugs' raid occurs at Keith Richard's Sussex home. Jagger and Richard are both arrested and charged. (12th)

US Billboard singles for the week ending February the 18th

 1 **Kind Of A Drag** - The Buckinghams
 2 I'm A Believer - The Monkees
 3 Ruby Tuesday - The Rolling Stones
 4 Georgy Girl - The Seekers
 5 (We Ain't Got) Nothin' Yet - The Blues Magoos
 6 Love Is Here And Now You're Gone - The Supremes
 7 98.6 - Keith
 8 Tell It Like It Is - Aaron Neville
 9 The Beat Goes On - Sonny & Cher
10 Gimme Some Lovin' - The Spencer Davis Group

1967

  1 **This Is My Song** - Petula Clark
  2 Release Me (And Let Me Love Again) - Engelbert Humperdinck
  3 I'm A Believer - The Monkees
  4 Here Comes My Baby - The Tremeloes
  5 Penny Lane/Strawberry Fields Forever - The Beatles
  6 Let's Spend The Night Together/Ruby Tuesday - The Rolling Stones
  7 Peek-A-Boo - The New Vaudeville Band
  8 Snoopy Vs. The Red Baron - The Royal Guardsmen
  9 Matthew And Son - Cat Stevens
10 Mellow Yellow - Donovan

UK Number One album: *The Monkees* - The Monkees
US Billboard Number One album: *More Of The Monkees* - The Monkees
US Cashbox Number One single: *Ruby Tuesday* - The Rolling Stones
Also this week: Police recapture the 'Boston Strangler'. (25th)

US Billboard singles for the week ending February the 25th
  1 **Kind Of A Drag** - The Buckinghams
  2 Love Is Here And Now You're Gone - The Supremes
  3 Ruby Tuesday - The Rolling Stones
  4 I'm A Believer - The Monkees
  5 Georgy Girl - The Seekers
  6 The Beat Goes On - Sonny & Cher
  7 Gimme Some Lovin' - The Spencer Davis Group
  8 Then You Can Tell Me Goodbye - The Casinos
  9 (We Ain't Got) Nothin' Yet - The Blues Magoos
10 Baby I Need Your Lovin' - Johnny Rivers

1967

1 **Release Me** (**And Let Me Love Again**) - Engelbert Humperdinck
2 Penny Lane/Strawberry Fields Forever - The Beatles
3 This Is My Song - Petula Clark
4 Here Comes My Baby - The Tremeloes
5 I'm A Believer - The Monkees
6 Edelweiss - Vince Hill
7 On A Carousel - The Hollies
8 Mellow Yellow - Donovan
9 Peek-A-Boo - The New Vaudeville Band
10 Snoopy Vs. The Red Baron - The Royal Guardsmen

UK Number One album: *The Monkees* - The Monkees
US Billboard Number One album: *More Of The Monkees* - The Monkees
US Cashbox Number One single: *Love Is Here And Now You're Gone* - The Supremes
Also this week: British troops shoot at rioters in Aden. (1st)

US Billboard singles for the week ending March the 4th
1 **Ruby Tuesday** - The Rolling Stones
2 Love Is Here And Now You're Gone - The Supremes
3 Kind Of A Drag - The Buckinghams
4 Baby I Need Your Lovin' - Johnny Rivers
5 Georgy Girl - The Seekers
6 The Beat Goes On - Sonny & Cher
7 Gimme Some Lovin' - The Spencer Davis Group
8 Then You Can Tell Me Goodbye - The Casinos
9 Sock It To Me - Baby! - Mitch Ryder & The Detroit Wheels
10 I'm A Believer - The Monkees

Engelbert Humperdinck ended a sequence of eleven UK Number Ones for the Beatles!

1967

UK singles chart for the week ending March the 11th

1 **Release Me (And Let Me Love Again)** - Engelbert Humperdinck
2 Penny Lane/Strawberry Fields Forever - The Beatles
3 This Is My Song - Petula Clark
4 Edelweiss - Vince Hill
5 On A Carousel - The Hollies
6 Here Comes My Baby - The Tremeloes
7 I'm A Believer - The Monkees
8 There's A Kind Of Hush - Herman's Hermits
9 Mellow Yellow - Donovan
10 Snoopy Vs. The Red Baron - The Royal Guardsmen

UK Number One album: *The Monkees* - The Monkees
US Billboard Number One album: *More Of The Monkees* - The Monkees
US Cashbox Number One single: *Ruby Tuesday* - The Rolling Stones
Also this week: Stalin's daughter, Svetlana, defects to the West. (9th)

US Billboard singles for the week ending March the 11th

1 **Love Is Here And Now You're Gone** - The Supremes
2 Ruby Tuesday - The Rolling Stones
3 Baby I Need Your Lovin' - Johnny Rivers
4 Kind Of A Drag - The Buckinghams
5 Penny Lane - The Beatles
6 Then You Can Tell Me Goodbye - The Casinos
7 Sock It To Me - Baby! - Mitch Ryder & The Detroit Wheels
8 Happy Together - The Turtles
9 My Cup Runneth Over - Ed Ames
10 Dedicated To The One I Love - The Mamas & The Papas

1967

1 **Release Me (And Let Me Love Again)** - Engelbert Humperdinck
2 Penny Lane/Strawberry Fields Forever - The Beatles
3 This Is My Song - Petula Clark
4 On A Carousel - The Hollies
5 Edelweiss - Vince Hill
6 Georgy Girl - The Seekers
7 There's A Kind Of Hush - Herman's Hermits
8 Detroit City - Tom Jones
9 Here Comes My Baby - The Tremeloes
10 Snoopy Vs. The Red Baron - The Royal Guardsmen

UK Number One album: *The Monkees* - The Monkees
US Billboard Number One album: *More Of The Monkees* - The Monkees
US Cashbox Number One single: *Penny Lane* - The Beatles
Also this week: London School of Economics students stage an all-night sit-in protest. (13th)

US Billboard singles for the week ending March the 18th
1 **Penny Lane** - The Beatles
2 Happy Together - The Turtles
3 Baby I Need Your Lovin' - Johnny Rivers
4 Love Is Here And Now You're Gone - The Supremes
5 Ruby Tuesday - The Rolling Stones
6 Dedicated To The One I Love - The Mamas & The Papas
7 Sock It To Me - Baby! - Mitch Ryder & The Detroit Wheels
8 There's A Kind Of Hush - Herman's Hermits
9 My Cup Runneth Over - Ed Ames
10 Then You Can Tell Me Goodbye - The Casinos

1967

1 **Release Me** (**And Let Me Love Again**) - Engelbert Humperdinck
2 Edelweiss - Vince Hill
3 Georgy Girl - The Seekers
4 This Is My Song - Petula Clark
5 Penny Lane/Strawberry Fields Forever - The Beatles
6 Simon Smith And The Dancing Bear - The Alan Price Set
7 On A Carousel - The Hollies
8 I Was Kaiser Bill's Batman - Whistling Jack Smith
9 This Is My Song - Harry Secombe
10 There's A Kind Of Hush - Herman's Hermits

UK Number One album: *The Sound Of Music* - Soundtrack
US Billboard Number One album: *More Of The Monkees* - The Monkees
US Cashbox Number One single: *Penny Lane* - The Beatles
Also this week: An oil tanker, the Torrey Canyon, runs aground off the coast of Cornwall, spilling much oil. (19th)

US Billboard singles for the week ending March the 25th

1 **Happy Together** - The Turtles
2 Dedicated To The One I Love - The Mamas & The Papas
3 Penny Lane - The Beatles
4 There's A Kind Of Hush - Herman's Hermits
5 Baby I Need Your Lovin' - Johnny Rivers
6 Sock It To Me - Baby! - Mitch Ryder & The Detroit Wheels
7 For What It's Worth (Stop, Hey What's That) - The Buffalo Springfield
8 My Cup Runneth Over - Ed Ames
9 Love Is Here And Now You're Gone - The Supremes
10 Ruby Tuesday - The Rolling Stones

1967

 1 **Release Me (And Let Me Love Again)** - Engelbert Humperdinck
 2 This Is My Song - Harry Secombe
 3 Edelweiss - Vince Hill
 4 Simon Smith And The Dancing Bear - The Alan Price Set
 5 I Was Kaiser Bill's Batman - Whistling Jack Smith
 6 Puppet On A String - Sandie Shaw
 7 Georgy Girl - The Seekers
 8 This Is My Song - Petula Clark
 9 Somethin' Stupid - Nancy Sinatra & Frank Sinatra
10 Penny Lane/Strawberry Fields Forever - The Beatles

UK Number One album: *The Sound Of Music* - Soundtrack
US Billboard Number One album: *More Of The Monkees* - The Monkees
US Cashbox Number One single: *Happy Together* - The Turtles
Also this week: Eighteen people die when a jet crashes in New Orleans. (30th)

US Billboard singles for the week ending April the 1st
 1 **Happy Together** - The Turtles
 2 Dedicated To The One I Love - The Mamas & The Papas
 3 Penny Lane - The Beatles
 4 There's A Kind Of Hush - Herman's Hermits
 5 Bernadette - The Four Tops
 6 This Is My Song - Petula Clark
 7 For What It's Worth (Stop, Hey What's That) - The Buffalo Springfield
 8 Strawberry Fields Forever - The Beatles
 9 Somethin' Stupid - Nancy Sinatra & Frank Sinatra
10 Western Union - The Five Americans

1967

  1 **Release Me** (**And Let Me Love Again**) - Engelbert Humperdinck
  2 Somethin' Stupid - Nancy Sinatra & Frank Sinatra
  3 This Is My Song - Harry Secombe
  4 Puppet On A String - Sandie Shaw
  5 Simon Smith And The Dancing Bear - The Alan Price Set
  6 I Was Kaiser Bill's Batman - Whistling Jack Smith
  7 Edelweiss - Vince Hill
  8 Penny Lane/Strawberry Fields Forever - The Beatles
  9 This Is My Song - Petula Clark
10 Georgy Girl - The Seekers

UK Number One album: *The Sound Of Music* - Soundtrack
US Billboard Number One album: *More Of The Monkees* - The Monkees
US Cashbox Number One single: *Happy Together* - The Turtles
Also this week: British troops clash with angry demonstrators in Aden. (3rd)

US Billboard singles for the week ending April the 8th
  1 **Happy Together** - The Turtles
  2 Dedicated To The One I Love - The Mamas & The Papas
  3 Somethin' Stupid - Nancy Sinatra & Frank Sinatra
  4 Bernadette - The Four Tops
  5 This Is My Song - Petula Clark
  6 Penny Lane - The Beatles
  7 Western Union - The Five Americans
  8 I Think We're Alone Now - Tommy James
  9 A Little Bit Me, A Little Bit You - The Monkees
10 There's A Kind Of Hush - Herman's Hermits

1967

1 **Somethin' Stupid** - Nancy Sinatra & Frank Sinatra
2 Release Me (And Let Me Love Again) - Engelbert Humperdinck
3 Puppet On A String - Sandie Shaw
4 A Little Bit Me, A Little Bit You - The Monkees
5 This Is My Song - Harry Secombe
6 Ha! Ha! Said The Clown - Manfred Mann
7 Simon Smith And The Dancing Bear - The Alan Price Set
8 I Was Kaiser Bill's Batman - Whistling Jack Smith
9 It's All Over - Cliff Richard
10 Edelweiss - Vince Hill

UK Number One album: *The Sound Of Music* - Soundtrack
US Billboard Number One album: *More Of The Monkees* - The Monkees
US Cashbox Number One single: *Somethin' Stupid* - Nancy Sinatra & Frank Sinatra
Also this week: Scotland beat England 3-2 at Wembley. (15th)

US Billboard singles for the week ending April the 15th
1 **Somethin' Stupid** - Nancy Sinatra & Frank Sinatra
2 Happy Together - The Turtles
3 This Is My Song - Petula Clark
4 Bernadette - The Four Tops
5 A Little Bit Me, A Little Bit You - The Monkees
6 Western Union - The Five Americans
7 I Think We're Alone Now - Tommy James
8 Dedicated To The One I Love - The Mamas & The Papas
9 I Never Loved A Man (The Way I Love You) - Aretha Franklin
10 Jimmy Mack - Martha & The Vandellas

1967

UK singles chart for the week ending April the 22nd
1 **Somethin' Stupid** - Nancy Sinatra & Frank Sinatra
2 Puppet On A String - Sandie Shaw
3 A Little Bit Me, A Little Bit You - The Monkees
4 Ha! Ha! Said The Clown - Manfred Mann
5 Release Me (And Let Me Love Again) - Engelbert
Humperdinck
6 Purple Haze - The Jimi Hendrix Experience
7 This Is My Song - Harry Secombe
8 Bernadette - The Four Tops
9 It's All Over - Cliff Richard
10 I'm Gonna Get Me A Gun - Cat Stevens

UK Number One album: *The Sound Of Music* - Soundtrack
US Billboard Number One album: *More Of The Monkees* - The
Monkees
US Cashbox Number One single: *A Little Bit Me, A Little Bit
You* - The Monkees
Also this week: Army colonels seize power in Greece. (21st)

US Billboard singles for the week ending April the 22nd
1 **Somethin' Stupid** - Nancy Sinatra & Frank Sinatra
2 Happy Together - The Turtles
3 A Little Bit Me, A Little Bit You - The Monkees
4 I Think We're Alone Now - Tommy James
5 Western Union - The Five Americans
6 This Is My Song - Petula Clark
7 Sweet Soul Music - Arthur Conley
8 Bernadette - The Four Tops
9 I Never Loved A Man (The Way I Love You) - Aretha
Franklin
10 Jimmy Mack - Martha & The Vandellas

1967

1 **Puppet On A String** - Sandie Shaw
2 Somethin' Stupid - Nancy Sinatra & Frank Sinatra
3 A Little Bit Me, A Little Bit You - The Monkees
4 Ha! Ha! Said The Clown - Manfred Mann
5 Purple Haze - The Jimi Hendrix Experience
6 I'm Gonna Get Me A Gun - Cat Stevens
7 I Can Hear The Grass Grow - The Move
8 Release Me (And Let Me Love Again) - Engelbert Humperdinck
9 Dedicated To The One I Love - The Mamas & The Papas
10 Bernadette - The Four Tops

UK Number One album: *The Sound Of Music* - Soundtrack
US Billboard Number One album: *More Of The Monkees* - The Monkees
US Cashbox Number One single: *A Little Bit Me, A Little Bit You* - The Monkees
Also this week: A Pablo Picasso painting is sold for over five hundred thousand dollars in London. (26th)

US Billboard singles for the week ending April the 29th

1 **Somethin' Stupid** - Nancy Sinatra & Frank Sinatra
2 A Little Bit Me, A Little Bit You - The Monkees
3 Happy Together - The Turtles
4 Sweet Soul Music - Arthur Conley
5 I Think We're Alone Now - Tommy James
6 Western Union - The Five Americans
7 This Is My Song - Petula Clark
8 The Happening - The Supremes
9 Bernadette - The Four Tops
10 Jimmy Mack - Martha & The Vandellas

1967

UK singles chart for the week ending May the 6th
 1 **Puppet On A String** - Sandie Shaw
 2 Somethin' Stupid - Nancy Sinatra & Frank Sinatra
 3 Purple Haze - The Jimi Hendrix Experience
 4 A Little Bit Me, A Little Bit You - The Monkees
 5 I Can Hear The Grass Grow - The Move
 6 Dedicated To The One I Love - The Mamas & The Papas
 7 Ha! Ha! Said The Clown - Manfred Mann
 8 I'm Gonna Get Me A Gun - Cat Stevens
 9 Funny Familiar Forgotten Feelings - Tom Jones
10 The Boat That I Row - Lulu

UK Number One album: *The Sound Of Music* - Soundtrack
US Billboard Number One album: *More Of The Monkees* - The Monkees
US Cashbox Number One single: *Somethin' Stupid* - Nancy Sinatra & Frank Sinatra
Also this week: Muhammad Ali is stripped of his World Heavyweight title for refusing to be drafted by the army. (30th)

US Billboard singles for the week ending May the 6th
 1 **Somethin' Stupid** - Nancy Sinatra & Frank Sinatra
 2 The Happening - The Supremes
 3 Sweet Soul Music - Arthur Conley
 4 A Little Bit Me, A Little Bit You - The Monkees
 5 Happy Together - The Turtles
 6 I Think We're Alone Now - Tommy James
 7 Don't You Care - The Buckinghams
 8 Close Your Eyes - Peaches & Herb
 9 You Got What It Takes - The Dave Clark Five
10 I'm A Man - The Spencer Davis Group

1967

1 **Puppet On A String** - Sandie Shaw
2 Somethin' Stupid - Nancy Sinatra & Frank Sinatra
3 Dedicated To The One I Love - The Mamas & The Papas
4 Silence Is Golden - The Tremeloes
5 Pictures Of Lily - The Who
6 The Boat That I Row - Lulu
7 Purple Haze - The Jimi Hendrix Experience
8 Funny Familiar Forgotten Feelings - Tom Jones
9 I Can Hear The Grass Grow - The Move
10 A Little Bit Me, A Little Bit You - The Monkees

UK Number One album: *More Of The Monkees* - The Monkees
US Billboard Number One album: *More Of The Monkees* - The Monkees
US Cashbox Number One single: *The Happening* - The Supremes
Also this week: Mick Jagger and Keith Richard appear at a court hearing facing drugs charges. (10th)

US Billboard singles for the week ending May the 13th

1 **The Happening** - The Supremes
2 Sweet Soul Music - Arthur Conley
3 Somethin' Stupid - Nancy Sinatra & Frank Sinatra
4 Groovin' - The Young Rascals
5 A Little Bit Me, A Little Bit You - The Monkees
6 Don't You Care - The Buckinghams
7 You Got What It Takes - The Dave Clark Five
8 Close Your Eyes - Peaches & Herb
9 I Got Rhythm - The Happenings
10 I Think We're Alone Now - Tommy James

Puppet On A String was the first song to win at Eurovision and achieve a UK Number 1.

1967

1 **Silence Is Golden** - The Tremeloes
2 Dedicated To The One I Love - The Mamas & The Papas
3 Puppet On A String - Sandie Shaw
4 Pictures Of Lily - The Who
5 Somethin' Stupid - Nancy Sinatra & Frank Sinatra
6 The Boat That I Row - Lulu
7 Funny Familiar Forgotten Feelings - Tom Jones
8 Seven Drunken Nights - The Dubliners
9 Waterloo Sunset - The Kinks
10 Purple Haze - The Jimi Hendrix Experience

UK Number One album: *The Sound Of Music* - Soundtrack
US Billboard Number One album: *More Of The Monkees* - The Monkees
US Cashbox Number One single: *Groovin'* - The Young Rascals
Also this week: Anti-British demonstrators march through the streets of Peking. (15th)

US Billboard singles for the week ending May the 20th
1 **Groovin'** - The Young Rascals
2 The Happening - The Supremes
3 Sweet Soul Music - Arthur Conley
4 Somethin' Stupid - Nancy Sinatra & Frank Sinatra
5 Respect - Aretha Franklin
6 I Got Rhythm - The Happenings
7 Release Me (And Let Me Love Again) - Engelbert Humperdinck
8 Close Your Eyes - Peaches & Herb
9 Don't You Care - The Buckinghams
10 You Got What It Takes - The Dave Clark Five

1967

UK singles chart for the week ending May the 27th
1 **Silence Is Golden** - The Tremeloes
2 Waterloo Sunset - The Kinks
3 Dedicated To The One I Love - The Mamas & The Papas
4 Then I Kissed Her - The Beach Boys
5 Puppet On A String - Sandie Shaw
6 Pictures Of Lily - The Who
7 Seven Drunken Nights - The Dubliners
8 The Boat That I Row - Lulu
9 The Wind Cries Mary - The Jimi Hendrix Experience
10 Somethin' Stupid - Nancy Sinatra & Frank Sinatra

UK Number One album: *More Of The Monkees* - The Monkees
US Billboard Number One album: *More Of The Monkees* - The Monkees
US Cashbox Number One single: *Groovin'* - The Young Rascals
Also this week: The 25th Amendment becomes US law. (25th)

US Billboard singles for the week ending May the 27th
1 **Groovin**' - The Young Rascals
2 Respect - Aretha Franklin
3 I Got Rhythm - The Happenings
4 Release Me (And Let Me Love Again) - Engelbert Humperdinck
5 The Happening - The Supremes
6 Sweet Soul Music - Arthur Conley
7 Him Or Me - What's It Gonna Be - Paul Revere
8 Creeque Alley - The Mamas & The Papas
9 Somethin' Stupid - Nancy Sinatra & Frank Sinatra
10 Girl, You'll Be A Woman Soon - Neil Diamond

1967

  1 **Silence Is Golden** - The Tremeloes
  2 Waterloo Sunset - The Kinks
  3 Dedicated To The One I Love - The Mamas & The Papas
  4 A Whiter Shade Of Pale - Procol Harum
  5 Then I Kissed Her - The Beach Boys
  6 The Wind Cries Mary - The Jimi Hendrix Experience
  7 There Goes My Everything - Engelbert Humperdinck
  8 The Happening - The Supremes
  9 Pictures Of Lily - The Who
10 Seven Drunken Nights - The Dubliners

UK Number One album: *The Sound Of Music* - Soundtrack
US Billboard Number One album: *More Of The Monkees* - The Monkees
US Cashbox Number One single: *I Got Rhythm* - The Happenings
Also this week: Francis Chichester returns to Plymouth after his round-the-world yacht solo voyage. (28th)

US Billboard singles for the week ending June the 3rd
  1 **Respect** - Aretha Franklin
  2 Groovin' - The Young Rascals
  3 I Got Rhythm - The Happenings
  4 Release Me (And Let Me Love Again) - Engelbert Humperdinck
  5 Creeque Alley - The Mamas & The Papas
  6 Him Or Me - What's It Gonna Be - Paul Revere
  7 The Happening - The Supremes
  8 Sweet Soul Music - Arthur Conley
  9 Somebody To Love - Jefferson Starship
10 All I Need - The Temptations

1967

1 **A Whiter Shade Of Pale** - Procol Harum
2 Silence Is Golden - The Tremeloes
3 Waterloo Sunset - The Kinks
4 There Goes My Everything - Engelbert Humperdinck
5 Then I Kissed Her - The Beach Boys
6 The Happening - The Supremes
7 Dedicated To The One I Love - The Mamas & The Papas
8 The Wind Cries Mary - The Jimi Hendrix Experience
9 Sweet Soul Music - Arthur Conley
10 Pictures Of Lily - The Who

UK Number One album: *Sgt Pepper's Lonely Hearts Club Band* - The Beatles
US Billboard Number One album: *More Of The Monkees* - The Monkees
US Cashbox Number One single: *Respect* - Aretha Franklin
Also this week: The six-day war between Egypt and Israel begins. (5th)

US Billboard singles for the week ending June the 10th

1 **Respect** - Aretha Franklin
2 Groovin' - The Young Rascals
3 I Got Rhythm - The Happenings
4 Release Me (And Let Me Love Again) - Engelbert Humperdinck
5 Him Or Me - What's It Gonna Be - Paul Revere
6 Somebody To Love - Jefferson Starship
7 She'd Rather Be With Me - The Turtles
8 Little Bit O'Soul - The Music Explosion
9 All I Need - The Temptations
10 Creeque Alley - The Mamas & The Papas

1967

1 **A Whiter Shade Of Pale** - Procol Harum
2 There Goes My Everything - Engelbert Humperdinck
3 Waterloo Sunset - The Kinks
4 Silence Is Golden - The Tremeloes
5 Carrie-Anne - The Hollies
6 The Happening - The Supremes
7 Sweet Soul Music - Arthur Conley
8 Then I Kissed Her - The Beach Boys
9 Dedicated To The One I Love - The Mamas & The Papas
10 Okay! - Dave Dee, Dozy, Beaky, Mick, And Tich

UK Number One album: *Sgt Pepper's Lonely Hearts Club Band* - The Beatles
US Billboard Number One album: *Sounds Like...* - Herb Alpert And The Tijuana Brass
US Cashbox Number One single: *Respect* - Aretha Franklin
Also this week: The first Chinese Hydrogen bomb is detonated. (17th)

US Billboard singles for the week ending June the 17th
1 **Groovin'** - The Young Rascals
2 Respect - Aretha Franklin
3 She'd Rather Be With Me - The Turtles
4 Release Me (And Let Me Love Again) - Engelbert Humperdinck
5 Somebody To Love - Jefferson Starship
6 Little Bit O'Soul - The Music Explosion
7 Windy - The Association
8 All I Need - The Temptations
9 I Got Rhythm - The Happenings
10 Mirage - Tommy James

1967

UK singles chart for the week ending June the 24th
1 **A Whiter Shade Of Pale** - Procol Harum
2 There Goes My Everything - Engelbert Humperdinck
3 Carrie-Anne - The Hollies
4 Silence Is Golden - The Tremeloes
5 Waterloo Sunset - The Kinks
6 Okay! - Dave Dee, Dozy, Beaky, Mick, And Tich
7 The Happening - The Supremes
8 Paper Sun -Traffic
9 Sweet Soul Music - Arthur Conley
10 Then I Kissed Her - The Beach Boys

UK Number One album: *Sgt Pepper's Lonely Hearts Club Band* - The Beatles
US Billboard Number One album: *Headquarters* - The Monkees
US Cashbox Number One single: *Groovin'* - The Young Rascals
Also this week: Alexei Kosygin meets Lyndon Johnson. (20th)

US Billboard singles for the week ending June the 24th
1 **Groovin**' - The Young Rascals
2 Respect - Aretha Franklin
3 She'd Rather Be With Me - The Turtles
4 Windy - The Association
5 Little Bit O'Soul - The Music Explosion
6 San Francisco (Be Sure To Wear Some Flowers In Your Hair) - Scott McKenzie
7 Somebody To Love - Jefferson Starship
8 Can't Take My Eyes Off You - Frankie Valli
9 Sunday Will Never Be The Same - Spanky And Our Gang
10 Let's Live For Today - The Grass Roots

1967

1 **A Whiter Shade Of Pale** - Procol Harum
2 There Goes My Everything - Engelbert Humperdinck
3 Carrie-Anne - The Hollies
4 Okay! - Dave Dee, Dozy, Beaky, Mick, And Tich
5 Paper Sun -Traffic
6 She'd Rather Be With Me - The Turtles
7 Alternate Title - The Monkees
8 Groovin' - The Young Rascals
9 Silence Is Golden - The Tremeloes
10 The Happening - The Supremes

UK Number One album: *Sgt Pepper's Lonely Hearts Club Band* - The Beatles
US Billboard Number One album: *Sgt Pepper's Lonely Hearts Club Band* - The Beatles
US Cashbox Number One single: *Windy* - The Association
Also this week: BBC 2 broadcasts in colour for the first time. (1st)

US Billboard singles for the week ending July the 1st

1 **Windy** - The Association
2 Groovin' - The Young Rascals
3 Little Bit O'Soul - The Music Explosion
4 San Francisco (Be Sure To Wear Some Flowers In Your Hair) - Scott McKenzie
5 She'd Rather Be With Me - The Turtles
6 Respect - Aretha Franklin
7 Can't Take My Eyes Off You - Frankie Valli
8 Let's Live For Today - The Grass Roots
9 Come On Down To My Boat - Every Mother's Son
10 Don't Sleep In The Subway - Petula Clark

1967

UK singles chart for the week ending July the 8th

1 **A Whiter Shade Of Pale** - Procol Harum
2 There Goes My Everything - Engelbert Humperdinck
3 Alternate Title - The Monkees
4 She'd Rather Be With Me - The Turtles
5 Carrie-Anne - The Hollies
6 It Must Be Him (Seul Sur Son Etoile) - Vikki Carr
7 Okay! - Dave Dee, Dozy, Beaky, Mick, And Tich
8 Paper Sun -Traffic
9 Groovin' - The Young Rascals
10 If I Were A Rich Man - Topol

UK Number One album: *Sgt Pepper's Lonely Hearts Club Band* - The Beatles
US Billboard Number One album: *Sgt Pepper's Lonely Hearts Club Band* - The Beatles
US Cashbox Number One single: *Windy* - The Association
Also this week: Nigerian troops invade the breakaway region of Biafra. (7th)

US Billboard singles for the week ending July the 8th

1 **Windy** - The Association
2 Little Bit O'Soul - The Music Explosion
3 Can't Take My Eyes Off You - Frankie Valli
4 San Francisco (Be Sure To Wear Some Flowers In Your Hair) - Scott McKenzie
5 Don't Sleep In The Subway - Petula Clark
6 Come On Down To My Boat - Every Mother's Son
7 Up - - Up And Away - The 5th Dimension
8 Let's Live For Today - The Grass Roots
9 Groovin' - The Young Rascals
10 The Tracks Of My Tears - Johnny Rivers

1967

UK singles chart for the week ending July the 15th
1 **A Whiter Shade Of Pale** - Procol Harum
2 All You Need Is Love - The Beatles
3 Alternate Title - The Monkees
4 There Goes My Everything - Engelbert Humperdinck
5 She'd Rather Be With Me - The Turtles
6 It Must Be Him (Seul Sur Son Etoile) - Vikki Carr
7 Carrie-Anne - The Hollies
8 See Emily Play - Pink Floyd
9 If I Were A Rich Man - Topol
10 Respect - Aretha Franklin

UK Number One album: *Sgt Pepper's Lonely Hearts Club Band* - The Beatles
US Billboard Number One album: *Sgt Pepper's Lonely Hearts Club Band* - The Beatles
US Cashbox Number One single: *Can't Take My Eyes Off You* - Frankie Valli
Also this week: Britain's MPs vote to legalise abortion. (14th)

US Billboard singles for the week ending July the 15th
1 **Windy** - The Association
2 Little Bit O'Soul - The Music Explosion
3 Can't Take My Eyes Off You - Frankie Valli
4 San Francisco (Be Sure To Wear Some Flowers In Your Hair) - Scott McKenzie
5 Don't Sleep In The Subway - Petula Clark
6 Come On Down To My Boat - Every Mother's Son
7 Up - - Up And Away - The 5th Dimension
8 Light My Fire - The Doors
9 C'mon Marianne - The Four Seasons
10 A Whiter Shade Of Pale - Procol Harum

1967

1 **All You Need Is Love** - The Beatles
2 Alternate Title - The Monkees
3 It Must Be Him (Seul Sur Son Etoile) - Vikki Carr
4 A Whiter Shade Of Pale - Procol Harum
5 San Francisco (Be Sure To Wear Some Flowers In Your Hair) - Scott McKenzie
6 There Goes My Everything - Engelbert Humperdinck
7 She'd Rather Be With Me - The Turtles
8 See Emily Play - Pink Floyd
9 If I Were A Rich Man - Topol
10 With A Little Help From My Friends - Young Idea

UK Number One album: *Sgt Pepper's Lonely Hearts Club Band* - The Beatles
US Billboard Number One album: *Sgt Pepper's Lonely Hearts Club Band* - The Beatles
US Cashbox Number One single: *Windy* - The Association
Also this week: A 'Legalise Pot' rally is held in London. (17th)

US Billboard singles for the week ending July the 22nd

1 **Windy** - The Association
2 Can't Take My Eyes Off You - Frankie Valli
3 Light My Fire - The Doors
4 San Francisco (Be Sure To Wear Some Flowers In Your Hair) - Scott McKenzie
5 Little Bit O'Soul - The Music Explosion
6 I Was Made To Love Her - Stevie Wonder
7 Up - - Up And Away - The 5th Dimension
8 A Whiter Shade Of Pale - Procol Harum
9 C'mon Marianne - The Four Seasons
10 Come On Down To My Boat - Every Mother's Son

1967

1 **All You Need Is Love** - The Beatles
2 It Must Be Him (Seul Sur Son Etoile) - Vikki Carr
3 San Francisco (Be Sure To Wear Some Flowers In Your Hair) - Scott McKenzie
4 Alternate Title - The Monkees
5 She'd Rather Be With Me - The Turtles
6 See Emily Play - Pink Floyd
7 A Whiter Shade Of Pale - Procol Harum
8 There Goes My Everything - Engelbert Humperdinck
9 Up, Up And Away - The Johnny Mann Singers
10 Death Of A Clown - Dave Davies

UK Number One album: *Sgt Pepper's Lonely Hearts Club Band* - The Beatles
US Billboard Number One album: *Sgt Pepper's Lonely Hearts Club Band* - The Beatles
US Cashbox Number One single: *Can't Take My Eyes Off You* - Frankie Valli
Also this week: The British Steel Corporation is created. (28th)

US Billboard singles for the week ending July the 29th

1 **Light My Fire** - The Doors
2 I Was Made To Love Her - Stevie Wonder
3 Windy - The Association
4 Can't Take My Eyes Off You - Frankie Valli
5 A Whiter Shade Of Pale - Procol Harum
6 Little Bit O'Soul - The Music Explosion
7 Mercy, Mercy, Mercy - The Buckinghams
8 White Rabbit - Jefferson Starship
9 Up - - Up And Away - The 5th Dimension
10 C'mon Marianne - The Four Seasons

1967

UK singles chart for the week ending August the 5th
 1 **All You Need Is Love** - The Beatles
 2 San Francisco (Be Sure To Wear Some Flowers In Your Hair) - Scott McKenzie
 3 Death Of A Clown - Dave Davies
 4 It Must Be Him (Seul Sur Son Etoile) - Vikki Carr
 5 Alternate Title - The Monkees
 6 I'll Never Fall In Love Again - Tom Jones
 7 She'd Rather Be With Me - The Turtles
 8 I Was Made To Love Her - Stevie Wonder
 9 See Emily Play - Pink Floyd
10 A Whiter Shade Of Pale - Procol Harum

UK Number One album: *Sgt Pepper's Lonely Hearts Club Band* - The Beatles
US Billboard Number One album: *Sgt Pepper's Lonely Hearts Club Band* - The Beatles
US Cashbox Number One single: *Light My Fire* - The Doors
Also this week: The Dartford Tunnel under the River Thames is opened. (2nd)

US Billboard singles for the week ending August the 5th
 1 **Light My Fire** - The Doors
 2 I Was Made To Love Her - Stevie Wonder
 3 All You Need Is Love - The Beatles
 4 Windy - The Association
 5 A Whiter Shade Of Pale - Procol Harum
 6 Can't Take My Eyes Off You - Frankie Valli
 7 Mercy, Mercy, Mercy - The Buckinghams
 8 White Rabbit - Jefferson Starship
 9 Pleasant Valley Sunday - The Monkees
10 Little Bit O'Soul - The Music Explosion

1967

 1 **San Francisco (Be Sure To Wear Some Flowers In Your Hair)** - Scott McKenzie
 2 All You Need Is Love - The Beatles
 3 Death Of A Clown - Dave Davies
 4 I'll Never Fall In Love Again - Tom Jones
 5 It Must Be Him (Seul Sur Son Etoile) - Vikki Carr
 6 She'd Rather Be With Me - The Turtles
 7 I Was Made To Love Her - Stevie Wonder
 8 Up, Up And Away - The Johnny Mann Singers
 9 Alternate Title - The Monkees
10 See Emily Play - Pink Floyd

UK Number One album: *Sgt Pepper's Lonely Hearts Club Band* - The Beatles
US Billboard Number One album: *Sgt Pepper's Lonely Hearts Club Band* - The Beatles
US Cashbox Number One single: *All You Need Is Love* - The Beatles
Also this week: China opts to give aid to North Vietnam. (7th)

US Billboard singles for the week ending August the 12th
 1 **Light My Fire** - The Doors
 2 All You Need Is Love - The Beatles
 3 I Was Made To Love Her - Stevie Wonder
 4 Pleasant Valley Sunday - The Monkees
 5 Mercy, Mercy, Mercy - The Buckinghams
 6 Can't Take My Eyes Off You - Frankie Valli
 7 A Whiter Shade Of Pale - Procol Harum
 8 Windy - The Association
 9 Carrie-Anne - The Hollies
10 A Girl Like You - The Rascals

1967

   1 **San Francisco (Be Sure To Wear Some Flowers In Your Hair**) - Scott McKenzie
   2 All You Need Is Love - The Beatles
   3 I'll Never Fall In Love Again - Tom Jones
   4 Death Of A Clown - Dave Davies
   5 I Was Made To Love Her - Stevie Wonder
   6 Up, Up And Away - The Johnny Mann Singers
   7 Just Loving You - Anita Harris
   8 Even The Bad Times Are Good - The Tremeloes
   9 The House That Jack Built - The Alan Price Set
   10 It Must Be Him (Seul Sur Son Etoile) - Vikki Carr

UK Number One album: *Sgt Pepper's Lonely Hearts Club Band* - The Beatles
US Billboard Number One album: *Sgt Pepper's Lonely Hearts Club Band* - The Beatles
US Cashbox Number One single: *All You Need Is Love* - The Beatles
Also this week: Pirate radio is now officially outlawed. (15th)

US Billboard singles for the week ending August the 19th
   1 **All You Need Is Love** - The Beatles
   2 Light My Fire - The Doors
   3 Pleasant Valley Sunday - The Monkees
   4 I Was Made To Love Her - Stevie Wonder
   5 Baby I Love You - Aretha Franklin
   6 Mercy, Mercy, Mercy - The Buckinghams
   7 Ode To Billie Joe - Bobbie Gentry
   8 Cold Sweat - Part 1 - James Brown
   9 A Whiter Shade Of Pale - Procol Harum
   10 A Girl Like You - The Rascals

1967

 1 **San Francisco (Be Sure To Wear Some Flowers In Your Hair**) - Scott McKenzie
 2 I'll Never Fall In Love Again - Tom Jones
 3 All You Need Is Love - The Beatles
 4 Even The Bad Times Are Good - The Tremeloes
 5 The House That Jack Built - The Alan Price Set
 6 Just Loving You - Anita Harris
 7 Death Of A Clown - Dave Davies
 8 I Was Made To Love Her - Stevie Wonder
 9 Creeque Alley - The Mamas & The Papas
10 Up, Up And Away - The Johnny Mann Singers

UK Number One album: *Sgt Pepper's Lonely Hearts Club Band* - The Beatles
US Billboard Number One album: *Sgt Pepper's Lonely Hearts Club Band* - The Beatles
US Cashbox Number One single: *Ode To Billie Joe* - Bobbie Gentry
Also this week: A truce is declared in Congo. (21st)

US Billboard singles for the week ending August the 26th
 1 **Ode To Billie Joe** - Bobbie Gentry
 2 All You Need Is Love - The Beatles
 3 Pleasant Valley Sunday - The Monkees
 4 Light My Fire - The Doors
 5 Baby I Love You - Aretha Franklin
 6 I Was Made To Love Her - Stevie Wonder
 7 Cold Sweat - Part 1 - James Brown
 8 Reflections - Diana Ross And The Supremes
 9 You're My Everything - The Temptations
10 A Whiter Shade Of Pale - Procol Harum

1967

1 **San Francisco (Be Sure To Wear Some Flowers In Your Hair)** - Scott McKenzie
2 I'll Never Fall In Love Again - Tom Jones
3 The Last Waltz - Engelbert Humperdinck
4 The House That Jack Built - The Alan Price Set
5 Even The Bad Times Are Good - The Tremeloes
6 All You Need Is Love - The Beatles
7 Just Loving You - Anita Harris
8 I Was Made To Love Her - Stevie Wonder
9 Death Of A Clown - Dave Davies
10 We Love You/Dandelion - The Rolling Stones

UK Number One album: *Sgt Pepper's Lonely Hearts Club Band* - The Beatles
US Billboard Number One album: *Sgt Pepper's Lonely Hearts Club Band* - The Beatles
US Cashbox Number One single: *Ode To Billie Joe* - Bobbie Gentry
Also this week: Paddy Bates creates the 'state' of Sealand. (2nd)

US Billboard singles for the week ending September the 2nd
1 **Ode To Billie Joe** - Bobbie Gentry
2 All You Need Is Love - The Beatles
3 Reflections - Diana Ross And The Supremes
4 Light My Fire - The Doors
5 Baby I Love You - Aretha Franklin
6 Come Back When You Grow Up - Bobby Vee
7 Cold Sweat - Part 1 - James Brown
8 Pleasant Valley Sunday - The Monkees
9 You're My Everything - The Temptations
10 I Was Made To Love Her - Stevie Wonder

1967

1 **The Last Waltz** - **Engelbert Humperdinck**
2 I'll Never Fall In Love Again - Tom Jones
3 San Francisco (Be Sure To Wear Some Flowers In Your Hair) - Scott McKenzie
4 Excerpt From 'A Teenage Opera' - Keith West
5 The House That Jack Built - The Alan Price Set
6 Even The Bad Times Are Good - The Tremeloes
7 Just Loving You - Anita Harris
8 We Love You/Dandelion - The Rolling Stones
9 I Was Made To Love Her - Stevie Wonder
10 Itchycoo Park - The Small Faces

UK Number One album: *Sgt Pepper's Lonely Hearts Club Band* - The Beatles
US Billboard Number One album: *Sgt Pepper's Lonely Hearts Club Band* - The Beatles
US Cashbox Number One single: *Ode To Billie Joe* - Bobbie Gentry
Also this week: The Fashion Island 'shopping mall' opens. (9th)

US Billboard singles for the week ending September the 9th
1 **Ode To Billie Joe** - Bobbie Gentry
2 Reflections - Diana Ross And The Supremes
3 Come Back When You Grow Up - Bobby Vee
4 Baby I Love You - Aretha Franklin
5 The Letter - The Box Tops
6 All You Need Is Love - The Beatles
7 You're My Everything - The Temptations
8 Light My Fire - The Doors
9 Apples, Peaches, Pumpkin Pie - Jay & The Techniques
10 San Franciscan Nights - Eric Burdon And The Animals

1967
UK singles chart for the week ending September the 16th
1 **The Last Waltz** - Engelbert Humperdinck
2 I'll Never Fall In Love Again - Tom Jones
3 San Francisco (Be Sure To Wear Some Flowers In Your Hair) - Scott McKenzie
4 Excerpt From 'A Teenage Opera' - Keith West
5 Let's Go To San Francisco - The Flower Pot Men
6 Itchycoo Park - The Small Faces
7 Even The Bad Times Are Good - The Tremeloes
8 Heroes And Villains - The Beach Boys
9 Just Loving You - Anita Harris
10 We Love You/Dandelion - The Rolling Stones

UK Number One album: *Sgt Pepper's Lonely Hearts Club Band* - The Beatles
US Billboard Number One album: *Sgt Pepper's Lonely Hearts Club Band* - The Beatles
US Cashbox Number One single: *Ode To Billie Joe* - Bobbie Gentry
Also this week: Gibraltar's people vote to remain British. (10th)

US Billboard singles for the week ending September the 16th
1 **Ode To Billie Joe** - Bobbie Gentry
2 Reflections - Diana Ross And The Supremes
3 Come Back When You Grow Up - Bobby Vee
4 The Letter - The Box Tops
5 Baby I Love You - Aretha Franklin
6 You're My Everything - The Temptations
7 Apples, Peaches, Pumpkin Pie - Jay & The Techniques
8 All You Need Is Love - The Beatles
9 San Franciscan Nights - Eric Burdon And The Animals
10 Funky Broadway - Wilson Pickett

1967

UK singles chart for the week ending September the 23rd
1 **The Last Waltz** - Engelbert Humperdinck
2 Excerpt From 'A Teenage Opera' - Keith West
3 Itchycoo Park - The Small Faces
4 Let's Go To San Francisco - The Flower Pot Men
5 I'll Never Fall In Love Again - Tom Jones
6 San Francisco (Be Sure To Wear Some Flowers In Your Hair) - Scott McKenzie
7 Reflections - Diana Ross And The Supremes
8 Flowers In The Rain - The Move
9 We Love You/Dandelion - The Rolling Stones
10 Hole In My Shoe - Traffic

UK Number One album: *Sgt Pepper's Lonely Hearts Club Band* - The Beatles
US Billboard Number One album: *Sgt Pepper's Lonely Hearts Club Band* - The Beatles
US Cashbox Number One single: *The Letter* - The Box Tops
Also this week: The Doors appear on Ed Sullivan's show. (17th)

US Billboard singles for the week ending September the 23rd
1 **The Letter** - The Box Tops
2 Ode To Billie Joe - Bobbie Gentry
3 Come Back When You Grow Up - Bobby Vee
4 Reflections - Diana Ross And The Supremes
5 Never My Love - The Association
6 Apples, Peaches, Pumpkin Pie - Jay & The Techniques
7 (Your Love Keeps Lifting Me) Higher And Higher - Jackie Wilson
8 You're My Everything - The Temptations
9 I Dig Rock And Roll Music - Peter, Paul, & Mary
10 Funky Broadway - Wilson Pickett

1967

 1 **The Last Waltz** - Engelbert Humperdinck
 2 Excerpt From 'A Teenage Opera' - Keith West
 3 Flowers In The Rain - The Move
 4 Itchycoo Park - The Small Faces
 5 Reflections - Diana Ross And The Supremes
 6 Let's Go To San Francisco - The Flower Pot Men
 7 Hole In My Shoe - Traffic
 8 I'll Never Fall In Love Again - Tom Jones
 9 San Francisco (Be Sure To Wear Some Flowers In Your
Hair) - Scott McKenzie
10 The Day I Met Marie - Cliff Richard

UK Number One album: *Sgt Pepper's Lonely Hearts Club
Band* - The Beatles
US Billboard Number One album: *Sgt Pepper's Lonely Hearts
Club Band* - The Beatles
US Cashbox Number One single: *The Letter* - The Box Tops
Also this week: BBC Radio 1, 2, 3, and 4 first go on air. (30th)

US Billboard singles for the week ending September the 30th
 1 **The Letter** - The Box Tops
 2 Ode To Billie Joe - Bobbie Gentry
 3 Never My Love - The Association
 4 Come Back When You Grow Up - Bobby Vee
 5 Reflections - Diana Ross And The Supremes
 6 Apples, Peaches, Pumpkin Pie - Jay & The Techniques
 7 (Your Love Keeps Lifting Me) Higher And Higher - Jackie
Wilson
 8 Funky Broadway - Wilson Pickett
 9 I Dig Rock And Roll Music - Peter, Paul, & Mary
10 Brown Eyed Girl - Van Morrison

1967

UK singles chart for the week ending October the 7th
  1 **The Last Waltz** - Engelbert Humperdinck
  2 Flowers In The Rain - The Move
  3 Hole In My Shoe - Traffic
  4 Excerpt From 'A Teenage Opera' - Keith West
  5 Reflections - Diana Ross And The Supremes
  6 Massachusetts (The Lights Went Out In) - The Bee Gees
  7 Itchycoo Park - The Small Faces
  8 Let's Go To San Francisco - The Flower Pot Men
  9 The Letter - The Box Tops
10 The Day I Met Marie - Cliff Richard

UK Number One album: *Sgt Pepper's Lonely Hearts Club Band* - The Beatles
US Billboard Number One album: *Sgt Pepper's Lonely Hearts Club Band* - The Beatles
US Cashbox Number One single: *The Letter* - The Box Tops
Also this week: North Vietnam rejects a USA offer of peace discussions. (3rd)

US Billboard singles for the week ending October the 7th
  1 **The Letter** - The Box Tops
  2 Never My Love - The Association
  3 Ode To Billie Joe - Bobbie Gentry
  4 Come Back When You Grow Up - Bobby Vee
  5 Little Ole Man (Uptight - Everything's Alright) - Bill Cosby
  6 (Your Love Keeps Lifting Me) Higher And Higher - Jackie Wilson
  7 Reflections - Diana Ross And The Supremes
  8 Apples, Peaches, Pumpkin Pie - Jay & The Techniques
  9 How Can I Be Sure - The Rascals
10 Gimme Little Sign - Brenton Wood

1967

1 **Massachusetts** (**The Lights Went Out In**) - The Bee Gees
2 Flowers In The Rain - The Move
3 The Last Waltz - Engelbert Humperdinck
4 Hole In My Shoe - Traffic
5 Excerpt From 'A Teenage Opera' - Keith West
6 There Must Be A Way - Frankie Vaughan
7 The Letter - The Box Tops
8 Reflections - Diana Ross And The Supremes
9 Homburg - Procol Harum
10 Itchycoo Park - The Small Faces

UK Number One album: *Sgt Pepper's Lonely Hearts Club Band* - The Beatles
US Billboard Number One album: *Ode To Billie Joe* - Bobbie Gentry
US Cashbox Number One single: *Never My Love* - The Association
Also this week: 66 die in an air crash west of Cyprus. (12th)

US Billboard singles for the week ending October the 14th
1 **The Letter** - The Box Tops
2 Never My Love - The Association
3 To Sir With Love - Lulu
4 Little Ole Man (Uptight - Everything's Alright) - Bill Cosby
5 Ode To Billie Joe - Bobbie Gentry
6 (Your Love Keeps Lifting Me) Higher And Higher - Jackie Wilson
7 Come Back When You Grow Up - Bobby Vee
8 How Can I Be Sure - The Rascals
9 Gimme Little Sign - Brenton Wood
10 Soul Man - Sam & Dave

1967

UK singles chart for the week ending October the 21st
1 **Massachusetts** (**The Lights Went Out In**) - The Bee Gees
2 Hole In My Shoe - Traffic
3 The Last Waltz - Engelbert Humperdinck
4 Flowers In The Rain - The Move
5 The Letter - The Box Tops
6 Homburg - Procol Harum
7 There Must Be A Way - Frankie Vaughan
8 From The Underworld - The Herd
9 Excerpt From 'A Teenage Opera' - Keith West
10 Reflections - Diana Ross And The Supremes

UK Number One album: *Sgt Pepper's Lonely Hearts Club Band* - The Beatles
US Billboard Number One album: *Ode To Billie Joe* - Bobbie Gentry
US Cashbox Number One single: *To Sir With Love* - Lulu
Also this week: The singer Joan Baez is arrested at an anti-Vietnam War protest. (16th)

US Billboard singles for the week ending October the 21st
1 **To Sir With Love** - Lulu
2 The Letter - The Box Tops
3 Never My Love - The Association
4 How Can I Be Sure - The Rascals
5 Expressway (To Your Heart) - Soul Survivors
6 It Must Be Him (Seul Sur Son Etoile) - Vikki Carr
7 Soul Man - Sam & Dave
8 Little Ole Man (Uptight - Everything's Alright) - Bill Cosby
9 Gimme Little Sign - Brenton Wood
10 Your Precious Love - Marvin Gaye & Tammi Terrell

1967

 1 **Massachusetts** (**The Lights Went Out In**) - The Bee Gees
 2 The Last Waltz - Engelbert Humperdinck
 3 Hole In My Shoe - Traffic
 4 Baby Now That I've Found You - The Foundations
 5 Flowers In The Rain - The Move
 6 The Letter - The Box Tops
 7 Zabadak! - Dave Dee, Dozy, Beaky, Mick, and Tich
 8 From The Underworld - The Herd
 9 Homburg - Procol Harum
10 There Must Be A Way - Frankie Vaughan

UK Number One album: *Sgt Pepper's Lonely Hearts Club Band* - The Beatles
US Billboard Number One album: *Diana Ross & The Supremes Greatest Hits* - Diana Ross & The Supremes
US Cashbox Number One single: *To Sir With Love* - Lulu
Also this week: The Abortion Bill becomes law in the United Kingdom. (27th)

US Billboard singles for the week ending October the 28th
 1 **To Sir With Love** - Lulu
 2 The Letter - The Box Tops
 3 Never My Love - The Association
 4 How Can I Be Sure - The Rascals
 5 Expressway (To Your Heart) - Soul Survivors
 6 It Must Be Him (Seul Sur Son Etoile) - Vikki Carr
 7 Soul Man - Sam & Dave
 8 Your Precious Love - Marvin Gaye & Tammi Terrell
 9 A Natural Woman (You Make Me Feel Like) - Aretha Franklin
10 Incense And Peppermints - Strawberry Alarm Clock

1967

 1 **Massachusetts** (**The Lights Went Out In**) - The Bee Gees
 2 Baby Now That I've Found You - The Foundations
 3 Zabadak! - Dave Dee, Dozy, Beaky, Mick, and Tich
 4 The Last Waltz - Engelbert Humperdinck
 5 Hole In My Shoe - Traffic
 6 From The Underworld - The Herd
 7 Homburg - Procol Harum
 8 Autumn Almanac - The Kinks
 9 Flowers In The Rain - The Move
10 The Letter - The Box Tops

UK Number One album: *Sgt Pepper's Lonely Hearts Club Band* - The Beatles
US Billboard Number One album: *Diana Ross & The Supremes Greatest Hits* - Diana Ross & The Supremes
US Cashbox Number One single: *To Sir With Love* - Lulu
Also this week: The Scottish Nationalist Winnie Ewing wins a by-election. (3rd)

US Billboard singles for the week ending November the 4th
 1 **To Sir With Love** - Lulu
 2 Soul Man - Sam & Dave
 3 It Must Be Him (Seul Sur Son Etoile) - Vikki Carr
 4 Expressway (To Your Heart) - Soul Survivors
 5 Your Precious Love - Marvin Gaye & Tammi Terrell
 6 Never My Love - The Association
 7 Incense And Peppermints - Strawberry Alarm Clock
 8 A Natural Woman (You Make Me Feel Like) - Aretha Franklin
 9 The Rain, The Park And Other Things - The Cowsills
10 Please Love Me Forever - Bobby Vinton

1967

1 **Baby Now That I've Found You** - The Foundations
2 Massachusetts (The Lights Went Out In) - The Bee Gees
3 Zabadak! - Dave Dee, Dozy, Beaky, Mick, and Tich
4 The Last Waltz - Engelbert Humperdinck
5 Autumn Almanac - The Kinks
6 From The Underworld - The Herd
7 Love Is All Around - The Troggs
8 San Franciscan Nights - Eric Burdon And The Animals
9 Homburg - Procol Harum
10 There Must Be A Way - Frankie Vaughan

UK Number One album: *Sgt Pepper's Lonely Hearts Club Band* - The Beatles
US Billboard Number One album: *Diana Ross & The Supremes Greatest Hits* - Diana Ross & The Supremes
US Cashbox Number One single: *Soul Man* - Sam & Dave
Also this week: More than fifty people are killed in a train crash at Hither Green, London. (5th)

US Billboard singles for the week ending November the 11th
1 **To Sir With Love** - Lulu
2 Soul Man - Sam & Dave
3 It Must Be Him (Seul Sur Son Etoile) - Vikki Carr
4 Incense And Peppermints - Strawberry Alarm Clock
5 Your Precious Love - Marvin Gaye & Tammi Terrell
6 The Rain, The Park And Other Things - The Cowsills
7 Please Love Me Forever - Bobby Vinton
8 A Natural Woman (You Make Me Feel Like) - Aretha Franklin
9 Expressway (To Your Heart) - Soul Survivors
10 Never My Love - The Association

1967

1 **Baby Now That I've Found You** - The Foundations
2 Massachusetts (The Lights Went Out In) - The Bee Gees
3 Autumn Almanac - The Kinks
4 Zabadak! - Dave Dee, Dozy, Beaky, Mick, and Tich
5 The Last Waltz - Engelbert Humperdinck
6 Love Is All Around - The Troggs
7 San Franciscan Nights - Eric Burdon And The Animals
8 There Is A Mountain - Donovan
9 Let The Heartaches Begin - Long John Baldry
10 I Can See For Miles - The Who

UK Number One album: *The Sound Of Music* - Soundtrack
US Billboard Number One album: *Diana Ross & The Supremes Greatest Hits* - Diana Ross & The Supremes
US Cashbox Number One single: *Incense And Peppermints* - Strawberry Alarm Clock
Also this week: The disgraced traitor Kim Philby is interviewed in the Soviet Union by western journalists. (14th)

US Billboard singles for the week ending November the 18th
1 **To Sir With Love** - Lulu
2 Soul Man - Sam & Dave
3 Incense And Peppermints - Strawberry Alarm Clock
4 The Rain, The Park And Other Things - The Cowsills
5 It Must Be Him (Seul Sur Son Etoile) - Vikki Carr
6 Please Love Me Forever - Bobby Vinton
7 Your Precious Love - Marvin Gaye & Tammi Terrell
8 I Say A Little Prayer - Dionne Warwick
9 Expressway (To Your Heart) - Soul Survivors
10 I Can See For Miles - The Who

1967

1 **Let The Heartaches Begin** - Long John Baldry
2 Baby Now That I've Found You - The Foundations
3 Everybody Knows - The Dave Clark Five
4 Massachusetts (The Lights Went Out In) - The Bee Gees
5 Love Is All Around - The Troggs
6 Autumn Almanac - The Kinks
7 Zabadak! - Dave Dee, Dozy, Beaky, Mick, and Tich
8 The Last Waltz - Engelbert Humperdinck
9 If The Whole World Stopped Loving - Val Doonican
10 There Is A Mountain - Donovan

UK Number One album: *Sgt Pepper's Lonely Hearts Club Band* - The Beatles
US Billboard Number One album: *Diana Ross & The Supremes Greatest Hits* - Diana Ross & The Supremes
US Cashbox Number One single: *The Rain, The Park And Other Things* - The Cowsills
Also this week: Harold Wilson goes on television to justify devaluation of the pound. (19th)

US Billboard singles for the week ending November the 25th
1 **Incense And Peppermints** - Strawberry Alarm Clock
2 To Sir With Love - Lulu
3 The Rain, The Park And Other Things - The Cowsills
4 Soul Man - Sam & Dave
5 Daydream Believer - The Monkees
6 Please Love Me Forever - Bobby Vinton
7 I Say A Little Prayer - Dionne Warwick
8 It Must Be Him (Seul Sur Son Etoile) - Vikki Carr
9 I Can See For Miles - The Who
10 Expressway (To Your Heart) - Soul Survivors

1967

UK singles chart for the week ending December the 2nd
1 **Let The Heartaches Begin** - Long John Baldry
2 Everybody Knows - The Dave Clark Five
3 If The Whole World Stopped Loving - Val Doonican
4 Baby Now That I've Found You - The Foundations
5 The Last Waltz - Engelbert Humperdinck
6 Love Is All Around - The Troggs
7 Something's Gotten Hold Of My Heart - Gene Pitney
8 All My Love - Cliff Richard
9 Hello Goodbye - The Beatles
10 Careless Hands - Des O'Connor

UK Number One album: *The Sound Of Music* - Soundtrack
US Billboard Number One album: *Pisces, Aquarius, Capricorn & Jones Ltd.* - The Monkees
US Cashbox Number One single: *Daydream Believer* - The Monkees
Also this week: Roy Jenkins becomes the new Chancellor of the Exchequer, replacing James Callaghan. (29th)

US Billboard singles for the week ending December the 2nd
1 **Daydream Believer** - The Monkees
2 The Rain, The Park And Other Things - The Cowsills
3 Incense And Peppermints - Strawberry Alarm Clock
4 To Sir With Love - Lulu
5 I Say A Little Prayer - Dionne Warwick
6 Please Love Me Forever - Bobby Vinton
7 Soul Man - Sam & Dave
8 I Heard It Through The Grapevine - Gladys Knight & The Pips
9 I Can See For Miles - The Who
10 An Open Letter - Victor Lundberg

1967

UK singles chart for the week ending December the 9th
 1 **Hello Goodbye** - The Beatles
 2 Let The Heartaches Begin - Long John Baldry
 3 Everybody Knows - The Dave Clark Five
 4 If The Whole World Stopped Loving - Val Doonican
 5 Something's Gotten Hold Of My Heart - Gene Pitney
 6 Careless Hands - Des O'Connor
 7 Love Is All Around - The Troggs
 8 Baby Now That I've Found You - The Foundations
 9 World - The Bee Gees
10 I'm Coming Home - Tom Jones

UK Number One album: *The Sound Of Music* - Soundtrack
US Billboard Number One album: *Pisces, Aquarius, Capricorn & Jones Ltd.* - The Monkees
US Cashbox Number One single: *Daydream Believer* - The Monkees
Also this week: The first heart transplant takes place in Cape Town, South Africa. (3rd)

US Billboard singles for the week ending December the 9th
 1 **Daydream Believer** - The Monkees
 2 The Rain, The Park And Other Things - The Cowsills
 3 Incense And Peppermints - Strawberry Alarm Clock
 4 I Say A Little Prayer - Dionne Warwick
 5 I Heard It Through The Grapevine - Gladys Knight & The Pips
 6 To Sir With Love - Lulu
 7 I Second That Emotion - The Miracles
 8 Hello Goodbye - The Beatles
 9 In And Out Of Love – Diana Ross & The Supremes
10 An Open Letter - Victor Lundberg

1967

 1 **Hello Goodbye** - The Beatles
 2 Everybody Knows - The Dave Clark Five
 3 Let The Heartaches Begin - Long John Baldry
 4 If The Whole World Stopped Loving - Val Doonican
 5 I'm Coming Home - Tom Jones
 6 Something's Gotten Hold Of My Heart - Gene Pitney
 7 Careless Hands - Des O'Connor
 8 Here We Go Round The Mulberry Bush - Traffic
 9 World - The Bee Gees
10 Thank U Very Much - Scaffold

UK Number One album: *The Sound Of Music* - Soundtrack
US Billboard Number One album: *Pisces, Aquarius, Capricorn & Jones Ltd.* - The Monkees
US Cashbox Number One single: *Daydream Believer* - The Monkees
Also this week: Rolling Stones' musician Brian Jones is put on probation for his drugs offence. (12th)

US Billboard singles for the week ending December the 16th
 1 **Daydream Believer** - The Monkees
 2 I Heard It Through The Grapevine - Gladys Knight & The Pips
 3 Hello Goodbye - The Beatles
 4 I Second That Emotion - The Miracles
 5 The Rain, The Park And Other Things - The Cowsills
 6 Incense And Peppermints - Strawberry Alarm Clock
 7 I Say A Little Prayer - Dionne Warwick
 8 Boogaloo Down Broadway - The Fantastic Johnny C
 9 In And Out Of Love – Diana Ross & The Supremes
10 You Better Sit Down Kids - Cher

1967

1 **Hello Goodbye** - The Beatles
2 I'm Coming Home - Tom Jones
3 Magical Mystery Tour (EP) - The Beatles
4 If The Whole World Stopped Loving - Val Doonican
5 Something's Gotten Hold Of My Heart - Gene Pitney
6 Let The Heartaches Begin - Long John Baldry
7 All My Love - Cliff Richard
8 Daydream Believer - The Monkees
9 Thank U Very Much - Scaffold
10 Here We Go Round The Mulberry Bush - Traffic

UK Number One album: *Sgt Pepper's Lonely Hearts Club Band* - The Beatles
US Billboard Number One album: *Pisces, Aquarius, Capricorn & Jones Ltd.* - The Monkees
US Cashbox Number One single: *Daydream Believer* - The Monkees
Also this week: Alec Rose's solo sail reaches Australia. (17th)

US Billboard singles for the week ending December the 23rd
1 **Daydream Believer** - The Monkees
2 I Heard It Through The Grapevine - Gladys Knight & The Pips
3 Hello Goodbye - The Beatles
4 I Second That Emotion - The Miracles
5 Woman, Woman - Gary Puckett & The Union Gap
6 The Rain, The Park And Other Things - The Cowsills
7 Boogaloo Down Broadway - The Fantastic Johnny C
8 Incense And Peppermints - Strawberry Alarm Clock
9 You Better Sit Down Kids - Cher
10 I Say A Little Prayer - Dionne Warwick

1967

 1 **Hello Goodbye** - The Beatles
 2 Magical Mystery Tour (EP) - The Beatles
 3 I'm Coming Home - Tom Jones
 4 If The Whole World Stopped Loving - Val Doonican
 5 Something's Gotten Hold Of My Heart - Gene Pitney
 6 All My Love - Cliff Richard
 7 Daydream Believer - The Monkees
 8 Let The Heartaches Begin - Long John Baldry
 9 Thank U Very Much - Scaffold
10 Walk Away Renee - The Four Tops

UK Number One album: *Sgt Pepper's Lonely Hearts Club Band* - The Beatles
US Billboard Number One album: *Pisces, Aquarius, Capricorn & Jones Ltd.* - The Monkees
US Cashbox Number One single: *Hello Goodbye* - The Beatles
Also this week: The Beatles' film, 'Magical Mystery Tour' is first broadcast on British television. (26th)

US Billboard singles for the week ending December the 30th
 1 **Hello Goodbye** - The Beatles
 2 I Heard It Through The Grapevine - Gladys Knight & The Pips
 3 Daydream Believer - The Monkees
 4 I Second That Emotion - The Miracles
 5 Woman, Woman - Gary Puckett & The Union Gap
 6 Judy In Disguise - John Fred And His Playboy Band
 7 Chain Of Fools - Aretha Franklin
 8 Bend Me, Shape Me - The American Breed
 9 Boogaloo Down Broadway - The Fantastic Johnny C
10 Skinny Legs And All - Joe Tex

THE BEST 10 SONGS OF 1967?

Death Of A Clown by Dave Davies

Having previously treated the airwaves to the superb 'Waterloo Sunset', Dave Davies emerged from the shadow of his brother Ray and the other Kinks to briefly fly solo on this delightful ditty. He followed up the success of this release with another admirable single, 'Susannah's Still Alive' before returning to further Kinks projects. Anyhow, let's all drink to this UK Top 3 hit with its la-la-la backing vocals.

Don't Sleep In The Subway by Petula Clark

'Downtown' is undoubtedly Petula's best-known song. It even reached the coveted Number One position on the US Billboard and Cashbox singles charts. However, I have a liking for this relatively minor hit. Petula Clark may have delivered a number of strong-selling singles, but her vocals and the musical accompaniment on this particular recording are worthy of repeated listens.

007 by Desmond Dekker And The Aces

Desmond Dekker was the first male Jamaican singing sensation to find international popularity. This recording may have been viewed in some quarters as something of a novelty song, but more hits followed. In this track Dekker makes reference to the rude boys of the shanty town. These were Jamaican gangsters whose deeds inspired some of the material at this time in Jamaica where the craze of blue beat and ska was in fashion. It also found a willing audience amongst inner-city Britain.

Excerpt From A Teenage Opera by Keith West

It wasn't exactly an opera song, though the subject matter was something of a soap opera as folks ponder the absence of the once-reliable grocer Jack. As we discover that poor old Jack's delivery days are over, we are treated to a wondrous tune. The backing vocals of the children would have attracted a young audience, but this single proved popular amongst the older age group who appreciated the strings of this unusual ballad. This was definitely one of the 1960s' best novelty records.

Let's Go To San Francisco by The Flower Pot Men

San Francisco was the happening place to be in 1967 as numerous flower people made pilgrimages to Haight-Ashbury to bask in the sunshine, the sea, the sounds, and the substances. The Flower Pot Men were one-hit wonders but they did leave the legacy of this fine museum piece from the 'summer of love'. Scott McKenzie and the Animals had also paid homage to San Francisco in their song titles, as the west coast of the USA became the Mecca for all self-respecting hippies.

THE BEST 10 SONGS OF 1967? (continued)

Light My Fire by The Doors

The Doors eclipsed both the Beach Boys and the Byrds in 1967 as the leading act from the west coast of the USA. They hit the ground running with a memorable debut album that featured the psychotic 'The End' as well as this lighter item. Ray Manzarek's keyboards are an absolute joy here as the charismatic Jim Morrison remains sufficiently sober to get playful. Hereafter Jim's behaviour would become erratic, but quality tunes continued to be delivered until his death in 1971.

Massachusetts (The Lights Went Out In) by The Bee Gees

Whilst other citizens of pop world were thinking about San Francisco, the Bee Gees were singing of a location on the opposite coast. A decade before they became the premier disco act, the Gibb brothers were issuing this two and a half minute piece of melancholy. Record buyers were suitably impressed by the orchestral arrangement and the vocals of this release to reward these new singing sensations with a British chart-topper. The USA were yet to be convinced.

She's A Rainbow by The Rolling Stones

1967 has been described as an 'annus horribilis' for the strolling ruins as they fell foul of the law and fell out with one another. Ultimately Brian, Keef, and Mick narrowly escaped porridge, but they didn't escape widespread scorn when they attempted their very own 'Pepper' album. The result was the sorely under-rated 'Their Satanic Majesties Request'. This LP featured the delightful 'She's A Rainbow'. Assisted by the piano, this was a colourful psychedelic Stones track.

Somethin' Stupid by Nancy Sinatra And Frank Sinatra

The Sinatras had been regular visitors to the Transatlantic charts in recent times, and each had enjoyed a Number One single in 1966. In fact they spent the turn of the year competing against one another in the midst of the Billboard's Top 10. Now at last, father and daughter joined ranks with this easy listening piece which predictably climbed to the top of the pop listings. It was a unique achievement for a family get-together. Maybe it inspired the Jacksons and the Osmonds.

Within You, Without You by The Beatles

George Harrison was among the first western pop artists to embrace the eastern sounds as demonstrated by the likes of India's sitar man, Ravi Shankar. Harrison brought this influence into his own compositions. A number of Asian instruments were drafted into the likes of John Lennon's 'Strawberry Fields Forever' and George's offering for the Pepper album, 'Within You Without You'. This five-minute wonder is a strong contender for the album's best song.

THE BEST ALBUM OF 1967?
Are You Experienced
by The Jimi Hendrix Experience
peaked in the UK charts at No.2
peaked in the US charts at No.5
produced by Chas Chandler
released in May

James Hendrix was languishing in New York, going
nowhere slowly, when ex-Animals' guitarist Chas Chandler
chanced upon him and correctly identified Hendrix as a
prodigious talent who was wasting himself. Chandler
persuaded the talented left-handed axeman to flee his native
land and find fame in the UK. In the winter of 1966/7, word
began to spread amongst the chattering classes of London town
about this extraordinary guitarist. Paul McCartney and Eric
Clapton were two such high-profile champions of Hendrix and
it therefore came as little surprise when Jimi and his two
excellent sidekicks, Mitch Mitchell and Noel Redding, began a
successful incursion of the airwaves in early 1967. During the
course of this year, Hendrix and his Experience would offload
two albums of startling sounds upon the British (and eventually
American) public. 'Axis: Bold As Love' has its merits, but I
believe 'Are You Experienced' lays a credible claim to being the
best debut album ever. Herein however lay a problem for
Hendrix. Had he peaked too soon? Could he maintain this
formidable sound? Would he have to re-invent himself to stay
ahead of the chasing pack? Whatever considerations played
upon his drugged mind, 1967 was regrettably his creative peak,
even if 'Electric Ladyland' possesses a handful of jaw-dropping
tracks. As for the debut album, Hendrix and his very competent

THE BEST ALBUM OF 1967? (continued)

rhythm section proceed to unleash a series of raw power chords that no-one had been prepared for. Are You Experienced? The listener was not, though Cream, Jeff Beck, and the Who were also in the vanguard of laying the foundations for what has become known as 'rock music'. Hendrix and his first album were certainly foremost in providing a heavy alternative to the lighter, easy listening sounds of pop music. Generation gaps were well and truly pronounced now as the youth tuned in to guitar feedback and their elders pined for the return of the Shadows. Popular music had clearly come a long way. Was it only two years earlier that groups adorning Moptops and suits, and aping the Mersey sound were in vogue? Not for nothing did Hendrix exclaim in 'Third Stone From The Sun' that "but then you'll never hear surf music again". This wasn't strictly true but what Hendrix was suggesting was that he and his Experience were flying their freak flag and ushering new sounds which challenged the traditional teeny pop music which had run its course. If ever the popular music scene was undergoing a transformation, it was here on this vinyl. 'Fire' highlighted Jimi's sense of humour whilst the title track underpinned the playfulness of a shy man who paradoxically had copious female conquests. Even an impressed Clapton felt obliged to grow his own Hendrix afro. For a while, Hendrix was the talk of the town. However, rock music is a dangerous pastime, and Jimi was out of the game permanently in September 1970.

The album's best song? - *Third Stone From The Sun*

SPORT IN 1967

English Division One soccer champions: Manchester United
English FA Cup final: Tottenham Hotspur 2 Chelsea 1
English League Cup winners: Queen's Park Rangers
Scottish Division One soccer champions: Glasgow Celtic
Scottish FA Cup final: Glasgow Celtic 2 Aberdeen 0
Scottish League Cup winners: Glasgow Celtic
Irish League soccer champions: Glentoran; Irish Cup winners:
Crusaders
League Of Ireland soccer champions: Dundalk; cup winners:
Shamrock Rovers
European Cup final: Glasgow Celtic 2 Inter Milan 1
European Cup-Winners' Cup final: Bayern Munich 1 Glasgow
Rangers 0
European Fairs' Cup final: Dynamo Zagreb beat Leeds United
2-0 on aggregate
English county cricket champions: Yorkshire
Five Nations' rugby union champions: France
Formula One world drivers' champion: Denny Hulme
Gaelic football All-Ireland champions: Galway; hurling
champions: Kilkenny
British Open golf champion: Roberto DeVicenzo
US Masters golf champion: Gay Brewer
US Open golf champion: Jack Nicklaus
USPGA golf champion: Don January
Rugby league Challenge Cup final: Featherstone Rovers 17
Barrow 12
Wimbledon men's singles tennis champion: John Newcombe
Wimbledon ladies' singles tennis champion: Billie Jean King
The Aintree Grand National steeplechase winner: Foinavon
The Epsom Derby winner: Royal Palace
The Ryder Cup: USA 23.5 Great Britain & Ireland 8.5

DEATHS IN 1967

January 3rd: Jack Leon Ruby (US assassin), aged 55
January 4th: Donald Campbell (British record-breaker), aged 45
February 3rd: Joe Meek (British music producer), aged 37
February 8th: Sir Victor Gollancz (British publisher), aged 73
February 18th: Dr J. Robert Oppenheimer (US nuclear scientist), aged 62
March 5th: Mohammed Mossadegh (ex-Iranian Prime Minister), aged 86
March 6th: Zoltan Kodaly (Hungarian composer), aged 84
April 19th: Konrad Adenauer (ex-West German Chancellor), aged 91
May 12th: John Masefield (British Poet Laureate), aged 88
May 30th: Claude Rains (British actor), aged 77
June 3rd: Arthur Mitchell Ransome (British author), aged 83
June 3rd: Lord Arthur William Tedder (British airman), aged 76
June 7th: Dorothy Parker (US author), aged 73
June 10th: Spencer Tracy (US actor), aged 67
June 29th: Jayne Mansfield (US actress), aged 35
July 8th: Vivien Leigh (British actress), aged 53
July 13th: Tommy Simpson (British cyclist) , aged 29
July 17th: John Coltrane (US saxophonist), aged 40
July 21st: Basil Rathbone (British actor), aged 75
July 21st: Albert Luthuli (South African ex-Nobel Prize winner), aged 69
August 1st: Siegfried Lorraine Sassoon (British poet), aged 80
August 9th: John Kingsley 'Joe' Orton (British playwright), aged 34
August 15th: Rene Magritte (Belgian artist), aged 68
August 25th: George Lincoln Rockwell (US agitator), aged 49
August 27th: Brian Epstein (British entrepreneur), aged 32
September 18th: Sir John Douglas Cockcroft (British scientist), aged 70
October 3rd: Woodrow Wilson 'Woody' Guthrie (US singer), aged 55
October 8th: Clement Richard Attlee (ex-British Prime Minister), aged 84
October 9th: Ernesto 'Che' Guevara (Cuban revolutionary), aged 39
October 17th: Pu Yi (ex-Chinese Emperor), aged 61
November 20th: Casimir Funk (US biochemist), aged 83
December 10th: Otis Ray Redding, Junior (US singer), aged 26
December 17th: Harold Holt (Australian Prime Minister), aged 59
December 29th: Paul Whiteman (US jazz musician), aged 77

1968

 1 **Hello Goodbye** - The Beatles
 2 Magical Mystery Tour (EP) - The Beatles
 3 I'm Coming Home - Tom Jones
 4 Thank U Very Much - Scaffold
 5 Walk Away Renee - The Four Tops
 6 Daydream Believer - The Monkees
 7 Something's Gotten Hold Of My Heart - Gene Pitney
 8 If The Whole World Stopped Loving - Val Doonican
 9 Kites - Simon Dupree And The Big Sound
10 The Ballad Of Bonnie And Clyde - Georgie Fame

UK Number One album: *Val Doonican Rocks* - Val Doonican
US Billboard Number One album: *Magical Mystery Tour* - The Beatles
US Cashbox Number One single: *Hello Goodbye* - The Beatles
Also this week: The actress Sharon Tate marries Roman Polanski. (2nd)

US Billboard singles for the week ending January the 6th
 1 **Hello Goodbye** - The Beatles
 2 Daydream Believer - The Monkees
 3 Judy In Disguise - John Fred And His Playboy Band
 4 I Heard It Through The Grapevine - Gladys Knight & The Pips
 5 Woman, Woman - Gary Puckett & The Union Gap
 6 I Second That Emotion - The Miracles
 7 Chain Of Fools - Aretha Franklin
 8 Bend Me, Shape Me - The American Breed
 9 Boogaloo Down Broadway - The Fantastic Johnny C
10 Skinny Legs And All - Joe Tex

1968

UK singles chart for the week ending January the 13th
1 **Hello Goodbye** - The Beatles
2 Magical Mystery Tour (EP) - The Beatles
3 Walk Away Renee - The Four Tops
4 The Ballad Of Bonnie And Clyde - Georgie Fame
5 Daydream Believer - The Monkees
6 Thank U Very Much - Scaffold
7 I'm Coming Home - Tom Jones
8 If The Whole World Stopped Loving - Val Doonican
9 Kites - Simon Dupree And The Big Sound
10 Here We Go Round The Mulberry Bush - Traffic

UK Number One album: *Val Doonican Rocks* - Val Doonican
US Billboard Number One album: *Magical Mystery Tour* - The Beatles
US Cashbox Number One single: *I Heard It Through The Grapevine* - Gladys Knight & The Pips
Also this week: John Gorton is chosen as Australia's new Prime Minister. (9th)

US Billboard singles for the week ending January the 13th
1 **Hello Goodbye** - The Beatles
2 Judy In Disguise - John Fred And His Playboy Band
3 Daydream Believer - The Monkees
4 Woman, Woman - Gary Puckett & The Union Gap
5 I Heard It Through The Grapevine - Gladys Knight & The Pips
6 Chain Of Fools - Aretha Franklin
7 Bend Me, Shape Me - The American Breed
8 I Second That Emotion - The Miracles
9 Green Tambourine - The Lemon Pipers
10 Skinny Legs And All - Joe Tex

1968

UK singles chart for the week ending January the 20th
1 **Hello Goodbye** - The Beatles
2 The Ballad Of Bonnie And Clyde - Georgie Fame
3 Everlasting Love - The Love Affair
4 Magical Mystery Tour (EP) - The Beatles
5 Walk Away Renee - The Four Tops
6 Daydream Believer - The Monkees
7 I'm Coming Home - Tom Jones
8 Am I That Easy To Forget - Engelbert Humperdinck
9 If The Whole World Stopped Loving - Val Doonican
10 Thank U Very Much - Scaffold

UK Number One album: *Val Doonican Rocks* - Val Doonican
US Billboard Number One album: *Magical Mystery Tour* - The Beatles
US Cashbox Number One single: *Chain Of Fools* - Aretha Franklin
Also this week: 41 Labour MPs vote against more cuts. (17th)

US Billboard singles for the week ending January the 20th
1 **Judy In Disguise** - John Fred And His Playboy Band
2 Chain Of Fools - Aretha Franklin
3 Hello Goodbye - The Beatles
4 Woman, Woman - Gary Puckett & The Union Gap
5 Green Tambourine - The Lemon Pipers
6 Daydream Believer - The Monkees
7 Bend Me, Shape Me - The American Breed
8 I Second That Emotion - The Miracles
9 I Heard It Through The Grapevine - Gladys Knight & The Pips
10 If I Could Build My Whole World Around You - Marvin Gaye & Tammi Terrell

1968

1 **The Ballad Of Bonnie And Clyde** - Georgie Fame
2 Everlasting Love - The Love Affair
3 Am I That Easy To Forget - Engelbert Humperdinck
4 Judy In Disguise - John Fred And His Playboy Band
5 Magical Mystery Tour (EP) - The Beatles
6 Daydream Believer - The Monkees
7 Walk Away Renee - The Four Tops
8 Hello Goodbye - The Beatles
9 Tin Soldier - The Small Faces
10 Everything I Am - Plastic Penny

UK Number One album: *The Sound Of Music* - Soundtrack
US Billboard Number One album: *Magical Mystery Tour* - The Beatles
US Cashbox Number One single: *Judy In Disguise* - John Fred And His Playboy Band
Also this week: A USA ship is seized in North Korea. (23rd)

US Billboard singles for the week ending January the 27th

1 **Judy In Disguise** - John Fred And His Playboy Band
2 Chain Of Fools - Aretha Franklin
3 Green Tambourine - The Lemon Pipers
4 Woman, Woman - Gary Puckett & The Union Gap
5 Bend Me, Shape Me - The American Breed
6 Hello Goodbye - The Beatles
7 Spooky - Classics IV
8 Daydream Believer - The Monkees
9 I Heard It Through The Grapevine - Gladys Knight & The Pips
10 If I Could Build My Whole World Around You - Marvin Gaye & Tammi Terrell

1968

1 **Everlasting Love** - The Love Affair
2 The Ballad Of Bonnie And Clyde - Georgie Fame
3 Am I That Easy To Forget - Engelbert Humperdinck
4 Judy In Disguise - John Fred And His Playboy Band
5 Bend Me Shape Me - Amen Corner
6 Everything I Am - Plastic Penny
7 Mighty Quinn (Quinn The Eskimo) - Manfred Mann
8 She Wears My Ring - Solomon King
9 Suddenly You Love Me - The Tremeloes
10 Tin Soldier - The Small Faces

UK Number One album: *Sgt Pepper's Lonely Hearts Club Band* - The Beatles
US Billboard Number One album: *Magical Mystery Tour* - The Beatles
US Cashbox Number One single: *Green Tambourine* - The Lemon Pipers
Also this week: The seemingly-defeated Viet Cong launch the Tet offensive. (31st)

US Billboard singles for the week ending February the 3rd
1 **Green Tambourine** - The Lemon Pipers
2 Judy In Disguise - John Fred And His Playboy Band
3 Chain Of Fools - Aretha Franklin
4 Spooky - Classics IV
5 Bend Me, Shape Me - The American Breed
6 Woman, Woman - Gary Puckett & The Union Gap
7 Love Is Blue (L'Amour Est Bleu) - Paul Mauriat Orchestra
8 Nobody But Me - The Human Beinz
9 Out Of My Head/Can't Take My Eyes - The Lettermen
10 I Wish It Would Rain - The Temptations

1968

1 **Everlasting Love** - The Love Affair
2 Mighty Quinn (Quinn The Eskimo) - Manfred Mann
3 Judy In Disguise - John Fred And His Playboy Band
4 Am I That Easy To Forget - Engelbert Humperdinck
5 Bend Me Shape Me - Amen Corner
6 Suddenly You Love Me - The Tremeloes
7 The Ballad Of Bonnie And Clyde - Georgie Fame
8 Gimme Little Sign - Brenton Wood
9 She Wears My Ring - Solomon King
10 Everything I Am - Plastic Penny

UK Number One album: *The Four Tops Greatest Hits* - The Four Tops
US Billboard Number One album: *Magical Mystery Tour* - The Beatles
US Cashbox Number One single: *Love Is Blue (L'Amour Est Bleu)* - Paul Mauriat Orchestra
Also this week: The Winter Olympics begin in Grenoble. (6th)

US Billboard singles for the week ending February the 10th

1 **Love Is Blue** (**L'Amour Est Bleu**) - Paul Mauriat Orchestra
2 Green Tambourine - The Lemon Pipers
3 Spooky - Classics IV
4 Judy In Disguise - John Fred And His Playboy Band
5 Chain Of Fools - Aretha Franklin
6 I Wish It Would Rain - The Temptations
7 Out Of My Head/Can't Take My Eyes - The Lettermen
8 Nobody But Me - The Human Beinz
9 Woman, Woman - Gary Puckett & The Union Gap
10 Bend Me, Shape Me - The American Breed

1968

1 **Mighty Quinn** (**Quinn The Eskimo**) - Manfred Mann
2 Everlasting Love - The Love Affair
3 Bend Me Shape Me - Amen Corner
4 Am I That Easy To Forget - Engelbert Humperdinck
5 She Wears My Ring - Solomon King
6 Judy In Disguise - John Fred And His Playboy Band
7 Suddenly You Love Me - The Tremeloes
8 Gimme Little Sign - Brenton Wood
9 Pictures Of Matchstick Men - Status Quo
10 Fire Brigade - The Move

UK Number One album: *Diana Ross & The Supremes Greatest Hits* - Diana Ross & The Supremes
US Billboard Number One album: *Magical Mystery Tour* - The Beatles
US Cashbox Number One single: *Love Is Blue (L'Amour Est Bleu)* - Paul Mauriat Orchestra
Also this week: The British test the new Polaris missile for the first time. (15th)

US Billboard singles for the week ending February the 17th
1 **Love Is Blue** (**L'Amour Est Bleu**) - Paul Mauriat Orchestra
2 Green Tambourine - The Lemon Pipers
3 Spooky - Classics IV
4 I Wish It Would Rain - The Temptations
5 (Theme From) Valley Of The Dolls - Dionne Warwick
6 The Dock Of The Bay - Otis Redding
7 Out Of My Head/Can't Take My Eyes - The Lettermen
8 Nobody But Me - The Human Beinz
9 Judy In Disguise - John Fred And His Playboy Band
10 I Wonder What She's Doing Tonite – Boyce & Hart

1968

UK singles chart for the week ending February the 24th
 1 **Mighty Quinn** (**Quinn The Eskimo**) - Manfred Mann
 2 Cinderella Rockefella - Esther And Abi Ofarim
 3 She Wears My Ring - Solomon King
 4 Everlasting Love - The Love Affair
 5 Bend Me Shape Me - Amen Corner
 6 Am I That Easy To Forget - Engelbert Humperdinck
 7 Pictures Of Matchstick Men - Status Quo
 8 Fire Brigade - The Move
 9 Judy In Disguise - John Fred And His Playboy Band
10 Gimme Little Sign - Brenton Wood

UK Number One album: *Diana Ross & The Supremes Greatest Hits* - Diana Ross & The Supremes
US Billboard Number One album: *Magical Mystery Tour* - The Beatles
US Cashbox Number One single: *Love Is Blue (L'Amour Est Bleu)* - Paul Mauriat Orchestra
Also this week: The British Labour government reveals plans to restrict immigration from the Commonwealth. (22nd)

US Billboard singles for the week ending February the 24th
 1 **Love Is Blue** (**L'Amour Est Bleu**) - Paul Mauriat Orchestra
 2 (Theme From) Valley Of The Dolls - Dionne Warwick
 3 Spooky - Classics IV
 4 I Wish It Would Rain - The Temptations
 5 The Dock Of The Bay - Otis Redding
 6 Simon Says - 1910 Fruitgum Co.
 7 Green Tambourine - The Lemon Pipers
 8 I Wonder What She's Doing Tonite – Boyce & Hart
 9 Out Of My Head/Can't Take My Eyes - The Lettermen
10 Nobody But Me - The Human Beinz

1968

UK singles chart for the week ending March the 2nd
 1 **Cinderella Rockefella** - Esther And Abi Ofarim
 2 Mighty Quinn (Quinn The Eskimo) - Manfred Mann
 3 The Legend Of Xanadu - Dave Dee, Dozy, Beaky, Mick, and Tich
 4 Bend Me Shape Me - Amen Corner
 5 She Wears My Ring - Solomon King
 6 Fire Brigade - The Move
 7 Pictures Of Matchstick Men - Status Quo
 8 Words - The Bee Gees
 9 Everlasting Love - The Love Affair
10 Suddenly You Love Me - The Tremeloes

UK Number One album: *Diana Ross & The Supremes Greatest Hits* - Diana Ross & The Supremes
US Billboard Number One album: *Blooming Hits* - Paul Mauriat And His Orchestra
US Cashbox Number One single: *Love Is Blue (L'Amour Est Bleu)* - Paul Mauriat Orchestra
Also this week: The 'Valle Giulia' protest begins in Rome. (1st)

US Billboard singles for the week ending March the 2nd
 1 **Love Is Blue** (**L'Amour Est Bleu**) - Paul Mauriat Orchestra
 2 (Theme From) Valley Of The Dolls - Dionne Warwick
 3 The Dock Of The Bay - Otis Redding
 4 I Wish It Would Rain - The Temptations
 5 Simon Says - 1910 Fruitgum Co.
 6 Spooky - Classics IV
 7 Just Dropped In - Kenny Rogers
 8 I Wonder What She's Doing Tonite - Boyce & Hart
 9 Bottle Of Wine - The Fireballs
10 Everything That Touches You - The Association

1968

1 **Cinderella Rockefella** - Esther And Abi Ofarim
2 The Legend Of Xanadu - Dave Dee, Dozy, Beaky, Mick, and Tich
3 Mighty Quinn (Quinn The Eskimo) - Manfred Mann
4 Fire Brigade - The Move
5 Rosie - Don Partridge
6 Jennifer Juniper - Donovan
7 Pictures Of Matchstick Men - Status Quo
8 Bend Me Shape Me - Amen Corner
9 She Wears My Ring - Solomon King
10 Green Tambourine - The Lemon Pipers

UK Number One album: *John Wesley Harding* - Bob Dylan
US Billboard Number One album: *Blooming Hits* - Paul Mauriat And His Orchestra
US Cashbox Number One single: *Love Is Blue (L'Amour Est Bleu)* - Paul Mauriat Orchestra
Also this week: Police clash with pro-democracy students in Poland. (8th)

US Billboard singles for the week ending March the 9th

1 **Love Is Blue** (**L'Amour Est Bleu**) - Paul Mauriat Orchestra
2 (Theme From) Valley Of The Dolls - Dionne Warwick
3 The Dock Of The Bay - Otis Redding
4 Simon Says - 1910 Fruitgum Co.
5 I Wish It Would Rain - The Temptations
6 Just Dropped In - Kenny Rogers
7 Spooky - Classics IV
8 I Wonder What She's Doing Tonite - Boyce & Hart
9 La-La-Means I Love You - The Delfonics
10 Everything That Touches You - The Association

1968

1 **Cinderella Rockefella** - Esther And Abi Ofarim
2 The Legend Of Xanadu - Dave Dee, Dozy, Beaky, Mick, and Tich
3 Fire Brigade - The Move
4 Rosie - Don Partridge
5 Jennifer Juniper - Donovan
6 Delilah - Tom Jones
7 Green Tambourine - The Lemon Pipers
8 Mighty Quinn (Quinn The Eskimo) - Manfred Mann
9 The Dock Of The Bay - Otis Redding
10 Me, The Peaceful Heart - Lulu

UK Number One album: *John Wesley Harding* - Bob Dylan
US Billboard Number One album: *Blooming Hits* - Paul Mauriat And His Orchestra
US Cashbox Number One single: *Love Is Blue (L'Amour Est Bleu)* - Paul Mauriat Orchestra
Also this week: Vietnam's My Lai massacre takes place. (16th)

US Billboard singles for the week ending March the 16th
1 **The Dock Of The Bay** - Otis Redding
2 (Theme From) Valley Of The Dolls - Dionne Warwick
3 Love Is Blue (L'Amour Est Bleu) - Paul Mauriat Orchestra
4 Simon Says - 1910 Fruitgum Co.
5 Just Dropped In - Kenny Rogers
6 I Wish It Would Rain - The Temptations
7 La-La-Means I Love You - The Delfonics
8 Valleri - The Monkees
9 Sweet Sweet Baby (Since You've Been Gone) - Aretha Franklin
10 I Thank You - Sam & Dave

1968

1 **The Legend Of Xanadu** - Dave Dee, Dozy, Beaky, Mick, and Tich

2 Cinderella Rockefella - Esther And Abi Ofarim

3 Delilah - Tom Jones

4 Rosie - Don Partridge

5 The Dock Of The Bay - Otis Redding

6 Jennifer Juniper - Donovan

7 Fire Brigade - The Move

8 Green Tambourine - The Lemon Pipers

9 Me, The Peaceful Heart - Lulu

10 What A Wonderful World/Cabaret - Louis Armstrong

<u>UK Number One album:</u> *John Wesley Harding* - Bob Dylan
<u>US Billboard Number One album:</u> *Blooming Hits* - Paul Mauriat And His Orchestra
<u>US Cashbox Number One single:</u> *Love Is Blue (L'Amour Est Bleu)* - Paul Mauriat Orchestra
<u>*Also this week:*</u> Anti-war protests are held in London. (17th)

US Billboard singles for the week ending March the 23rd

1 **The Dock Of The Bay** - Otis Redding

2 Love Is Blue (L'Amour Est Bleu) - Paul Mauriat Orchestra

3 (Theme From) Valley Of The Dolls - Dionne Warwick

4 Simon Says - 1910 Fruitgum Co.

5 Just Dropped In - Kenny Rogers

6 La-La-Means I Love You - The Delfonics

7 Valleri - The Monkees

8 Sweet Sweet Baby (Since You've Been Gone) - Aretha Franklin

9 I Thank You - Sam & Dave

10 The Ballad Of Bonnie And Clyde - Georgie Fame

1968

UK singles chart for the week ending March the 30th
1 **Lady Madonna** - The Beatles
2 Delilah - Tom Jones
3 The Dock Of The Bay - Otis Redding
4 Cinderella Rockefella - Esther And Abi Ofarim
5 The Legend Of Xanadu - Dave Dee, Dozy, Beaky, Mick, and Tich
6 What A Wonderful World/Cabaret - Louis Armstrong
7 Rosie - Don Partridge
8 Congratulations - Cliff Richard
9 Jennifer Juniper - Donovan
10 If I Were A Carpenter - The Four Tops

UK Number One album: *John Wesley Harding* - Bob Dylan
US Billboard Number One album: *Blooming Hits* - Paul Mauriat And His Orchestra
US Cashbox Number One single: *Valleri* - The Monkees
Also this week: Rolls-Royce wins Britain's biggest aviation contract. (29th)

US Billboard singles for the week ending March the 30th
1 **The Dock Of The Bay** - Otis Redding
2 Love Is Blue (L'Amour Est Bleu) - Paul Mauriat Orchestra
3 Valleri - The Monkees
4 Simon Says - 1910 Fruitgum Co.
5 Sweet Sweet Baby (Since You've Been Gone) - Aretha Franklin
6 La-La-Means I Love You - The Delfonics
7 Young Girl - Gary Puckett & The Union Gap
8 The Ballad Of Bonnie And Clyde - Georgie Fame
9 Lady Madonna - The Beatles
10 (Theme From) Valley Of The Dolls - Dionne Warwick

1968

1 **Lady Madonna** - The Beatles
2 Delilah - Tom Jones
3 Congratulations - Cliff Richard
4 The Dock Of The Bay - Otis Redding
5 What A Wonderful World/Cabaret - Louis Armstrong
6 Cinderella Rockefella - Esther And Abi Ofarim
7 If I Were A Carpenter - The Four Tops
8 The Legend Of Xanadu - Dave Dee, Dozy, Beaky, Mick, and Tich
9 Step Inside Love - Cilla Black
10 Rosie - Don Partridge

UK Number One album: *John Wesley Harding* - Bob Dylan
US Billboard Number One album: *The Graduate* - Simon And Garfunkel/Soundtrack
US Cashbox Number One single: *Valleri* - The Monkees
Also this week: President Johnson announces his intention to stand down and not seek re-election in November. (31st)

US Billboard singles for the week ending April the 6th
1 **The Dock Of The Bay** - Otis Redding
2 Young Girl - Gary Puckett & The Union Gap
3 Valleri - The Monkees
4 La-La-Means I Love You - The Delfonics
5 Sweet Sweet Baby (Since You've Been Gone) - Aretha Franklin
6 Cry Like A Baby - The Box Tops
7 Lady Madonna - The Beatles
8 The Ballad Of Bonnie And Clyde - Georgie Fame
9 Love Is Blue (L'Amour Est Bleu) - Paul Mauriat Orchestra
10 Honey - Bobby Goldsboro

1968

1 **Congratulations** - Cliff Richard
2 Delilah - Tom Jones
3 What A Wonderful World/Cabaret - Louis Armstrong
4 Lady Madonna - The Beatles
5 If I Only Had Time - John Rowles
6 The Dock Of The Bay - Otis Redding
7 Simon Says - 1910 Fruitgum Co.
8 Step Inside Love - Cilla Black
9 If I Were A Carpenter - The Four Tops
10 Jennifer Eccles - The Hollies

UK Number One album: *John Wesley Harding* - Bob Dylan
US Billboard Number One album: *The Graduate* - Simon And Garfunkel/Soundtrack
US Cashbox Number One single: *Young Girl* - Gary Puckett & The Union Gap
Also this week: Thousands of students riot in West Germany. (12th)

US Billboard singles for the week ending April the 13th

1 **Honey** - Bobby Goldsboro
2 Young Girl - Gary Puckett & The Union Gap
3 The Dock Of The Bay - Otis Redding
4 Cry Like A Baby - The Box Tops
5 Sweet Sweet Baby (Since You've Been Gone) - Aretha Franklin
6 Lady Madonna - The Beatles
7 The Ballad Of Bonnie And Clyde - Georgie Fame
8 La-La-Means I Love You - The Delfonics
9 Valleri - The Monkees
10 Mighty Quinn (Quinn The Eskimo) - Manfred Mann

1968

UK singles chart for the week ending April the 20th
1 **Congratulations** - Cliff Richard
2 What A Wonderful World/Cabaret - Louis Armstrong
3 If I Only Had Time - John Rowles
4 Delilah - Tom Jones
5 Simon Says - 1910 Fruitgum Co.
6 Lady Madonna - The Beatles
7 Jennifer Eccles - The Hollies
8 The Dock Of The Bay - Otis Redding
9 Step Inside Love - Cilla Black
10 Can't Take My Eyes Off You - Andy Williams

UK Number One album: *John Wesley Harding* - Bob Dylan
US Billboard Number One album: *The Graduate* - Simon And Garfunkel/Soundtrack
US Cashbox Number One single: *Honey* - Bobby Goldsboro
Also this week: 122 people are killed when an airliner crashes in South Africa. (20th)

US Billboard singles for the week ending April the 20th
1 **Honey** - Bobby Goldsboro
2 Young Girl - Gary Puckett & The Union Gap
3 Cry Like A Baby - The Box Tops
4 Lady Madonna - The Beatles
5 Sweet Sweet Baby (Since You've Been Gone) - Aretha Franklin
6 The Dock Of The Bay - Otis Redding
7 The Ballad Of Bonnie And Clyde - Georgie Fame
8 Dance To The Music - Sly & The Family Stone
9 I Got The Feelin' - James Brown
10 Mighty Quinn (Quinn The Eskimo) - Manfred Mann
The once-prolific Cliff Richard had to wait eleven years until his next UK Number One.

1968
1 **What A Wonderful World/Cabaret** - Louis Armstrong
2 Congratulations - Cliff Richard
3 Simon Says - 1910 Fruitgum Co.
4 If I Only Had Time - John Rowles
5 Delilah - Tom Jones
6 Can't Take My Eyes Off You - Andy Williams
7 Jennifer Eccles - The Hollies
8 I Can't Let Maggie Go - Honeybus
9 Lady Madonna - The Beatles
10 Lazy Sunday - The Small Faces

UK Number One album: *John Wesley Harding* - Bob Dylan
US Billboard Number One album: *The Graduate* - Simon And Garfunkel/Soundtrack
US Cashbox Number One single: *Honey* - Bobby Goldsboro
Also this week: A political storm erupts after an Enoch Powell speech predicts "rivers of blood". (21st)

US Billboard singles for the week ending April the 27th
1 **Honey** - Bobby Goldsboro
2 Cry Like A Baby - The Box Tops
3 Young Girl - Gary Puckett & The Union Gap
4 Lady Madonna - The Beatles
5 Sweet Sweet Baby (Since You've Been Gone) - Aretha Franklin
6 I Got The Feelin' - James Brown
7 The Dock Of The Bay - Otis Redding
8 Dance To The Music - Sly & The Family Stone
9 Tighten Up - Archie Bell & The Drells
10 The Ballad Of Bonnie And Clyde - Georgie Fame
Louis Armstrong became the oldest artist to achieve a UK Number 1 at the age of 66 !

1968

 1 **What A Wonderful World/Cabaret** - Louis Armstrong
 2 Simon Says - 1910 Fruitgum Co.
 3 Lazy Sunday - The Small Faces
 4 If I Only Had Time - John Rowles
 5 Can't Take My Eyes Off You - Andy Williams
 6 Congratulations - Cliff Richard
 7 A Man Without Love - Engelbert Humperdinck
 8 Jennifer Eccles - The Hollies
 9 I Can't Let Maggie Go - Honeybus
10 Delilah - Tom Jones

UK Number One album: *John Wesley Harding* - Bob Dylan
US Billboard Number One album: *The Graduate* - Simon And Garfunkel/Soundtrack
US Cashbox Number One single: *Honey* - Bobby Goldsboro
Also this week: Britain's first human liver transplant takes place. (2nd)

US Billboard singles for the week ending May the 4th

 1 **Honey** - Bobby Goldsboro
 2 Cry Like A Baby - The Box Tops
 3 Young Girl - Gary Puckett & The Union Gap
 4 Lady Madonna - The Beatles
 5 Tighten Up - Archie Bell & The Drells
 6 I Got The Feelin' - James Brown
 7 Cowboys To Girls - The Intruders
 8 The Good, The Bad And The Ugly - Hugo Montenegro
 9 A Beautiful Morning - The Rascals
10 The Unicorn - The Irish Rovers

1968

1 **What A Wonderful World/Cabaret** - Louis Armstrong
2 Lazy Sunday - The Small Faces
3 Simon Says - 1910 Fruitgum Co.
4 A Man Without Love - Engelbert Humperdinck
5 I Don't Want Our Loving To Die - The Herd
6 Can't Take My Eyes Off You - Andy Williams
7 Young Girl - Gary Puckett & The Union Gap
8 If I Only Had Time - John Rowles
9 Honey - Bobby Goldsboro
10 Jennifer Eccles - The Hollies

UK Number One album: *John Wesley Harding* - Bob Dylan
US Billboard Number One album: *The Graduate* - Simon And
Garfunkel/Soundtrack
US Cashbox Number One single: *Honey* - Bobby Goldsboro
Also this week: Three Kray brothers are arrested again in
London. (8th)

US Billboard singles for the week ending May the 11th
1 **Honey** - Bobby Goldsboro
2 Tighten Up - Archie Bell & The Drells
3 Young Girl - Gary Puckett & The Union Gap
4 The Good, The Bad And The Ugly - Hugo Montenegro
5 Cry Like A Baby - The Box Tops
6 A Beautiful Morning - The Rascals
7 Cowboys To Girls - The Intruders
8 The Unicorn - The Irish Rovers
9 Mrs Robinson - Simon And Garfunkel
10 Lady Madonna - The Beatles

1968

 1 **What A Wonderful World/Cabaret** - Louis Armstrong
 2 A Man Without Love - Engelbert Humperdinck
 3 Young Girl - Gary Puckett & The Union Gap
 4 Lazy Sunday - The Small Faces
 5 Honey - Bobby Goldsboro
 6 Simon Says - 1910 Fruitgum Co.
 7 I Don't Want Our Loving To Die - The Herd
 8 If I Only Had Time - John Rowles
 9 Can't Take My Eyes Off You - Andy Williams
10 White Horses - Jacky

UK Number One album: *Scott 2* - Scott Walker
US Billboard Number One album: *The Graduate* - Simon And Garfunkel/Soundtrack
US Cashbox Number One single: *Tighten Up* - Archie Bell & The Drells
Also this week: Bobby Kennedy wins a second successive primary contest. (14th)

US Billboard singles for the week ending May the 18th
 1 **Tighten Up** - Archie Bell & The Drells
 2 Mrs Robinson - Simon And Garfunkel
 3 Honey - Bobby Goldsboro
 4 The Good, The Bad And The Ugly - Hugo Montenegro
 5 A Beautiful Morning - The Rascals
 6 Cowboys To Girls - The Intruders
 7 Love Is All Around - The Troggs
 8 The Unicorn - The Irish Rovers
 9 Young Girl - Gary Puckett & The Union Gap
10 Do You Know The Way To San Jose - Dionne Warwick

1968

  1 **Young Girl** - Gary Puckett & The Union Gap
  2 A Man Without Love - Engelbert Humperdinck
  3 Honey - Bobby Goldsboro
  4 Lazy Sunday - The Small Faces
  5 What A Wonderful World/Cabaret - Louis Armstrong
  6 I Don't Want Our Loving To Die - The Herd
  7 Simon Says - 1910 Fruitgum Co.
  8 Can't Take My Eyes Off You - Andy Williams
  9 Rainbow Valley - The Love Affair
10 White Horses - Jacky

UK Number One album: *John Wesley Harding* - Bob Dylan
US Billboard Number One album: *Bookends* - Simon And Garfunkel
US Cashbox Number One single: *Mrs Robinson* - Simon And Garfunkel
Also this week: A French policeman is killed amidst more student riots. (24th)

US Billboard singles for the week ending May the 25th

  1 **Tighten Up** - Archie Bell & The Drells
  2 Mrs Robinson - Simon And Garfunkel
  3 A Beautiful Morning - The Rascals
  4 The Good, The Bad And The Ugly - Hugo Montenegro
  5 Honey - Bobby Goldsboro
  6 Cowboys To Girls - The Intruders
  7 The Unicorn - The Irish Rovers
  8 Ain't Nothing Like The Real Thing - Marvin Gaye And Tammi Terrell
  9 Shoo-Be-Doo-Be-Doo-Da-Day - Stevie Wonder
10 Do You Know The Way To San Jose - Dionne Warwick

1968

1 **Young Girl** - Gary Puckett & The Union Gap
2 Honey - Bobby Goldsboro
3 A Man Without Love - Engelbert Humperdinck
4 What A Wonderful World/Cabaret - Louis Armstrong
5 Lazy Sunday - The Small Faces
6 I Don't Want Our Loving To Die - The Herd
7 Rainbow Valley - The Love Affair
8 Joanna - Scott Walker
9 Do You Know The Way To San Jose - Dionne Warwick
10 This Wheel's On Fire - Julie Driscoll, Brian Auger, And The Trinity

UK Number One album: *John Wesley Harding* - Bob Dylan
US Billboard Number One album: *Bookends* - Simon And Garfunkel
US Cashbox Number One single: *Mrs Robinson* - Simon And Garfunkel
Also this week: The Beatles begin recording a new LP.(30th)

US Billboard singles for the week ending June the 1st

1 **Mrs Robinson** - Simon And Garfunkel
2 The Good, The Bad And The Ugly - Hugo Montenegro
3 A Beautiful Morning - The Rascals
4 Tighten Up - Archie Bell & The Drells
5 Honey - Bobby Goldsboro
6 Yummy Yummy Yummy - Ohio Express
7 Mony Mony - Tommy James And The Shondells
8 Ain't Nothing Like The Real Thing - Marvin Gaye And Tammi Terrell
9 Cowboys To Girls - The Intruders
10 Do You Know The Way To San Jose - Dionne Warwick

1968

1 **Young Girl** - Gary Puckett & The Union Gap
2 A Man Without Love - Engelbert Humperdinck
3 Honey - Bobby Goldsboro
4 Jumpin' Jack Flash - The Rolling Stones
5 Rainbow Valley - The Love Affair
6 I Don't Want Our Loving To Die - The Herd
7 Joanna - Scott Walker
8 Do You Know The Way To San Jose - Dionne Warwick
9 Lazy Sunday - The Small Faces
10 This Wheel's On Fire - Julie Driscoll, Brian Auger, And The Trinity

UK Number One album: *John Wesley Harding* - Bob Dylan
US Billboard Number One album: *Bookends* - Simon And Garfunkel
US Cashbox Number One single: *Mrs Robinson* - Simon And Garfunkel
Also this week: Sirhan Sirhan is charged with the recent murder of Robert Kennedy. (7th)

US Billboard singles for the week ending June the 8th

1 **Mrs Robinson** - Simon And Garfunkel
2 Tighten Up - Archie Bell & The Drells
3 This Guy's In Love With You - Herb Alpert
4 The Good, The Bad And The Ugly - Hugo Montenegro
5 Mony Mony - Tommy James And The Shondells
6 Yummy Yummy Yummy - Ohio Express
7 MacArthur Park - Richard Harris
8 A Beautiful Morning - The Rascals
9 Think - Aretha Franklin
10 Honey - Bobby Goldsboro

1968

1 **Young Girl** - Gary Puckett & The Union Gap
2 Jumpin' Jack Flash - The Rolling Stones
3 Honey - Bobby Goldsboro
4 A Man Without Love - Engelbert Humperdinck
5 Rainbow Valley - The Love Affair
6 This Wheel's On Fire - Julie Driscoll, Brian Auger, And The Trinity
7 Blue Eyes - Don Partridge
8 Hurdy Gurdy Man - Donovan
9 Do You Know The Way To San Jose - Dionne Warwick
10 I Don't Want Our Loving To Die - The Herd

UK Number One album: *Love Andy* - Andy Williams
US Billboard Number One album: *The Graduate* - Simon And Garfunkel/Soundtrack
US Cashbox Number One single: *Mrs Robinson* - Simon And Garfunkel
Also this week: President de Gaulle bans open-air demonstrations. (12th)

US Billboard singles for the week ending June the 15th

1 **Mrs Robinson** - Simon And Garfunkel
2 This Guy's In Love With You - Herb Alpert
3 Mony Mony - Tommy James And The Shondells
4 Yummy Yummy Yummy - Ohio Express
5 MacArthur Park - Richard Harris
6 Tighten Up - Archie Bell & The Drells
7 Think - Aretha Franklin
8 A Beautiful Morning - The Rascals
9 The Good, The Bad And The Ugly - Hugo Montenegro
10 The Look Of Love - Sergio Mendes

1968

UK singles chart for the week ending June the 22nd
 1 **Jumpin' Jack Flash** - The Rolling Stones
 2 Young Girl - Gary Puckett & The Union Gap
 3 Blue Eyes - Don Partridge
 4 Hurdy Gurdy Man - Donovan
 5 This Wheel's On Fire - Julie Driscoll, Brian Auger, And The Trinity
 6 Honey - Bobby Goldsboro
 7 Baby Come Back - The Equals
 8 Do You Know The Way To San Jose - Dionne Warwick
 9 I Pretend - Des O'Connor
10 A Man Without Love - Engelbert Humperdinck

UK Number One album: *The Dock Of The Bay* - Otis Redding
US Billboard Number One album: *The Graduate* - Simon And Garfunkel/Soundtrack
US Cashbox Number One single: *This Guy's In Love With You* - Herb Alpert
Also this week: Sprinter Jim Hines of the USA sets a new 100 metres world record. (20th)

US Billboard singles for the week ending June the 22nd
 1 **This Guy's In Love With You** - Herb Alpert
 2 MacArthur Park - Richard Harris
 3 Mrs Robinson - Simon And Garfunkel
 4 Yummy Yummy Yummy - Ohio Express
 5 The Look Of Love - Sergio Mendes
 6 Mony Mony - Tommy James And The Shondells
 7 Think - Aretha Franklin
 8 Angel Of The Morning - Merrilee Rush & The Turnabouts
 9 Tighten Up - Archie Bell & The Drells
10 Reach Out Of The Darkness - Friend & Lover

1968

1 **Jumpin' Jack Flash** - The Rolling Stones
2 Young Girl - Gary Puckett & The Union Gap
3 Baby Come Back - The Equals
4 Hurdy Gurdy Man - Donovan
5 Blue Eyes - Don Partridge
6 I Pretend - Des O'Connor
7 The Son Of Hickory Holler's Tramp - O.C. Smith
8 This Wheel's On Fire - Julie Driscoll, Brian Auger, And The Trinity
9 Lovin' Things - Marmalade
10 Honey - Bobby Goldsboro

UK Number One album: *Ogden's Nut Gone Flake* - The Small Faces
US Billboard Number One album: *Bookends* - Simon And Garfunkel
US Cashbox Number One single: *This Guy's In Love With You* - Herb Alpert
Also this week: The Liberals win Canada's election. (25th)

US Billboard singles for the week ending June the 29th

1 **This Guy's In Love With You** - Herb Alpert
2 The Horse - Cliff Nobles & Co.
3 MacArthur Park - Richard Harris
4 Yummy Yummy Yummy - Ohio Express
5 The Look Of Love - Sergio Mendes
6 Mony Mony - Tommy James And The Shondells
7 Angel Of The Morning - Merrilee Rush & The Turnabouts
8 Think - Aretha Franklin
9 Here Comes The Judge - Shorty Long
10 Reach Out Of The Darkness - Friend & Lover

1968

  1 **Baby Come Back** - The Equals
  2 The Son Of Hickory Holler's Tramp - O.C. Smith
  3 Jumpin' Jack Flash - The Rolling Stones
  4 Hurdy Gurdy Man - Donovan
  5 I Pretend - Des O'Connor
  6 Lovin' Things - Marmalade
  7 Blue Eyes - Don Partridge
  8 Yesterday Has Gone - Cupid's Inspiration
  9 My Name Is Jack - Manfred Mann
 10 Young Girl - Gary Puckett & The Union Gap

UK Number One album: *Ogden's Nut Gone Flake* - The Small Faces
US Billboard Number One album: *Bookends* - Simon And Garfunkel
US Cashbox Number One single: *This Guy's In Love With You* - Herb Alpert
Also this week: Alec Rose ends his 354-day sea voyage. (4th)

US Billboard singles for the week ending July the 6th
  1 **This Guy's In Love With You** - Herb Alpert
  2 The Horse - Cliff Nobles & Co.
  3 Jumpin' Jack Flash - The Rolling Stones
  4 The Look Of Love - Sergio Mendes
  5 Grazing In The Grass - Hugh Masekela
  6 Lady Willpower - Gary Puckett & The Union Gap
  7 Angel Of The Morning - Merrilee Rush & The Turnabouts
  8 Here Comes The Judge - Shorty Long
  9 MacArthur Park - Richard Harris
 10 Reach Out Of The Darkness - Friend & Lover

Eddy Grant earned a UK No. 1 with the Equals. 14 years would pass before his next No.1.

1968

 1 **Baby Come Back** - The Equals
 2 The Son Of Hickory Holler's Tramp - O.C. Smith
 3 I Pretend - Des O'Connor
 4 Yesterday Has Gone - Cupid's Inspiration
 5 Jumpin' Jack Flash - The Rolling Stones
 6 Hurdy Gurdy Man - Donovan
 7 Lovin' Things - Marmalade
 8 My Name Is Jack - Manfred Mann
 9 Yummy Yummy Yummy - Ohio Express
10 Blue Eyes - Don Partridge

UK Number One album: *Ogden's Nut Gone Flake* - The Small Faces
US Billboard Number One album: *Bookends* - Simon And Garfunkel
US Cashbox Number One single: *This Guy's In Love With You* - Herb Alpert
Also this week: The Queen opens the Hayward Gallery in central London. (10th)

US Billboard singles for the week ending July the 13th

 1 **This Guy's In Love With You** - Herb Alpert
 2 The Horse - Cliff Nobles & Co.
 3 Jumpin' Jack Flash - The Rolling Stones
 4 Lady Willpower - Gary Puckett & The Union Gap
 5 Grazing In The Grass - Hugh Masekela
 6 The Look Of Love - Sergio Mendes
 7 Angel Of The Morning - Merrilee Rush & The Turnabouts
 8 Stoned Soul Picnic - The 5th Dimension
 9 Here Comes The Judge - Shorty Long
10 Indian Lake - The Cowsills

1968

 1 **Baby Come Back** - The Equals
 2 The Son Of Hickory Holler's Tramp - O.C. Smith
 3 I Pretend - Des O'Connor
 4 Yesterday Has Gone - Cupid's Inspiration
 5 Yummy Yummy Yummy - Ohio Express
 6 Mony Mony - Tommy James And The Shondells
 7 MacArthur Park - Richard Harris
 8 Fire - The Crazy World Of Arthur Brown
 9 Jumpin' Jack Flash - The Rolling Stones
10 My Name Is Jack - Manfred Mann

UK Number One album: *Ogden's Nut Gone Flake* - The Small Faces
US Billboard Number One album: *Bookends* - Simon And Garfunkel
US Cashbox Number One single: *Jumpin' Jack Flash* - The Rolling Stones
Also this week: Five Warsaw Pact leaders meet to discuss the growing unrest in Czechoslovakia. (15th)

US Billboard singles for the week ending July the 20th
 1 **Grazing In The Grass** - Hugh Masekela
 2 Lady Willpower - Gary Puckett & The Union Gap
 3 Jumpin' Jack Flash - The Rolling Stones
 4 This Guy's In Love With You - Herb Alpert
 5 The Horse - Cliff Nobles & Co.
 6 Stoned Soul Picnic - The 5th Dimension
 7 Hurdy Gurdy Man - Donovan
 8 Classical Gas - Mason Williams
 9 Hello, I Love You - The Doors
10 Indian Lake - The Cowsills

1968

UK singles chart for the week ending July the 27th
  1 **I Pretend** - Des O'Connor
  2 Mony Mony - Tommy James And The Shondells
  3 Baby Come Back - The Equals
  4 MacArthur Park - Richard Harris
  5 Yummy Yummy Yummy - Ohio Express
  6 The Son Of Hickory Holler's Tramp - O.C. Smith
  7 Yesterday Has Gone - Cupid's Inspiration
  8 Fire! - The Crazy World Of Arthur Brown
  9 This Guy's In Love With You - Herb Alpert
10 Mrs Robinson - Simon And Garfunkel

UK Number One album: *Ogden's Nut Gone Flake* - The Small
Faces
US Billboard Number One album: *The Beat Of The Brass* -
Herb Alpert And The Tijuana Brass
US Cashbox Number One single: *Grazing In The Grass* - Hugh
Masekela
Also this week: Barclays Bank merges with Martins Bank.
(25th)

US Billboard singles for the week ending July the 27th
  1 **Grazing In The Grass** - Hugh Masekela
  2 Lady Willpower - Gary Puckett & The Union Gap
  3 Stoned Soul Picnic - The 5th Dimension
  4 Jumpin' Jack Flash - The Rolling Stones
  5 The Horse - Cliff Nobles & Co.
  6 Hurdy Gurdy Man - Donovan
  7 This Guy's In Love With You - Herb Alpert
  8 Classical Gas - Mason Williams
  9 Hello, I Love You - The Doors
10 Indian Lake - The Cowsills

1968

UK singles chart for the week ending August the 3rd

 1 **Mony Mony** - Tommy James And The Shondells
 2 I Pretend - Des O'Connor
 3 Fire! - The Crazy World Of Arthur Brown
 4 MacArthur Park - Richard Harris
 5 Mrs Robinson - Simon And Garfunkel
 6 Baby Come Back - The Equals
 7 I Close My Eyes And Count To Ten - Dusty Springfield
 8 Last Night In Soho - Dave Dee, Dozy, Beaky, Mick, and Tich
 9 The Son Of Hickory Holler's Tramp - O.C. Smith
10 Yummy Yummy Yummy - Ohio Express

UK Number One album: *Ogden's Nut Gone Flake* - The Small Faces
US Billboard Number One album: *The Beat Of The Brass* - Herb Alpert And The Tijuana Brass
US Cashbox Number One single: *Lady Willpower* - Gary Puckett & The Union Gap
Also this week: Thames Television begins broadcasting.(30th)

US Billboard singles for the week ending August the 3rd

 1 **Hello, I Love You** - The Doors
 2 Classical Gas - Mason Williams
 3 Stoned Soul Picnic - The 5th Dimension
 4 Grazing In The Grass - Hugh Masekela
 5 Hurdy Gurdy Man - Donovan
 6 Jumpin' Jack Flash - The Rolling Stones
 7 Lady Willpower - Gary Puckett & The Union Gap
 8 The Horse - Cliff Nobles & Co.
 9 Turn Around, Look At Me - The Vogues
10 Sunshine Of Your Love - Cream

1968

1 **Mony Mony** - Tommy James And The Shondells
2 Fire! - The Crazy World Of Arthur Brown
3 I Pretend - Des O'Connor
4 Mrs Robinson - Simon And Garfunkel
5 This Guy's In Love With You - Herb Alpert
6 I Close My Eyes And Count To Ten - Dusty Springfield
7 Help Yourself - Tom Jones
8 MacArthur Park - Richard Harris
9 Last Night In Soho - Dave Dee, Dozy, Beaky, Mick, and Tich
10 Sunshine Girl - Herman's Hermits

UK Number One album: *Delilah* - Tom Jones
US Billboard Number One album: *Wheels Of Fire* - Cream
US Cashbox Number One single: *Classical Gas* - Mason Williams
Also this week: 48 people are killed when a British airliner crashes in West Germany. (9th)

US Billboard singles for the week ending August the 10th
1 **Hello, I Love You** - The Doors
2 Classical Gas - Mason Williams
3 Stoned Soul Picnic - The 5th Dimension
4 Grazing In The Grass - Hugh Masekela
5 People Got To Be Free - The Rascals
6 Hurdy Gurdy Man - Donovan
7 Lady Willpower - Gary Puckett & The Union Gap
8 Turn Around, Look At Me - The Vogues
9 Sunshine Of Your Love - Cream
10 Jumpin' Jack Flash - The Rolling Stones

The Doors achieved 2 Billboard No.1 hits, but their singles never reached the UK Top Ten.

1968

1 **Mony Mony** - Tommy James And The Shondells
2 Fire! - The Crazy World Of Arthur Brown
3 This Guy's In Love With You - Herb Alpert
4 I Close My Eyes And Count To Ten - Dusty Springfield
5 I Pretend - Des O'Connor
6 Mrs Robinson - Simon And Garfunkel
7 Dance To The Music - Sly & The Family Stone
8 Sunshine Girl - Herman's Hermits
9 Help Yourself - Tom Jones
10 Last Night In Soho - Dave Dee, Dozy, Beaky, Mick, and Tich

UK Number One album: *Bookends* - Simon And Garfunkel
US Billboard Number One album: *Wheels Of Fire* - Cream
US Cashbox Number One single: *Hello, I Love You* - The Doors
Also this week: Rioting erupts again in the Watts ghetto of Los Angeles, California. (12th)

US Billboard singles for the week ending August the 17th
1 **People Got To Be Free** - The Rascals
2 Hello, I Love You - The Doors
3 Classical Gas - Mason Williams
4 Born To Be Wild - Steppenwolf
5 Light My Fire - Jose Feliciano
6 Stoned Soul Picnic - The 5th Dimension
7 Turn Around, Look At Me - The Vogues
8 Sunshine Of Your Love - Cream
9 Grazing In The Grass - Hugh Masekela
10 Hurdy Gurdy Man - Donovan

1968

1 **Mony Mony** - Tommy James And The Shondells
2 Fire! - The Crazy World Of Arthur Brown
3 This Guy's In Love With You - Herb Alpert
4 Do It Again - The Beach Boys
5 Help Yourself - Tom Jones
6 I Close My Eyes And Count To Ten - Dusty Springfield
7 I've Gotta Get A Message To You - The Bee Gees
8 Sunshine Girl - Herman's Hermits
9 High In The Sky - Amen Corner
10 Dance To The Music - Sly & The Family Stone

UK Number One album: *Bookends* - Simon And Garfunkel
US Billboard Number One album: *Wheels Of Fire* - Cream
US Cashbox Number One single: *People Got To Be Free* - The Rascals
Also this week: Tanks enter Czechoslovakia on the orders of the USSR. (21st)

US Billboard singles for the week ending August the 24th
1 **People Got To Be Free** - The Rascals
2 Born To Be Wild - Steppenwolf
3 Hello, I Love You - The Doors
4 Light My Fire - Jose Feliciano
5 Classical Gas - Mason Williams
6 Sunshine Of Your Love - Cream
7 Turn Around, Look At Me - The Vogues
8 Stoned Soul Picnic - The 5th Dimension
9 I Can't Stop Dancing - Archie Bell & The Drells
10 Stay In My Corner - The Dells

1968

1 **Do It Again** - The Beach Boys
2 I've Gotta Get A Message To You - The Bee Gees
3 This Guy's In Love With You - Herb Alpert
4 Mony Mony - Tommy James And The Shondells
5 Help Yourself - Tom Jones
6 Fire! - The Crazy World Of Arthur Brown
7 High In The Sky - Amen Corner
8 I Say A Little Prayer - Aretha Franklin
9 Sunshine Girl - Herman's Hermits
10 Dance To The Music - Sly & The Family Stone

UK Number One album: *Bookends* - Simon And Garfunkel
US Billboard Number One album: *Wheels Of Fire* - Cream
US Cashbox Number One single: P*eople Got To Be Free* - The
Rascals
Also this week: England win at the Oval and draw cricket's
Ashes series 1-1, but Australia retain the Ashes. (27th)

US Billboard singles for the week ending August the 31st
1 **People Got To Be Free** - The Rascals
2 Born To Be Wild - Steppenwolf
3 Light My Fire - Jose Feliciano
4 Hello, I Love You - The Doors
5 Sunshine Of Your Love - Cream
6 You Keep Me Hangin' On - Vanilla Fudge
7 Harper Valley P.T.A. - Jeannie C. Riley
8 You're All I Need To Get By - Marvin Gaye And Tammi
Terrell
9 I Can't Stop Dancing - Archie Bell & The Drells
10 Stay In My Corner - The Dells

1968

1 **I've Gotta Get A Message To You** - The Bee Gees
2 Do It Again - The Beach Boys
3 This Guy's In Love With You - Herb Alpert
4 I Say A Little Prayer - Aretha Franklin
5 Help Yourself - Tom Jones
6 High In The Sky - Amen Corner
7 Hold Me Tight - Johnny Nash
8 Fire! - The Crazy World Of Arthur Brown
9 Mony Mony - Tommy James And The Shondells
10 On The Road Again - Canned Heat

UK Number One album: *Bookends* - Simon And Garfunkel
US Billboard Number One album: *Waiting For The Sun* - The Doors
US Cashbox Number One single: *People Got To Be Free* - The Rascals
Also this week: The London Underground's Victoria Line is opened. (1st)

US Billboard singles for the week ending September the 7th
1 **People Got To Be Free** - The Rascals
2 Born To Be Wild - Steppenwolf
3 Light My Fire - Jose Feliciano
4 Harper Valley P.T.A. - Jeannie C. Riley
5 Hello, I Love You - The Doors
6 The House That Jack Built - Aretha Franklin
7 1,2,3, Red Light - 1910 Fruitgum Co.
8 You're All I Need To Get By - Marvin Gaye And Tammi Terrell
9 I Can't Stop Dancing - Archie Bell & The Drells
10 Stay In My Corner - The Dells

1968

UK singles chart for the week ending September the 14th

1 **Hey Jude** - The Beatles
2 I've Gotta Get A Message To You - The Bee Gees
3 Do It Again - The Beach Boys
4 I Say A Little Prayer - Aretha Franklin
5 Hold Me Tight - Johnny Nash
6 This Guy's In Love With You - Herb Alpert
7 Those Were The Days - Mary Hopkin
8 Help Yourself - Tom Jones
9 High In The Sky - Amen Corner
10 On The Road Again - Canned Heat

UK Number One album: *Bookends* - Simon And Garfunkel
US Billboard Number One album: *Waiting For The Sun* - The Doors
US Cashbox Number One single: *Harper Valley P.T.A.* - Jeannie C. Riley
Also this week: Press censorship is reimposed in Czechoslovakia after the Prague Spring's demise. (13th)

US Billboard singles for the week ending September the 14th

1 **People Got To Be Free** - The Rascals
2 Harper Valley P.T.A. - Jeannie C. Riley
3 Light My Fire - Jose Feliciano
4 Born To Be Wild - Steppenwolf
5 1,2,3, Red Light - 1910 Fruitgum Co.
6 The House That Jack Built - Aretha Franklin
7 You're All I Need To Get By - Marvin Gaye And Tammi Terrell
8 Hush - Deep Purple
9 Hello, I Love You - The Doors
10 Hey Jude - The Beatles

1968

1 **Hey Jude** - The Beatles
2 Those Were The Days - Mary Hopkin
3 I've Gotta Get A Message To You - The Bee Gees
4 I Say A Little Prayer - Aretha Franklin
5 Do It Again - The Beach Boys
6 Jesamine - The Casuals
7 Hold Me Tight - Johnny Nash
8 On The Road Again - Canned Heat
9 Lady Willpower - Gary Puckett & The Union Gap
10 This Guy's In Love With You - Herb Alpert

UK Number One album: *Delilah* - Tom Jones
US Billboard Number One album: *Waiting For The Sun* - The Doors
US Cashbox Number One single: *Hey Jude* - The Beatles
Also this week: South Africa bans the England cricket team's forthcoming tour because Basil D'Oliveira was selected. (17th)

US Billboard singles for the week ending September the 21st
1 **Harper Valley P.T.A**. - Jeannie C. Riley
2 People Got To Be Free - The Rascals
3 Hey Jude - The Beatles
4 Hush - Deep Purple
5 1,2,3, Red Light - 1910 Fruitgum Co.
6 Light My Fire - Jose Feliciano
7 Born To Be Wild - Steppenwolf
8 The Fool On The Hill - Sergio Mendes
9 I've Gotta Get A Message To You - The Bee Gees
10 The House That Jack Built - Aretha Franklin

Hey Jude enabled the Beatles to match Elvis Presley's haul of fifteen UK Number Ones..

1968

1 **Those Were The Days** - Mary Hopkin
2 Hey Jude - The Beatles
3 Jesamine - The Casuals
4 I've Gotta Get A Message To You - The Bee Gees
5 Hold Me Tight - Johnny Nash
6 I Say A Little Prayer - Aretha Franklin
7 Do It Again - The Beach Boys
8 On The Road Again - Canned Heat
9 Little Arrows - Leapy Lee
10 Lady Willpower - Gary Puckett & The Union Gap

UK Number One album: *Bookends* - Simon And Garfunkel
US Billboard Number One album: *Time Peace: The Rascals' Greatest Hits* - The Rascals
US Cashbox Number One single: *Hey Jude* - The Beatles
Also this week: Jaguar Motors unveils the new XJ-6 luxury saloon car. (26th)

US Billboard singles for the week ending September the 28th
1 **Hey Jude** - The Beatles
2 Harper Valley P.T.A. - Jeannie C. Riley
3 People Got To Be Free - The Rascals
4 Hush - Deep Purple
5 Fire! - The Crazy World Of Arthur Brown
6 The Fool On The Hill - Sergio Mendes
7 1,2,3, Red Light - 1910 Fruitgum Co.
8 I've Gotta Get A Message To You - The Bee Gees
9 Girl Watcher - The O'Kaysions
10 Slip Away - Clarence Carter

1968

UK singles chart for the week ending October the 5th
1 **Those Were The Days** - Mary Hopkin
2 Hey Jude - The Beatles
3 Jesamine - The Casuals
4 Little Arrows - Leapy Lee
5 Hold Me Tight - Johnny Nash
6 I've Gotta Get A Message To You - The Bee Gees
7 Lady Willpower - Gary Puckett & The Union Gap
8 I Say A Little Prayer - Aretha Franklin
9 The Red Balloon - The Dave Clark Five
10 High In The Sky - Amen Corner

UK Number One album: *Bookends* - Simon And Garfunkel
US Billboard Number One album: *Waiting For The Sun* - The Doors
US Cashbox Number One single: *Hey Jude* - The Beatles
Also this week: A Red Cross DC-4 crashes, killing fifty-five Nigerian soldiers. (29th)

US Billboard singles for the week ending October the 5th
1 **Hey Jude** - The Beatles
2 Harper Valley P.T.A. - Jeannie C. Riley
3 Fire! - The Crazy World Of Arthur Brown
4 Little Green Apples - O.C. Smith
5 Girl Watcher - The O'Kaysions
6 Slip Away - Clarence Carter
7 People Got To Be Free - The Rascals
8 I've Gotta Get A Message To You - The Bee Gees
9 1,2,3, Red Light - 1910 Fruitgum Co.
10 I Say A Little Prayer - Aretha Franklin

1968

1 **Those Were The Days** - Mary Hopkin
2 Little Arrows - Leapy Lee
3 Jesamine - The Casuals
4 Hey Jude - The Beatles
5 Lady Willpower - Gary Puckett & The Union Gap
6 My Little Lady - The Tremeloes
7 The Red Balloon - The Dave Clark Five
8 Ice In The Sun - Status Quo
9 Classical Gas - Mason Williams
10 Hold Me Tight - Johnny Nash

UK Number One album: *The Hollies' Greatest* - The Hollies
US Billboard Number One album: *Cheap Thrills* - Big Brother
And The Holding Company
US Cashbox Number One single: *Hey Jude* - The Beatles
Also this week: The summer Olympics begin in Mexico City.
(12th)

US Billboard singles for the week ending October the 12th
1 **Hey Jude** - The Beatles
2 Harper Valley P.T.A. - Jeannie C. Riley
3 Fire! - The Crazy World Of Arthur Brown
4 Little Green Apples - O.C. Smith
5 Girl Watcher - The O'Kaysions
6 Midnight Confessions - The Grass Roots
7 My Special Angel - The Vogues
8 I've Gotta Get A Message To You - The Bee Gees
9 Over You - Gary Puckett & The Union Gap
10 Slip Away - Clarence Carter

1968

1 **Those Were The Days** - Mary Hopkin
2 Jesamine - The Casuals
3 Hey Jude - The Beatles
4 Little Arrows - Leapy Lee
5 Lady Willpower - Gary Puckett & The Union Gap
6 My Little Lady - The Tremeloes
7 Les Bicyclettes De Belsize - Engelbert Humperdinck
8 The Red Balloon - The Dave Clark Five
9 A Day Without Love - The Love Affair
10 Light My Fire - Jose Feliciano

UK Number One album: *The Hollies' Greatest* - The Hollies
US Billboard Number One album: *Cheap Thrills* - Big Brother
And The Holding Company
US Cashbox Number One single: *Hey Jude* - The Beatles
Also this week: John Lennon and Yoko Ono are arrested on
drugs charges. (18th)

US Billboard singles for the week ending October the 19th

1 **Hey Jude** - The Beatles
2 Fire! - The Crazy World Of Arthur Brown
3 Little Green Apples - O.C. Smith
4 Harper Valley P.T.A. - Jeannie C. Riley
5 Girl Watcher - The O'Kaysions
6 Midnight Confessions - The Grass Roots
7 My Special Angel - The Vogues
8 I've Gotta Get A Message To You - The Bee Gees
9 Over You - Gary Puckett & The Union Gap
10 Say It Loud - I'm Black And Proud - James Brown

1968

1 **Those Were The Days** - Mary Hopkin
2 Hey Jude - The Beatles
3 Jesamine - The Casuals
4 Little Arrows - Leapy Lee
5 Les Bicyclettes De Belsize - Engelbert Humperdinck
6 A Day Without Love - The Love Affair
7 The Good, The Bad And The Ugly - Hugo Montenegro
8 My Little Lady - The Tremeloes
9 Lady Willpower - Gary Puckett & The Union Gap
10 Light My Fire - Jose Feliciano

UK Number One album: *The Hollies' Greatest* - The Hollies
US Billboard Number One album: *Cheap Thrills* - Big Brother
And The Holding Company
US Cashbox Number One single: *Hey Jude* - The Beatles
Also this week: Australian businessman Rupert Murdoch makes
a bid to buy the News of the World. (23rd)

US Billboard singles for the week ending October the 26th
1 **Hey Jude** - The Beatles
2 Little Green Apples - O.C. Smith
3 Fire! - The Crazy World Of Arthur Brown
4 Those Were The Days - Mary Hopkin
5 Girl Watcher - The O'Kaysions
6 Midnight Confessions - The Grass Roots
7 Over You - Gary Puckett & The Union Gap
8 Harper Valley P.T.A. - Jeannie C. Riley
9 Elenore - The Turtles
10 I've Gotta Get A Message To You - The Bee Gees

1968

  1 **Those Were The Days** - Mary Hopkin
  2 With A Little Help From My Friends - Joe Cocker
  3 The Good, The Bad And The Ugly - Hugo Montenegro
  4 Little Arrows - Leapy Lee
  5 Only One Woman - The Marbles
  6 Light My Fire - Jose Feliciano
  7 Hey Jude - The Beatles
  8 Jesamine - The Casuals
  9 Les Bicyclettes De Belsize - Engelbert Humperdinck
10 My Little Lady - The Tremeloes

UK Number One album: *The Hollies' Greatest* - The Hollies
US Billboard Number One album: *Cheap Thrills* - Big Brother
And The Holding Company
US Cashbox Number One single: *Hey Jude* - The Beatles
Also this week: Thousands of Czechs protest against Soviet
occupation. (28th)

  1 **Hey Jude** - The Beatles
  2 Those Were The Days - Mary Hopkin
  3 Little Green Apples - O.C. Smith
  4 Fire! - The Crazy World Of Arthur Brown
  5 Midnight Confessions - The Grass Roots
  6 Elenore - The Turtles
  7 Over You - Gary Puckett & The Union Gap
  8 Hold Me Tight - Johnny Nash
  9 Love Child - Diana Ross And The Supremes
10 White Room - Cream

1968

UK singles chart for the week ending November the 9th

1 **With A Little Help From My Friends** - Joe Cocker
2 Those Were The Days - Mary Hopkin
3 The Good, The Bad And The Ugly - Hugo Montenegro
4 Eloise - Barry Ryan
5 This Old Heart Of Mine - The Isley Brothers
6 Only One Woman - The Marbles
7 Light My Fire - Jose Feliciano
8 Little Arrows - Leapy Lee
9 All Along The Watchtower - The Jimi Hendrix Experience
10 Hey Jude - The Beatles

UK Number One album: *The Hollies' Greatest* - The Hollies
US Billboard Number One album: *Cheap Thrills* - Big Brother And The Holding Company
US Cashbox Number One single: *Those Were The Days* - Mary Hopkin
Also this week: Richard Nixon wins the USA Presidential election, defeating the Democrats' Hubert Humphrey. (6th)

US Billboard singles for the week ending November the 9th

1 **Hey Jude** - The Beatles
2 Those Were The Days - Mary Hopkin
3 Love Child - Diana Ross And The Supremes
4 Little Green Apples - O.C. Smith
5 Hold Me Tight - Johnny Nash
6 White Room - Cream
7 Magic Carpet Ride - Steppenwolf
8 Elenore - The Turtles
9 Fire! - The Crazy World Of Arthur Brown
10 Midnight Confessions - The Grass Roots

White Room was Cream's second US Top 10 hit. They never reached the Top 10 in the UK

1968

 1 **The Good, The Bad And The Ugly** - Hugo Montenegro
 2 With A Little Help From My Friends - Joe Cocker
 3 Eloise - Barry Ryan
 4 This Old Heart Of Mine - The Isley Brothers
 5 Those Were The Days - Mary Hopkin
 6 All Along The Watchtower - The Jimi Hendrix Experience
 7 Light My Fire - Jose Feliciano
 8 Only One Woman - The Marbles
 9 Breakin' Down The Walls Of Heartache - Bandwagon
10 Jesamine - The Casuals

UK Number One album: *The Hollies' Greatest* - The Hollies
US Billboard Number One album: *Electric Ladyland* - The Jimi Hendrix Experience
US Cashbox Number One single: *Those Were The Days* - Mary Hopkin
Also this week: Edward Heath appoints Margaret Thatcher as the Shadow Transport Minister. (14th)

US Billboard singles for the week ending November the 16th

 1 **Hey Jude** - The Beatles
 2 Those Were The Days - Mary Hopkin
 3 Love Child - Diana Ross And The Supremes
 4 Magic Carpet Ride - Steppenwolf
 5 Hold Me Tight - Johnny Nash
 6 White Room - Cream
 7 Little Green Apples - O.C. Smith
 8 Who's Making Love - Johnnie Taylor
 9 Abraham, Martin And John - Dion
10 Elenore - The Turtles

1968

1 **The Good, The Bad And The Ugly** - Hugo Montenegro
2 Eloise - Barry Ryan
3 This Old Heart Of Mine - The Isley Brothers
4 Breakin' Down The Walls Of Heartache - Bandwagon
5 With A Little Help From My Friends - Joe Cocker
6 All Along The Watchtower - The Jimi Hendrix Experience
7 Elenore - The Turtles
8 Only One Woman - The Marbles
9 Those Were The Days - Mary Hopkin
10 Ain't Got No - I Got Life/Do What You Gotta Do - Nina Simone

UK Number One album: *The Sound Of Music* - Soundtrack
US Billboard Number One album: *Electric Ladyland* - The Jimi Hendrix Experience
US Cashbox Number One single: *Love Child* - Diana Ross And The Supremes
Also this week: A Glasgow warehouse fire kills over 20. (18th)

US Billboard singles for the week ending November the 23rd

1 **Hey Jude** - The Beatles
2 Love Child - Diana Ross And The Supremes
3 Those Were The Days - Mary Hopkin
4 Magic Carpet Ride - Steppenwolf
5 Abraham, Martin And John - Dion
6 White Room - Cream
7 Hold Me Tight - Johnny Nash
8 Who's Making Love - Johnnie Taylor
9 Little Green Apples - O.C. Smith
10 Wichita Lineman - Glen Campbell

The Sound Of Music soundtrack is now the UK No.1 album for a staggering 70th week!

1968

UK singles chart for the week ending November the 30th
1 **The Good, The Bad And The Ugly** - Hugo Montenegro
2 Eloise - Barry Ryan
3 This Old Heart Of Mine - The Isley Brothers
4 Lily The Pink - Scaffold
5 All Along The Watchtower - The Jimi Hendrix Experience
6 Breakin' Down The Walls Of Heartache - Bandwagon
7 Ain't Got No - I Got Life/Do What You Gotta Do - Nina Simone
8 Elenore - The Turtles
9 I'm A Tiger - Lulu
10 With A Little Help From My Friends - Joe Cocker

UK Number One album: *The Hollies' Greatest* - The Hollies
US Billboard Number One album: *Cheap Thrills* - Big Brother And The Holding Company
US Cashbox Number One single: *Love Child* - Diana Ross And The Supremes
Also this week: The Race Relations Act becomes law throughout the United Kingdom. (26th)

US Billboard singles for the week ending November the 30th
1 **Love Child** - Diana Ross And The Supremes
2 Hey Jude - The Beatles
3 Magic Carpet Ride - Steppenwolf
4 Those Were The Days - Mary Hopkin
5 Abraham, Martin And John - Dion
6 Who's Making Love - Johnnie Taylor
7 For Once In My Life - Stevie Wonder
8 Wichita Lineman - Glen Campbell
9 Hold Me Tight - Johnny Nash
10 White Room - Cream

1968

1 **The Good, The Bad And The Ugly** - Hugo Montenegro
2 Lily The Pink - Scaffold
3 Eloise - Barry Ryan
4 This Old Heart Of Mine - The Isley Brothers
5 Breakin' Down The Walls Of Heartache - Bandwagon
6 One, Two, Three O'Leary - Des O'Connor
7 Ain't Got No - I Got Life/Do What You Gotta Do - Nina Simone
8 May I Have The Next Dream With You - Malcolm Roberts
9 I'm A Tiger - Lulu
10 Elenore - The Turtles

UK Number One album: *The Beatles* - The Beatles
US Billboard Number One album: *Cheap Thrills* - Big Brother And The Holding Company
US Cashbox Number One single: *Love Child* - Diana Ross And The Supremes
Also this week: Israeli raiders destroy Jordanian bridges. (1st)

US Billboard singles for the week ending December the 7th
1 **Love Child** - Diana Ross And The Supremes
2 Hey Jude - The Beatles
3 For Once In My Life - Stevie Wonder
4 I Heard It Through The Grapevine - Marvin Gaye
5 Who's Making Love - Johnnie Taylor
6 Magic Carpet Ride - Steppenwolf
7 Abraham, Martin And John - Dion
8 Wichita Lineman - Glen Campbell
9 Stormy - Classics IV
10 Those Were The Days - Mary Hopkin

1968

UK singles chart for the week ending December the 14th
1 **Lily The Pink** - Scaffold
2 The Good, The Bad And The Ugly - Hugo Montenegro
3 Ain't Got No - I Got Life/Do What You Gotta Do - Nina Simone
4 One, Two, Three O'Leary - Des O'Connor
5 Build Me Up Buttercup - The Foundations
6 I'm The Urban Spaceman - Bonzo Dog Doo-Dah Band
7 This Old Heart Of Mine - The Isley Brothers
8 Eloise - Barry Ryan
9 May I Have The Next Dream With You - Malcolm Roberts
10 Breakin' Down The Walls Of Heartache - Bandwagon

UK Number One album: *The Beatles* - The Beatles
US Billboard Number One album: *Cheap Thrills* - Big Brother And The Holding Company
US Cashbox Number One single: *For Once In My Life* - Stevie Wonder
Also this week: Rene Cassin of France receives the Nobel Peace Prize. (10th)

US Billboard singles for the week ending December the 14th
1 **I Heard It Through The Grapevine** - Marvin Gaye
2 Love Child - Diana Ross And The Supremes
3 For Once In My Life - Stevie Wonder
4 Abraham, Martin And John - Dion
5 Who's Making Love - Johnnie Taylor
6 Hey Jude - The Beatles
7 Wichita Lineman - Glen Campbell
8 Stormy - Classics IV
9 I Love How You Love Me - Bobby Vinton
10 Magic Carpet Ride - Steppenwolf

1968

1 **Lily The Pink** - Scaffold
2 Ain't Got No - I Got Life/Do What You Gotta Do - Nina Simone
3 Build Me Up Buttercup - The Foundations
4 One, Two, Three O'Leary - Des O'Connor
5 I'm The Urban Spaceman - Bonzo Dog Doo-Dah Band
6 The Good, The Bad And The Ugly - Hugo Montenegro
7 Sabre Dance - Love Sculpture
8 Race With The Devil - Gun
9 Ob-La-Di, Ob-La-Da - Marmalade
10 This Old Heart Of Mine - The Isley Brothers

UK Number One album: *The Beatles* - The Beatles
US Billboard Number One album: *Wichita Lineman* - Glen Campbell
US Cashbox Number One single: *I Heard It Through The Grapevine* - Marvin Gaye
Also this week: An eleven-day sit-in at the University of Bristol finally ends. (16th)

US Billboard singles for the week ending December the 21st
1 **I Heard It Through The Grapevine** - Marvin Gaye
2 Love Child - Diana Ross And The Supremes
3 For Once In My Life - Stevie Wonder
4 Abraham, Martin And John - Dion
5 Wichita Lineman - Glen Campbell
6 Stormy - Classics IV
7 Who's Making Love - Johnnie Taylor
8 Both Sides Now - Judy Collins
9 I Love How You Love Me - Bobby Vinton
10 Magic Carpet Ride - Steppenwolf

1968

UK singles chart for the week ending December the 28th
1 **Lily The Pink** - Scaffold
2 Build Me Up Buttercup - The Foundations
3 Ain't Got No - I Got Life/Do What You Gotta Do - Nina Simone
4 One, Two, Three O'Leary - Des O'Connor
5 Sabre Dance - Love Sculpture
6 I'm The Urban Spaceman - Bonzo Dog Doo-Dah Band
7 Ob-La-Di, Ob-La-Da - Marmalade
8 The Good, The Bad And The Ugly - Hugo Montenegro
9 Albatross - Fleetwood Mac
10 Race With The Devil - Gun

UK Number One album: *The Beatles* - The Beatles
US Billboard Number One album: *The Beatles* - The Beatles
US Cashbox Number One single: *I Heard It Through The Grapevine* - Marvin Gaye
Also this week: The crew of the US 'intelligence' ship Pueblo are released from captivity. (24th)

US Billboard singles for the week ending December the 28th
1 **I Heard It Through The Grapevine** - Marvin Gaye
2 For Once In My Life - Stevie Wonder
3 Love Child - Diana Ross And The Supremes
4 Wichita Lineman - Glen Campbell
5 Stormy - Classics IV
6 Abraham, Martin And John - Dion
7 I'm Gonna Make You Love Me - Diana Ross & The Supremes & The Temptations
8 Who's Making Love - Johnnie Taylor
9 I Love How You Love Me - Bobby Vinton
10 Cloud Nine - The Temptations

THE BEST 10 SONGS OF 1968?

Build Me Up Buttercup by The Foundations

Having enjoyed a marvellous chart-topper in 1967 with 'Baby, Now That I've Found You', the Foundations journeyed up the hit parade again with the toe-tapper 'Build Me Up Buttercup'. It still deservedly receives airplay many decades later, a testimony to its timeless impact. Although this single climbed to the top spot on the US Cashbox chart in early 1969, the Foundations did not build upon the foundations of this commercial triumph.

Burning Of The Midnight Lamp by The Jimi Hendrix Experience

"Loneliness is such a drag" wailed Hendrix on this remarkable track from the double album 'Electric Ladyland'. Here the guitar virtuoso treats us to some wah-wah guitar, and throw in the harpsichord plus the rhythm of Mitch and Noel, and the outcome is pretty spectacular. It was such a pity that Hendrix would part company with Chas Chandler, and in time with his bass player and drummer too. Jimi never matched this excellence again. What a waste.

Can Blue Men Sing The Whites? by The Bonzo Dog Band

Having initially guested on the Beatles' 'Magical Mystery Tour' film fiasco, the Bonzos were back in the limelight in 1968 with the suitably ludicrous 'I'm The Urban Spaceman'. These urban spacemen also released an album entitled 'The Doughnut In Granny's Greenhouse'. This project included the spoof song which in its own weird way questioned whether English white boys should be singing the blues. It's a frantic little number with guitar and harmonica to the fore. It's worth checking out.

Crossroads by Cream

In-fighting amongst the trio's rhythm section ensured that Cream would be a short-lived phenomenon. Before they bade their 'fond' farewells at the Royal Albert Hall, they weighed in with an outstanding live interpretation of Robert Johnson's 'Crossroads'. This must surely rank alongside 'My Back Pages' and 'All Along The Watchtower' as the best cover version of the decade. Take four minutes to bask in Eric Clapton on guitar and vocals here. It's time well spent.

Lazy Sunday by The Small Faces

The cockney mods had really found their feet with the splendid 'Ogden's Nut Gone Flake'. The LP included this UK Number Two smash. It's a real slice of joie de vivre from that artful dodger Steve Marriott, assisted by Ian McLagen on keyboards, bemoaning intolerant neighbours who have no time for ravers! The Small Faces were really starting to go places, but regrettably Marriott jumped ship, leaving les autres to form the Faces with Rod and Woody, a rock group-cum-drinking club.

THE BEST 10 SONGS OF 1968? (continued)

Old Friends by Simon And Garfunkel

The old friends of Paul Simon and Art Garfunkel had spent enough time together that by the late 'sixties, their old friendship was becoming strained. Before they took a prolonged leave of one another, they recorded their penultimate studio album, 'Bookends'. The LP takes its name from the track 'Old Friends', a gentle, reflective piece with an orchestral arrangement thrown in. It may not be one of their toe-tappers, but this easy listening item is worth several listens.

Pictures Of Matchstick Men by Status Quo

Status Quo were the latest English male guitar group to emerge on planet pop. Their debut single was very much in keeping with its time, a slice of psychedelia which would be a far cry from much of their output in the rockin' seventies. Francis Rossi for the time being was sporting a moustache and hadn't yet re-invented himself as a good time rocker. He was however the lead vocalist on one of the best songs of its era, and that was more than good for starters.

Rainbow Valley by The Love Affair

Young Steve Ellis and his group helped themselves to a brilliant UK Number One with 'Everlasting Love'. Although its follow-up, 'Rainbow Valley', failed to reach the 'top of the pops', it was a hugely commendable single. Ellis longs for the safe haven of Rainbow Valley accompanied by fine female vocals and a notable contribution from the brass section. Deservedly, this release found a place in the UK Top 5. It is without doubt among the best singles of not only 1968, but of all-time.

Set The Controls For The Heart Of The Sun by Pink Floyd

With the wayward genius of Syd Barrett beginning to lose his marbles on account of his acid consumption, the other three were resigned to having to cut their umbilical cord and go it alone without the charismatic Syd. Recruiting new guitarist, Dave Gilmour, they opted for space rock on 'Set The Controls For The Heart Of The Sun'. This was one of the first occasions when Roger Waters took over song-writing duties. The result was sufficiently impressive to encourage him to write more tunes.

The Way Young Lovers Do by Van Morrison

Van the man served his musical apprenticeship with Them who were welcome visitors to the airwaves with the likes of 'Here Comes The Night'. Belfast's most famous singer then chose to go it alone and came forth with a remarkable eight-track album entitled 'Astral Weeks'. Although this project was something of an acquired taste, it did possess this obscure gem which, assisted by an excellent horns accompaniment, was a bit more energetic than most of the other laid-back tunes on the LP.

THE BEST ALBUM OF 1968?

The Beatles

by **The Beatles**

peaked in the UK charts at No.1
peaked in the US charts at No.1
produced by George Martin
released in November

By 1968, all was not well on planet Beatles. Brian Epstein's
untimely death in August 1967 prompted the seemingly
unsinkable quartet to go it alone and manage their own affairs
for the next eighteen months. However, musicians they were;
businessmen they were not. This state of affairs was
compounded by a revolving door of girlfriends as Cynthia
Lennon was obliged to trade places with the avant-garde
Japanese artist, Yoko Ono, while Jane Asher abandoned her
role as Paul McCartney's significant other, a vacancy that was
quickly filled by the American Linda Eastman. On top of all
this emotional upheaval, even the Fab Four were becoming
increasingly tired of one another. Having decided to quit
touring in the summer of 1966, this in hindsight was the
precursor to the eventual break-up, and the decision to spend
more time cooped up together in the recording studio was itself
partially counter-productive, as many long hours together
perfecting their art would have tried anyone's long-standing
friendships. The Beatles sought spiritual relief in the
Himalayan foothills in the company of their favourite guru, the
Maharishi Mahesh Yogi, but even this experience proved less
than fruitful, prompting a typically acidic Lennon to compose
the majestic put-down of 'Sexy Sadie', his less-than-subtle
revelation that the Maharishi was a fraud, or at least a self-

THE BEST ALBUM OF 1968? (continued)

proclaimed holy man who allegedly expressed an unholy interest in one of the Farrow sisters. If nothing else, their retreat to India provided a fertile ground for more songs which would surface later in the year on what came to be known as the 'White Album'. Here, the kings of pop made their own daring statement of providing an album cover that was the very antithesis of Sergeant Pepper. There was no colourful, all-singing, all-dancing album cover with a cast of thousands. Hell, there wasn't even a clever album title. Instead, the famous four were intent on letting their music do the talking and to steer clear of any fancy packaging or marketing. It remains a testimony to their ever-constant popularity that this ninety-minute delight was able to thrive in the absence of an accompanying tour. Here again, as with Pepper, the Beatles were making their own rules. In my semi-humble opinion, the 'White Album' contains songs that far surpass the majority of Pepper tunes, but effectively each song was a solo track, with the composer singing his own song, accompanied sometimes merely by an orchestra. Nevertheless, there are some terrific moments that reminded us of their camaraderie as an exhausted Ringo exclaims "I've got blisters on my fingers" at the conclusion of the raucous 'Helter Skelter'. Eric Clapton also made a welcome contribution on 'While My Guitar Gently Weeps'. Even as group harmony began to unravel, the Beatles were still remarkably capable of delivering an album of unquestioned greatness.

The album's best song? - *Sexy Sadie*

SPORT IN 1968

English Division One soccer champions: Manchester City
English FA Cup final: West Bromwich Albion 1 Everton 0
English League Cup winners: Leeds United
Scottish Division One soccer champions: Glasgow Celtic
Scottish FA Cup final: Dunfermline Athletic 3 Heart of
Midlothian 1
Scottish League Cup winners: Glasgow Celtic
Irish League soccer champions: Glentoran; Irish Cup winners:
Crusaders
League Of Ireland soccer champions: Waterford; cup winners:
Shamrock Rovers
European Cup final: Manchester United 4 Benfica 1
European Cup-Winners' Cup final: AC Milan 2 SV Hamburg 0
European Fairs' Cup final: Leeds United beat Ferencvaros 1-0
on aggregate
English county cricket champions: Yorkshire
Five Nations' rugby union champions: France (grand slam)
Formula One world drivers' champion: Graham Hill
Gaelic football All-Ireland champions: Down; hurling
champions: Wexford
British Open golf champion: Gary Player
US Masters golf champion: Bob Goalby
US Open golf champion: Lee Trevino
USPGA golf champion: Julius Boros
Rugby league Challenge Cup final: Leeds 11 Wakefield Trinity
10
Wimbledon men's singles tennis champion: Rod Laver
Wimbledon ladies' singles tennis champion: Billie Jean King
The Aintree Grand National steeplechase winner: Red Alligator
The Epsom Derby winner: Sir Ivor
The European Championship soccer final: Italy 2 Yugoslavia 0

DEATHS IN 1968

February 17th: Sir Donald Wolfit (British actor-manager), aged 65
February 20th: Anthony Asquith (British film director), aged 65
February 27th: Franklin Joseph 'Frankie' Lymon (US singer), aged 25
March 27th: Yuri Gagarin (Soviet cosmonaut), aged 34
April 4th: Dr Martin Luther King (US civil rights leader), aged 39
April 7th: Jim Clark (British racing driver), aged 32
June 6th: Robert Fitzgerald Kennedy (US politician), aged 42
June 14th: Salvatore Quasimodo (Italian 1959 Nobel Prize winner), aged 66
June 24th: Anthony John Hancock (British comedian), aged 44
July 21st: Ruth St.Denis (US dancer), aged 90
July 28th: Otto Hahn (German nuclear physicist), aged 89
October 13th: Sir Stanley Unwin (British publisher), aged 83
October 20th: Chaim Reeven 'Bud Flanagan' Weintrop (British comedian), aged 71
November 6th: Charles Munch (French conductor), aged 77
November 17th: Mervyn Laurence Peake (British author), aged 57
November 25th: Upton Sinclair (US author), aged 90
November 28th: Enid Mary Blyton (British author), aged 71
December 20th: John Steinbeck (US author), aged 66

COMMERCIAL BREAK:

The Ashes, 1945-2005, A Complete Record
by Tony Wagtar

The book is a statistical history of the Ashes conflicts from the 1946 tour to Australia through to the 2005 series, though there is also a page dedicated to the 2006-7 whitewash, as well as pages on non-Ashes test matches; and the County Championship and Sheffield Shield winners from 1945-2005. The book ends with a fascinating piece on the importance or otherwise of winning the toss in Ashes test matches.

However the bulk of the book concerns itself with the 160+ test matches and merely records all the scorecards. No such volume contains all Ashes scorecards in chronological order in such an accessible way. Whilst the fielders change ends between overs and during other momentary pauses in play, this reference book is ideal for leafing through. Although it is 90% facts and figures, there are brief comments which accompany each test match. Interesting facts include the following:

- Don Bradman's last-ever innings in test cricket in 1948
- Graham Gooch's baptism of fire in 1975
- The test in 1989 when Australia batted all day without conceding a wicket
- The batting partnership of Botham and Tavare at Old Trafford in 1981
- The test in 1981 when Australia slid from 56-1 to 75-8
- The 'sixties test when debutant Tom Cartwright had to bowl 77 overs
- The finely balanced test in 1975 that was ended by a vandalised pitch
- The 'fifties test when Australia were reduced to 32 for 7
- The Melbourne nail-biters of 1974 and 1982
- The Edgbaston and Old Trafford nail-biters of 2005

1969

  1 **Ob-La-Di**, **Ob-La-Da** - Marmalade
  2 Lily The Pink - Scaffold
  3 Build Me Up Buttercup - The Foundations
  4 Albatross - Fleetwood Mac
  5 I'm The Urban Spaceman - Bonzo Dog Doo-Dah Band
  6 Sabre Dance - Love Sculpture
  7 Ain't Got No - I Got Life/Do What You Gotta Do - Nina Simone
  8 One, Two, Three O'Leary - Des O'Connor
  9 Son-Of-A Preacher Man - Dusty Springfield
10 Something's Happening - Herman's Hermits

UK Number One album: *The Beatles* - The Beatles
US Billboard Number One album: *The Beatles* - The Beatles
US Cashbox Number One single: *I Heard It Through The Grapevine* - Marvin Gaye
Also this week: Civil rights marchers clash with the 'B Specials' police reserves near Derry. (3rd)

US Billboard singles for the week ending January the 4th
  1 **I Heard It Through The Grapevine -** Marvin Gaye
  2 For Once In My Life - Stevie Wonder
  3 I'm Gonna Make You Love Me - Diana Ross & The Supremes & The Temptations
  4 Soulful Strut - Young-Holt Unlimited
  5 Wichita Lineman - Glen Campbell
  6 Cloud Nine - The Temptations
  7 Love Child - Diana Ross And The Supremes
  8 Stormy - Classics IV
  9 Who's Making Love - Johnnie Taylor
10 Hooked On A Feeling - B.J. Thomas

1969

1 **Lily The Pink** - Scaffold
2 Build Me Up Buttercup - The Foundations
3 Ob-La-Di, Ob-La-Da - Marmalade
4 Albatross - Fleetwood Mac
5 I'm The Urban Spaceman - Bonzo Dog Doo-Dah Band
6 Sabre Dance - Love Sculpture
7 Ain't Got No - I Got Life/Do What You Gotta Do - Nina Simone
8 Something's Happening - Herman's Hermits
9 Son-Of-A Preacher Man - Dusty Springfield
10 For Once In My Life - Stevie Wonder

UK Number One album: *The Beatles* - The Beatles
US Billboard Number One album: *The Beatles* - The Beatles
US Cashbox Number One single: *I Heard It Through The Grapevine* - Marvin Gaye
Also this week: NASA chooses Buzz Aldrin and Neil Armstrong to take the space mission to land on the moon. (9th)

US Billboard singles for the week ending January the 11th

1 **I Heard It Through The Grapevine** - Marvin Gaye
2 I'm Gonna Make You Love Me - Diana Ross & The Supremes & The Temptations
3 Wichita Lineman - Glen Campbell
4 Soulful Strut - Young-Holt Unlimited
5 Hooked On A Feeling - B.J. Thomas
6 Cloud Nine - The Temptations
7 For Once In My Life - Stevie Wonder
8 Crimson And Clover - Tommy James And The Shondells
9 Love Child - Diana Ross And The Supremes
10 I Love How You Love Me - Bobby Vinton

1969

1 **Ob-La-Di, Ob-La-Da** - Marmalade
2 Albatross - Fleetwood Mac
3 Build Me Up Buttercup - The Foundations
4 Lily The Pink - Scaffold
5 For Once In My Life - Stevie Wonder
6 Something's Happening - Herman's Hermits
7 I'm The Urban Spaceman - Bonzo Dog Doo-Dah Band
8 Sabre Dance - Love Sculpture
9 Ain't Got No - I Got Life/Do What You Gotta Do - Nina Simone
10 Private Number - Judy Clay And William Bell

UK Number One album: *The Beatles* - The Beatles
US Billboard Number One album: *The Beatles* - The Beatles
US Cashbox Number One single: *I Heard It Through The Grapevine* - Marvin Gaye
Also this week: The White Paper, 'In Place Of Strife', is published. It aims to tackle industrial relations.(17th)

US Billboard singles for the week ending January the 18th
1 **I Heard It Through The Grapevine** - Marvin Gaye
2 I'm Gonna Make You Love Me - Diana Ross & The Supremes & The Temptations
3 Soulful Strut - Young-Holt Unlimited
4 Crimson And Clover - Tommy James And The Shondells
5 Hooked On A Feeling - B.J. Thomas
6 Wichita Lineman - Glen Campbell
7 For Once In My Life - Stevie Wonder
8 Touch Me - The Doors
9 Worst That Could Happen - Brooklyn Bridge
10 Son-Of-A Preacher Man - Dusty Springfield

1969

  1 **Ob-La-Di, Ob-La-Da** - Marmalade
  2 Albatross - Fleetwood Mac
  3 For Once In My Life - Stevie Wonder
  4 Lily The Pink - Scaffold
  5 Blackberry Way - The Move
  6 Build Me Up Buttercup - The Foundations
  7 Something's Happening - Herman's Hermits
  8 Private Number - Judy Clay And William Bell
  9 I'm The Urban Spaceman - Bonzo Dog Doo-Dah Band
10 Fox On The Run - Manfred Mann

UK Number One album: *The Best Of The Seekers* - The Seekers
US Billboard Number One album: *The Beatles* - The Beatles
US Cashbox Number One single: *I'm Gonna Make You Love Me* - Diana Ross & The Supremes & The Temptations
Also this week: The former Vice-President Richard Nixon is sworn in as the new USA President. (20th)

US Billboard singles for the week ending January the 25th
  1 **I Heard It Through The Grapevine** - Marvin Gaye
  2 Crimson And Clover - Tommy James And The Shondells
  3 I'm Gonna Make You Love Me - Diana Ross & The Supremes & The Temptations
  4 Soulful Strut - Young-Holt Unlimited
  5 Everyday People - Sly And The Family Stone
  6 Hooked On A Feeling - B.J. Thomas
  7 Touch Me - The Doors
  8 Worst That Could Happen - Brooklyn Bridge
  9 I Started A Joke - The Bee Gees
10 Son-Of-A Preacher Man - Dusty Springfield

1969

UK singles chart for the week ending February the 1st

1 **Albatross** - Fleetwood Mac
2 Blackberry Way - The Move
3 For Once In My Life - Stevie Wonder
4 Ob-La-Di, Ob-La-Da - Marmalade
5 Fox On The Run - Manfred Mann
6 Something's Happening - Herman's Hermits
7 Lily The Pink - Scaffold
8 Private Number - Judy Clay And William Bell
9 You Got Soul - Johnny Nash
10 Build Me Up Buttercup - The Foundations

UK Number One album: *The Beatles* - The Beatles
US Billboard Number One album: *The Beatles* - The Beatles
US Cashbox Number One single: *Crimson And Clover* - Tommy James And The Shondells
Also this week: London School of Economics students cause further campus unrest. (27th)

US Billboard singles for the week ending February the 1st

1 **Crimson And Clover** - Tommy James And The Shondells
2 Everyday People - Sly And The Family Stone
3 Worst That Could Happen - Brooklyn Bridge
4 Touch Me - The Doors
5 I Heard It Through The Grapevine - Marvin Gaye
6 I'm Gonna Make You Love Me - Diana Ross & The Supremes & The Temptations
7 I Started A Joke - The Bee Gees
8 Hooked On A Feeling - B.J. Thomas
9 Soulful Strut - Young-Holt Unlimited
10 Build Me Up Buttercup - The Foundations

FleetwoodMac's Albatross would climb to Number Two in the UK when re-issued in 1973.

1969

UK singles chart for the week ending February the 8th
  1 **Blackberry Way** - The Move
  2 Albatross - Fleetwood Mac
  3 For Once In My Life - Stevie Wonder
  4 Dancing In The Street - Martha & The Vandellas
  5 To Love Somebody - Nina Simone
  6 You Got Soul - Johnny Nash
  7 I'm Gonna Make You Love Me - Diana Ross & The
Supremes & The Temptations
  8 Please Don't Go - Donald Peers
  9 Mrs Robinson (EP) - Simon And Garfunkel
10 Ob-La-Di, Ob-La-Da - Marmalade

UK Number One album: *The Best Of The Seekers* - The
Seekers
US Billboard Number One album: *TCB* - Diana Ross & The
Supremes and The Temptations
US Cashbox Number One single: *Touch Me* - The Doors
Also this week: Yassir Arafat becomes leader of the PLO. (3rd)

US Billboard singles for the week ending February the 8th
  1 **Crimson And Clover** - Tommy James And The Shondells
  2 Everyday People - Sly And The Family Stone
  3 Worst That Could Happen - Brooklyn Bridge
  4 Touch Me - The Doors
  5 Build Me Up Buttercup - The Foundations
  6 I Started A Joke - The Bee Gees
  7 I Heard It Through The Grapevine - Marvin Gaye
  8 I'm Gonna Make You Love Me - Diana Ross & The
Supremes & The Temptations
  9 Hang 'Em High - Booker T. & The MGs
10 Can I Change My Mind - Tyrone Davis

1969

1 (**If Paradise Is**) **Half As Nice** - Amen Corner
2 Albatross - Fleetwood Mac
3 Blackberry Way - The Move
4 For Once In My Life - Stevie Wonder
5 Dancing In The Street - Martha & The Vandellas
6 Please Don't Go - Donald Peers
7 You Got Soul - Johnny Nash
8 I'm Gonna Make You Love Me - Diana Ross & The
Supremes & The Temptations
9 Ob-La-Di, Ob-La-Da - Marmalade
10 To Love Somebody - Nina Simone

UK Number One album: *Diana Ross & The Supremes Join The*
Temptations - Diana Ross & The Supremes
US Billboard Number One album: *The Beatles* - The Beatles
US Cashbox Number One single: *Everyday People* - Sly And
The Family Stone
Also this week: Ford's women workers win equal pay. (11th)

US Billboard singles for the week ending February the 15th
1 **Everyday People** - Sly And The Family Stone
2 Crimson And Clover - Tommy James And The Shondells
3 Touch Me - The Doors
4 Build Me Up Buttercup - The Foundations
5 Worst That Could Happen - Brooklyn Bridge
6 Can I Change My Mind - Tyrone Davis
7 You Showed Me - The Turtles
8 I Heard It Through The Grapevine - Marvin Gaye
9 Hang 'Em High - Booker T. & The MGs
10 I'm Gonna Make You Love Me - Diana Ross & The
Supremes & The Temptations

1969

1 (**If Paradise Is**) **Half As Nice** - Amen Corner
2 Where Do You Go To (My Lovely) - Peter Sarstedt
3 I'm Gonna Make You Love Me - Diana Ross & The Supremes & The Temptations
4 Please Don't Go - Donald Peers
5 Blackberry Way - The Move
6 Albatross - Fleetwood Mac
7 Dancing In The Street - Martha & The Vandellas
8 You Got Soul - Johnny Nash
9 The Way It Used To Be - Engelbert Humperdinck
10 For Once In My Life - Stevie Wonder

UK Number One album: *Diana Ross & The Supremes Join The Temptations* - Diana Ross & The Supremes
US Billboard Number One album: *The Beatles* - The Beatles
US Cashbox Number One single: *Everyday People* - Sly And The Family Stone
Also this week: Scottish female pop singer Lulu marries Maurice Gibb of the Bee Gees. (18th)

US Billboard singles for the week ending February the 22nd

1 **Everyday People** - Sly And The Family Stone
2 Crimson And Clover - Tommy James And The Shondells
3 Build Me Up Buttercup - The Foundations
4 Touch Me - The Doors
5 Can I Change My Mind - Tyrone Davis
6 Worst That Could Happen - Brooklyn Bridge
7 You Showed Me - The Turtles
8 This Magic Moment - Jay & The Americans
9 Proud Mary - Creedence Clearwater Revival
10 I'm Livin' In Shame - Diana Ross & The Supremes

1969

UK singles chart for the week ending March the 1st
1 **Where Do You Go To** (**My Lovely**) - Peter Sarstedt
2 (If Paradise Is) Half As Nice - Amen Corner
3 I'm Gonna Make You Love Me - Diana Ross & The
Supremes & The Temptations
4 Please Don't Go - Donald Peers
5 The Way It Used To Be - Engelbert Humperdinck
6 Dancing In The Street - Martha & The Vandellas
7 Blackberry Way - The Move
8 Albatross - Fleetwood Mac
9 Wichita Lineman - Glen Campbell
10 I'll Pick A Rose For My Rose - Marv Johnson

UK Number One album: *Diana Ross & The Supremes Join The Temptations* - Diana Ross & The Supremes
US Billboard Number One album: *The Beatles* - The Beatles
US Cashbox Number One single: *Build Me Up Buttercup* - The Foundations
Also this week: Richard Nixon visits Harold Wilson in Downing Street. (24th)

US Billboard singles for the week ending March the 1st
1 **Everyday People** - Sly And The Family Stone
2 Crimson And Clover - Tommy James And The Shondells
3 Build Me Up Buttercup - The Foundations
4 Touch Me - The Doors
5 Proud Mary - Creedence Clearwater Revival
6 You Showed Me - The Turtles
7 This Magic Moment - Jay & The Americans
8 Baby, Baby Don't Cry - The Miracles
9 Worst That Could Happen - Brooklyn Bridge
10 Dizzy - Tommy Roe

1969

  1 **Where Do You Go To** (**My Lovely**) - Peter Sarstedt
  2 (If Paradise Is) Half As Nice - Amen Corner
  3 Please Don't Go - Donald Peers
  4 Surround Yourself With Sorrow - Cilla Black
  5 I Heard It Through The Grapevine - Marvin Gaye
  6 I'm Gonna Make You Love Me - Diana Ross & The Supremes & The Temptations
  7 Wichita Lineman - Glen Campbell
  8 Monsieur Dupont - Sandie Shaw
  9 The Way It Used To Be - Engelbert Humperdinck
 10 Gentle On My Mind - Dean Martin

UK Number One album: *Diana Ross & The Supremes Join The Temptations* - Diana Ross & The Supremes
US Billboard Number One album: *Wichita Lineman* - Glen Campbell
US Cashbox Number One single: *Build Me Up Buttercup* - The Foundations
Also this week: The Concorde takes its maiden flight. (2nd)

US Billboard singles for the week ending March the 8th
  1 **Everyday People** - Sly And The Family Stone
  2 Proud Mary - Creedence Clearwater Revival
  3 Build Me Up Buttercup - The Foundations
  4 Dizzy - Tommy Roe
  5 Crimson And Clover - Tommy James And The Shondells
  6 This Magic Moment - Jay & The Americans
  7 This Girl's In Love With You - Dionne Warwick
  8 Baby, Baby Don't Cry - The Miracles
  9 Touch Me - The Doors
 10 Indian Giver - 1910 Fruitgum Co.

1969

UK singles chart for the week ending March the 15th
  1 **Where Do You Go To (My Lovely**) - Peter Sarstedt
  2 I Heard It Through The Grapevine - Marvin Gaye
  3 The Way It Used To Be - Engelbert Humperdinck
  4 Surround Yourself With Sorrow - Cilla Black
  5 Gentle On My Mind - Dean Martin
  6 First Of May - The Bee Gees
  7 Monsieur Dupont - Sandie Shaw
  8 Wichita Lineman - Glen Campbell
  9 I'm Gonna Make You Love Me - Diana Ross & The Supremes & The Temptations
10 Please Don't Go - Donald Peers

UK Number One album: *Goodbye* - Cream
US Billboard Number One album: *Wichita Lineman* - Glen Campbell
US Cashbox Number One single: *Dizzy* - Tommy Roe
Also this week: Paul McCartney marries the American photographer Linda Eastman. (12th)

US Billboard singles for the week ending March the 15th
  1 **Dizzy** - Tommy Roe
  2 Proud Mary - Creedence Clearwater Revival
  3 Everyday People - Sly And The Family Stone
  4 Build Me Up Buttercup - The Foundations
  5 Traces - Classics IV
  6 Crimson And Clover - Tommy James And The Shondells
  7 This Girl's In Love With You - Dionne Warwick
  8 Indian Giver - 1910 Fruitgum Co.
  9 Time Of The Season - The Zombies
10 This Magic Moment - Jay & The Americans

1969

1 **Where Do You Go To** (**My Lovely**) - Peter Sarstedt
2 I Heard It Through The Grapevine - Marvin Gaye
3 The Way It Used To Be - Engelbert Humperdinck
4 Gentle On My Mind - Dean Martin
5 Please Don't Go - Donald Peers
6 Surround Yourself With Sorrow - Cilla Black
7 Monsieur Dupont - Sandie Shaw
8 Wichita Lineman - Glen Campbell
9 First Of May - The Bee Gees
10 You've Lost That Lovin' Feelin' - The Righteous Brothers

UK Number One album: *Goodbye* - Cream
US Billboard Number One album: *Wichita Lineman* - Glen Campbell
US Cashbox Number One single: *Dizzy* - Tommy Roe
Also this week: Golda Meir takes office as Israel's new Prime Minister. (17th)

US Billboard singles for the week ending March the 22nd

1 **Dizzy** - Tommy Roe
2 Proud Mary - Creedence Clearwater Revival
3 Traces - Classics IV
4 Build Me Up Buttercup - The Foundations
5 Indian Giver - 1910 Fruitgum Co.
6 Time Of The Season - The Zombies
7 This Girl's In Love With You - Dionne Warwick
8 Everyday People - Sly And The Family Stone
9 Crimson And Clover - Tommy James And The Shondells
10 Run Away Child, Running Wild - The Temptations

1969

1 **I Heard It Through The Grapevine** - Marvin Gaye
2 Where Do You Go To (My Lovely) - Peter Sarstedt
3 Surround Yourself With Sorrow - Cilla Black
4 Sorry Suzanne - The Hollies
5 Gentle On My Mind - Dean Martin
6 Games People Play - Joe South
7 First Of May - The Bee Gees
8 Monsieur Dupont - Sandie Shaw
9 Boom Bang-A-Bang - Lulu
10 Get Ready - The Temptations

UK Number One album: *The Best Of The Seekers* - The Seekers
US Billboard Number One album: *Blood, Sweat & Tears* - Blood, Sweat & Tears
US Cashbox Number One single: *Time Of The Season* - The Zombies
Also this week: Yahya Khan seizes power in Pakistan. (25th)

US Billboard singles for the week ending March the 29th
1 **Dizzy** - Tommy Roe
2 Traces - Classics IV
3 Time Of The Season - The Zombies
4 Aquarius/Let The Sunshine In (The Flesh Failures) - 5th Dimension
5 Proud Mary - Creedence Clearwater Revival
6 Run Away Child, Running Wild - The Temptations
7 Indian Giver - 1910 Fruitgum Co.
8 Galveston -Glen Campbell
9 My World Ended (The Moment You Left) - David Ruffin
10 Only The Strong Survive - Jerry Butler

1969

 1 **I Heard It Through The Grapevine** - Marvin Gaye
 2 Gentle On My Mind - Dean Martin
 3 Sorry Suzanne - The Hollies
 4 Boom Bang-A-Bang - Lulu
 5 Israelites - Desmond Dekker & The Aces
 6 Monsieur Dupont - Sandie Shaw
 7 Where Do You Go To (My Lovely) - Peter Sarstedt
 8 Games People Play - Joe South
 9 In The Bad, Bad Old Days - The Foundations
10 First Of May - The Bee Gees

UK Number One album: *The Best Of The Seekers* - The Seekers
US Billboard Number One album: *Wichita Lineman* - Glen Campbell
US Cashbox Number One single: *Aquarius/Let The Sunshine In (The Flesh Failures)* - 5th Dimension
Also this week: The first artificial heart is implanted. (4th)

US Billboard singles for the week ending April the 5th
 1 **Dizzy** - Tommy Roe
 2 Aquarius/Let The Sunshine In (The Flesh Failures) - 5th Dimension
 3 Time Of The Season - The Zombies
 4 You've Made Me So Very Happy - Blood, Sweat & Tears
 5 Galveston -Glen Campbell
 6 Run Away Child, Running Wild - The Temptations
 7 Only The Strong Survive - Jerry Butler
 8 Traces - Classics IV
 9 My World Ended (The Moment You Left) - David Ruffin
10 Proud Mary - Creedence Clearwater Revival

1969

UK singles chart for the week ending April the 12th
 1 **I Heard It Through The Grapevine** - Marvin Gaye
 2 Boom Bang-A-Bang - Lulu
 3 Israelites - Desmond Dekker & The Aces
 4 Gentle On My Mind - Dean Martin
 5 Sorry Suzanne - The Hollies
 6 Goodbye - Mary Hopkin
 7 Games People Play - Joe South
 8 In The Bad, Bad Old Days - The Foundations
 9 Pinball Wizard - The Who
10 I Can Hear Music - The Beach Boys

UK Number One album: *Goodbye* - Cream
US Billboard Number One album: *Blood, Sweat & Tears* - Blood, Sweat & Tears
US Cashbox Number One single: *Aquarius/Let The Sunshine In (The Flesh Failures)* - 5th Dimension
Also this week: 25 valuable paintings are stolen from Sir Roland Penrose's home. (7th)

US Billboard singles for the week ending April the 12th
 1 **Aquarius/Let The Sunshine In** (**The Flesh Failures**) - 5th Dimension
 2 You've Made Me So Very Happy - Blood, Sweat & Tears
 3 Dizzy - Tommy Roe
 4 Galveston -Glen Campbell
 5 Time Of The Season - The Zombies
 6 Only The Strong Survive - Jerry Butler
 7 It's Your Thing - The Isley Brothers
 8 Hair - The Cowsills
 9 Run Away Child, Running Wild - The Temptations
10 Twenty-Five Miles - Edwin Starr

1969

1 **Israelites** - Desmond Dekker & The Aces
2 Goodbye - Mary Hopkin
3 I Heard It Through The Grapevine - Marvin Gaye
4 Boom Bang-A-Bang - Lulu
5 Gentle On My Mind - Dean Martin
6 Pinball Wizard - The Who
7 Sorry Suzanne - The Hollies
8 In The Bad, Bad Old Days - The Foundations
9 Games People Play - Joe South
10 The Windmills Of Your Mind - Noel Harrison

UK Number One album: *The Best Of The Seekers* - The Seekers
US Billboard Number One album: *Blood, Sweat & Tears* - Blood, Sweat & Tears
US Cashbox Number One single: *Aquarius/Let The Sunshine In (The Flesh Failures)* - 5th Dimension
Also this week: Bernadette Devlin, 22, is elected MP. (18th)

US Billboard singles for the week ending April the 19th

1 **Aquarius/Let The Sunshine In** (**The Flesh Failures**) - 5th Dimension
2 You've Made Me So Very Happy - Blood, Sweat & Tears
3 It's Your Thing - The Isley Brothers
4 Only The Strong Survive - Jerry Butler
5 Dizzy - Tommy Roe
6 Galveston -Glen Campbell
7 Hair - The Cowsills
8 Twenty-Five Miles - Edwin Starr
9 Time Of The Season - The Zombies
10 Rock Me -Steppenwolf

1969

1 **Get Back** - The Beatles with Billy Preston
2 Israelites - Desmond Dekker & The Aces
3 Goodbye - Mary Hopkin
4 Pinball Wizard - The Who
5 Gentle On My Mind - Dean Martin
6 I Heard It Through The Grapevine - Marvin Gaye
7 Boom Bang-A-Bang - Lulu
8 Come Back And Shake Me - Clodagh Rodgers
9 The Windmills Of Your Mind - Noel Harrison
10 In The Bad, Bad Old Days - The Foundations

UK Number One album: *Goodbye* - Cream
US Billboard Number One album: *Hair* - Original Cast
US Cashbox Number One single: *Aquarius/Let The Sunshine In (The Flesh Failures)* - 5th Dimension
Also this week: The QE2 sets sail on her first commercial voyage. (22nd)

US Billboard singles for the week ending April the 26th

1 **Aquarius/Let The Sunshine In** (**The Flesh Failures**) - 5th Dimension
2 You've Made Me So Very Happy - Blood, Sweat & Tears
3 It's Your Thing - The Isley Brothers
4 Hair - The Cowsills
5 Only The Strong Survive - Jerry Butler
6 Twenty-Five Miles - Edwin Starr
7 Galveston -Glen Campbell
8 Time Is Tight - Booker T. & The MGs
9 Dizzy - Tommy Roe
10 Sweet Cherry Wine - Tommy James

Get Back became the first single to enter the UK charts straight in at Number One.

1969

UK singles chart for the week ending May the 3rd
1 **Get Back** - The Beatles with Billy Preston
2 Goodbye - Mary Hopkin
3 Israelites - Desmond Dekker & The Aces
4 Pinball Wizard - The Who
5 Come Back And Shake Me - Clodagh Rodgers
6 Cupid - Johnny Nash
7 Harlem Shuffle - Bob And Earl
8 The Windmills Of Your Mind - Noel Harrison
9 I Heard It Through The Grapevine - Marvin Gaye
10 Boom Bang-A-Bang - Lulu

UK Number One album: *The Best Of The Seekers* - The Seekers
US Billboard Number One album: *Hair* - Original Cast
US Cashbox Number One single: *Aquarius/Let The Sunshine In (The Flesh Failures)* - 5th Dimension
Also this week: Charles de Gaulle resigns as President of France, having occupied the office for eleven years. (28th)

US Billboard singles for the week ending May the 3rd
1 **Aquarius/Let The Sunshine In (The Flesh Failures)** - 5th Dimension
2 It's Your Thing - The Isley Brothers
3 Hair - The Cowsills
4 You've Made Me So Very Happy - Blood, Sweat & Tears
5 Only The Strong Survive - Jerry Butler
6 Time Is Tight - Booker T. & The MGs
7 Sweet Cherry Wine - Tommy James
8 Hawaii Five-O - The Ventures
9 The Boxer - Simon And Garfunkel
10 Galveston -Glen Campbell

1969

1 **Get Back** - The Beatles with Billy Preston
2 Goodbye - Mary Hopkin
3 Come Back And Shake Me - Clodagh Rodgers
4 Pinball Wizard - The Who
5 My Sentimental Friend - Herman's Hermits
6 Israelites - Desmond Dekker & The Aces
7 Man Of The World - Fleetwood Mac
8 Behind A Painted Smile - The Isley Brothers
9 My Way - Frank Sinatra
10 Cupid - Johnny Nash

UK Number One album: *On The Threshold Of A Dream* - The Moody Blues
US Billboard Number One album: *Hair* - Original Cast
US Cashbox Number One single: *Hair* - The Cowsills
Also this week: The Labour Party suffers an ominous backlash at the local elections. (9th)

US Billboard singles for the week ending May the 10th

1 **Aquarius/Let The Sunshine In** (**The Flesh Failures**) - 5th Dimension
2 Hair - The Cowsills
3 It's Your Thing - The Isley Brothers
4 Hawaii Five-O - The Ventures
5 You've Made Me So Very Happy - Blood, Sweat & Tears
6 Time Is Tight - Booker T. & The MGs
7 Sweet Cherry Wine - Tommy James
8 The Boxer - Simon And Garfunkel
9 Atlantis - Donovan
10 Get Back - The Beatles with Billy Preston

1969

1 **Get Back** - The Beatles with Billy Preston
2 My Sentimental Friend - Herman's Hermits
3 Man Of The World - Fleetwood Mac
4 Come Back And Shake Me - Clodagh Rodgers
5 Goodbye - Mary Hopkin
6 My Way - Frank Sinatra
7 Behind A Painted Smile - The Isley Brothers
8 Israelites - Desmond Dekker & The Aces
9 The Boxer - Simon And Garfunkel
10 Pinball Wizard - The Who

UK Number One album: *On The Threshold Of A Dream* - The Moody Blues
US Billboard Number One album: *Hair* - Original Cast
US Cashbox Number One single: *Hair* - The Cowsills
Also this week: The Soviets' Venera 5 crashes on the planet of Venus. (16th)

US Billboard singles for the week ending May the 17th

1 **Aquarius/Let The Sunshine In** (**The Flesh Failures**) - 5th Dimension
2 Hair - The Cowsills
3 Get Back - The Beatles with Billy Preston
4 It's Your Thing - The Isley Brothers
5 Love (Can Make You Happy) - Mercy
6 Hawaii Five-O - The Ventures
7 The Boxer - Simon And Garfunkel
8 Atlantis - Donovan
9 Gitarzan - Ray Stevens
10 These Eyes - The Guess Who

1969

 1 **Get Back** - The Beatles with Billy Preston
 2 My Sentimental Friend - Herman's Hermits
 3 Man Of The World - Fleetwood Mac
 4 Dizzy - Tommy Roe
 5 Behind A Painted Smile - The Isley Brothers
 6 My Way - Frank Sinatra
 7 Come Back And Shake Me - Clodagh Rodgers
 8 Goodbye - Mary Hopkin
 9 The Boxer - Simon And Garfunkel
10 Ragamuffin Man - Manfred Mann

UK Number One album: *Nashville Skyline* - Bob Dylan
US Billboard Number One album: *Hair* - Original Cast
US Cashbox Number One single: *Get Back* - The Beatles with Billy Preston
Also this week: Former world champion Graham Hill wins the prestigious Monaco Grand Prix for a fifth time. (18th)

US Billboard singles for the week ending May the 24th
 1 **Get Back** - The Beatles with Billy Preston
 2 Aquarius/Let The Sunshine In (The Flesh Failures) - 5th Dimension
 3 Love (Can Make You Happy) - Mercy
 4 Hair - The Cowsills
 5 Oh Happy Day - The Edwin Hawkins Singers
 6 It's Your Thing - The Isley Brothers
 7 Atlantis - Donovan
 8 The Boxer - Simon And Garfunkel
 9 Gitarzan - Ray Stevens
10 These Eyes - The Guess Who

1969

1 **Get Back** - The Beatles with Billy Preston
2 Man Of The World - Fleetwood Mac
3 Dizzy - Tommy Roe
4 My Sentimental Friend - Herman's Hermits
5 My Way - Frank Sinatra
6 Behind A Painted Smile - The Isley Brothers
7 The Boxer - Simon And Garfunkel
8 Ragamuffin Man - Manfred Mann
9 Love Me Tonight - Tom Jones
10 Come Back And Shake Me - Clodagh Rodgers

UK Number One album: *Nashville Skyline* - Bob Dylan
US Billboard Number One album: *Hair* - Original Cast
US Cashbox Number One single: *Get Back* - The Beatles with Billy Preston
Also this week: Sudan's government is overthrown by a military coup. (25th)

US Billboard singles for the week ending May the 31st
1 **Get Back** - The Beatles with Billy Preston
2 Love (Can Make You Happy) - Mercy
3 Aquarius/Let The Sunshine In (The Flesh Failures) - 5th Dimension
4 Oh Happy Day - The Edwin Hawkins Singers
5 Hair - The Cowsills
6 These Eyes - The Guess Who
7 Atlantis - Donovan
8 Gitarzan - Ray Stevens
9 In The Ghetto - Elvis Presley
10 Grazing In The Grass - The Friends Of Distinction

1969

 1 **Dizzy** - Tommy Roe
 2 Get Back - The Beatles with Billy Preston
 3 Man Of The World - Fleetwood Mac
 4 The Ballad Of John And Yoko - The Beatles
 5 My Way - Frank Sinatra
 6 The Boxer - Simon And Garfunkel
 7 My Sentimental Friend - Herman's Hermits
 8 Behind A Painted Smile - The Isley Brothers
 9 Oh Happy Day - The Edwin Hawkins Singers
10 Ragamuffin Man - Manfred Mann

UK Number One album: *Nashville Skyline* - Bob Dylan
US Billboard Number One album: *Hair* - Original Cast
US Cashbox Number One single: *Get Back* - The Beatles with
Billy Preston
Also this week: Fifty-six American sailors are reported missing
after a collision at sea. (1st)

US Billboard singles for the week ending June the 7th
 1 **Get Back** - The Beatles with Billy Preston
 2 Love (Can Make You Happy) - Mercy
 3 Grazing In The Grass - The Friends Of Distinction
 4 Oh Happy Day - The Edwin Hawkins Singers
 5 Bad Moon Rising - Creedence Clearwater Revival
 6 In The Ghetto - Elvis Presley
 7 Aquarius/Let The Sunshine In (The Flesh Failures) - 5th
Dimension
 8 Love Theme From 'Romeo And Juliet' - Henry Mancini &
Orchestra
 9 These Eyes - The Guess Who
10 Too Busy Thinking About My Baby - Marvin Gaye

1969

1 **The Ballad Of John And Yoko** - The Beatles
2 Dizzy - Tommy Roe
3 Oh Happy Day - The Edwin Hawkins Singers
4 Man Of The World - Fleetwood Mac
5 Get Back - The Beatles with Billy Preston
6 Time Is Tight - Booker T. & The MGs
7 My Way - Frank Sinatra
8 The Boxer - Simon And Garfunkel
9 The Tracks Of My Tears - Smokey Robinson & The Miracles
10 Ragamuffin Man - Manfred Mann

UK Number One album: *Nashville Skyline* - Bob Dylan
US Billboard Number One album: *Hair* - Original Cast
US Cashbox Number One single: *Get Back* - The Beatles with Billy Preston
Also this week: Spain launches a blockade of Gibraltar. (8th)

US Billboard singles for the week ending June the 14th
1 **Get Back** - The Beatles with Billy Preston
2 Love Theme From 'Romeo And Juliet' - Henry Mancini & Orchestra
3 In The Ghetto - Elvis Presley
4 Bad Moon Rising - Creedence Clearwater Revival
5 Love (Can Make You Happy) - Mercy
6 Grazing In The Grass - The Friends Of Distinction
7 Oh Happy Day - The Edwin Hawkins Singers
8 Too Busy Thinking About My Baby - Marvin Gaye
9 These Eyes - The Guess Who
10 One - Three Dog Night
The Beatles spend two weeks at Number 1 in the UK and the USA with 2 different songs!

1969

1 **The Ballad Of John And Yoko** - The Beatles
2 Oh Happy Day - The Edwin Hawkins Singers
3 Dizzy - Tommy Roe
4 Time Is Tight - Booker T. & The MGs
5 Living In The Past - Jethro Tull
6 Get Back - The Beatles with Billy Preston
7 My Way - Frank Sinatra
8 Big Ship - Cliff Richard
9 In The Ghetto - Elvis Presley
10 The Boxer - Simon And Garfunkel

UK Number One album: *His Orchestra, His Chorus, His Singers, His Sound* - Ray Conniff
US Billboard Number One album: *Hair* - Original Cast
US Cashbox Number One single: *Get Back* - The Beatles with Billy Preston
Also this week: The Gaullist Georges Pompidou is elected as the new President of France. (15th)

US Billboard singles for the week ending June the 21st
1 **Get Back** - The Beatles with Billy Preston
2 Love Theme From 'Romeo And Juliet' - Henry Mancini & Orchestra
3 Bad Moon Rising - Creedence Clearwater Revival
4 In The Ghetto - Elvis Presley
5 Too Busy Thinking About My Baby - Marvin Gaye
6 One - Three Dog Night
7 Love (Can Make You Happy) - Mercy
8 Grazing In The Grass - The Friends Of Distinction
9 Good Morning Starshine - Oliver
10 Spinning Wheel - Blood, Sweat & Tears

1969

1 **The Ballad Of John And Yoko** - The Beatles
2 Oh Happy Day - The Edwin Hawkins Singers
3 Living In The Past - Jethro Tull
4 Time Is Tight - Booker T. & The MGs
5 In The Ghetto - Elvis Presley
6 Dizzy - Tommy Roe
7 Something In The Air - Thunderclap Newman
8 Breakaway - The Beach Boys
9 Proud Mary - Creedence Clearwater Revival
10 The Tracks Of My Tears - Smokey Robinson & The Miracles

UK Number One album: *His Orchestra, His Chorus, His Singers, His Sound* - Ray Conniff
US Billboard Number One album: *Hair* - Original Cast
US Cashbox Number One single: *In The Ghetto* - Elvis Presley
Also this week: Pancho Gonzales wins Wimbledon's longest singles match, defeating Pasarell 11-9 in the final set. (25th)

US Billboard singles for the week ending June the 28th
1 **Love Theme From 'Romeo And Juliet'** - Henry Mancini & Orchestra
2 Bad Moon Rising - Creedence Clearwater Revival
3 Get Back - The Beatles with Billy Preston
4 Too Busy Thinking About My Baby - Marvin Gaye
5 One - Three Dog Night
6 Spinning Wheel - Blood, Sweat & Tears
7 In The Ghetto - Elvis Presley
8 Good Morning Starshine - Oliver
9 Israelites - Desmond Dekker & The Aces
10 Grazing In The Grass - The Friends Of Distinction

1969

UK singles chart for the week ending July the 5th
1 **Something In The Air** - Thunderclap Newman
2 In The Ghetto - Elvis Presley
3 The Ballad Of John And Yoko - The Beatles
4 Living In The Past - Jethro Tull
5 Oh Happy Day - The Edwin Hawkins Singers
6 Time Is Tight - Booker T. & The MGs
7 Breakaway - The Beach Boys
8 A Way Of Life - Family Dogg
9 Proud Mary - Creedence Clearwater Revival
10 Frozen Orange Juice - Peter Sarstedt

UK Number One album: *His Orchestra, His Chorus, His Singers, His Sound* - Ray Conniff
US Billboard Number One album: *Hair* - Original Cast
US Cashbox Number One single: *Love Theme From 'Romeo And Juliet'* - Henry Mancini & Orchestra
Also this week: Nigeria permits relief drops into Biafra. (30th)

US Billboard singles for the week ending July the 5th
1 **Love Theme From 'Romeo And Juliet'** - Henry Mancini & Orchestra
2 Spinning Wheel - Blood, Sweat & Tears
3 Bad Moon Rising - Creedence Clearwater Revival
4 Good Morning Starshine - Oliver
5 One - Three Dog Night
6 Get Back - The Beatles with Billy Preston
7 Crystal Blue Persuasion - Tommy James
8 In The Year 2525 (Exordium And Terminus) - Zager And Evans
9 Color Him Father - The Winstons
10 Too Busy Thinking About My Baby - Marvin Gaye

1969

UK singles chart for the week ending July the 12th
1 **Something In The Air** - Thunderclap Newman
2 In The Ghetto - Elvis Presley
3 The Ballad Of John And Yoko - The Beatles
4 Hello Suzie - Amen Corner
5 Living In The Past - Jethro Tull
6 Breakaway - The Beach Boys
7 A Way Of Life - Family Dogg
8 Proud Mary - Creedence Clearwater Revival
9 Honky Tonk Women - The Rolling Stones
10 Time Is Tight - Booker T. & The MGs

UK Number One album: *According To My Heart* - Jim Reeves
US Billboard Number One album: *Hair* - Original Cast
US Cashbox Number One single: *Love Theme From 'Romeo And Juliet'* - Henry Mancini & Orchestra
Also this week: Many parades take place in Ulster amidst rising tension. (12th)

US Billboard singles for the week ending July the 12th
1 **In The Year 2525 (Exordium And Terminus)** - Zager And Evans
2 Spinning Wheel - Blood, Sweat & Tears
3 Good Morning Starshine - Oliver
4 Love Theme From 'Romeo And Juliet' - Henry Mancini & Orchestra
5 One - Three Dog Night
6 Crystal Blue Persuasion - Tommy James
7 Bad Moon Rising - Creedence Clearwater Revival
8 The Ballad Of John And Yoko - The Beatles
9 Color Him Father - The Winstons
10 What Does It Take - Jr. Walker & The All Stars

1969

UK singles chart for the week ending July the 19th
1 **Something In The Air** - Thunderclap Newman
2 In The Ghetto - Elvis Presley
3 Honky Tonk Women - The Rolling Stones
4 Give Peace A Chance - John Lennon & Plastic Ono Band
5 Hello Suzie - Amen Corner
6 A Way Of Life - Family Dogg
7 It Miek - Desmond Dekker & The Aces
8 Breakaway - The Beach Boys
9 Baby Make It Soon - Marmalade
10 Proud Mary - Creedence Clearwater Revival

UK Number One album: *According To My Heart* - Jim Reeves
US Billboard Number One album: *Hair* - Original Cast
US Cashbox Number One single: *In The Year 2525 (Exordium And Terminus)* - Zager And Evans
Also this week: The moon mission, Apollo 11, lifts off from Cape Kennedy. (16th)

US Billboard singles for the week ending July the 19th
1 **In The Year 2525** (**Exordium And Terminus**) - Zager And Evans
2 Spinning Wheel - Blood, Sweat & Tears
3 Good Morning Starshine - Oliver
4 Crystal Blue Persuasion - Tommy James
5 What Does It Take - Jr. Walker & The All Stars
6 One - Three Dog Night
7 Color Him Father - The Winstons
8 The Ballad Of John And Yoko - The Beatles
9 My Cherie Amour - Stevie Wonder
10 Love Theme From 'Romeo And Juliet' - Henry Mancini & Orchestra

1969

UK singles chart for the week ending July the 26th
1 **Honky Tonk Women** - The Rolling Stones
2 Give Peace A Chance - John Lennon & Plastic Ono Band
3 Something In The Air - Thunderclap Newman
4 In The Ghetto - Elvis Presley
5 Saved By The Bell - Robin Gibb
6 Hello Suzie - Amen Corner
7 It Miek - Desmond Dekker & The Aces
8 Goodnight Midnight - Clodagh Rodgers
9 Baby Make It Soon - Marmalade
10 A Way Of Life - Family Dogg

UK Number One album: *According To My Heart* - Jim Reeves
US Billboard Number One album: *Blood, Sweat & Tears* -
Blood, Sweat & Tears
US Cashbox Number One single: *In The Year 2525 (Exordium
And Terminus)* - Zager And Evans
Also this week: Neil Armstrong steps onto the moon. (21st)

US Billboard singles for the week ending July the 26th
1 **In The Year 2525** (**Exordium And Terminus**) - Zager And
Evans
2 Crystal Blue Persuasion - Tommy James
3 Spinning Wheel - Blood, Sweat & Tears
4 My Cherie Amour - Stevie Wonder
5 What Does It Take - Jr. Walker & The All Stars
6 Good Morning Starshine - Oliver
7 One - Three Dog Night
8 The Ballad Of John And Yoko - The Beatles
9 Baby, I Love You - Andy Kim
10 Love Theme From 'Romeo And Juliet' - Henry Mancini &
Orchestra

1969

 1 **Honky Tonk Women** - The Rolling Stones
 2 Give Peace A Chance - John Lennon & Plastic Ono Band
 3 Saved By The Bell - Robin Gibb
 4 In The Ghetto - Elvis Presley
 5 Something In The Air - Thunderclap Newman
 6 Goodnight Midnight - Clodagh Rodgers
 7 Make Me An Island - Joe Dolan
 8 It Miek - Desmond Dekker & The Aces
 9 Baby Make It Soon - Marmalade
10 Hello Suzie - Amen Corner

UK Number One album: *According To My Heart* - Jim Reeves
US Billboard Number One album: *Blood, Sweat & Tears* -
Blood, Sweat & Tears
US Cashbox Number One single: *In The Year 2525 (Exordium And Terminus)* - Zager And Evans
Also this week: Mariner 6 sends back close-up pictures of the planet Mars. (31st)

US Billboard singles for the week ending August the 2nd

 1 **In The Year 2525** (**Exordium And Terminus**) - Zager And Evans
 2 Crystal Blue Persuasion - Tommy James
 3 Spinning Wheel - Blood, Sweat & Tears
 4 My Cherie Amour - Stevie Wonder
 5 What Does It Take - Jr. Walker & The All Stars
 6 Ruby, Don't Take Your Love To Town - Kenny Rogers
 7 Sweet Caroline - Neil Diamond
 8 Honky Tonk Women - The Rolling Stones
 9 Baby, I Love You - Andy Kim
10 The Ballad Of John And Yoko - The Beatles

1969

UK singles chart for the week ending August the 9th

1 **Honky Tonk Women** - The Rolling Stones
2 Give Peace A Chance - John Lennon & Plastic Ono Band
3 Saved By The Bell - Robin Gibb
4 Goodnight Midnight - Clodagh Rodgers
5 In The Ghetto - Elvis Presley
6 My Cherie Amour - Stevie Wonder
7 Make Me An Island - Joe Dolan
8 Conversations - Cilla Black
9 Baby Make It Soon - Marmalade
10 It Miek - Desmond Dekker & The Aces

UK Number One album: *Stand Up* - Jethro Tull
US Billboard Number One album: *Blood, Sweat & Tears* - Blood, Sweat & Tears
US Cashbox Number One single: I*n The Year 2525 (Exordium And Terminus)* - Zager And Evans
Also this week: The Beatles cross an Abbey Road 'zebra' for a photograph which surfaces on their next album cover. (8th)

US Billboard singles for the week ending August the 9th

1 **In The Year 2525 (Exordium And Terminus**) - Zager And Evans
2 Crystal Blue Persuasion - Tommy James
3 Honky Tonk Women - The Rolling Stones
4 What Does It Take - Jr. Walker & The All Stars
5 Sweet Caroline - Neil Diamond
6 Ruby, Don't Take Your Love To Town - Kenny Rogers
7 A Boy Named Sue - Johnny Cash
8 My Cherie Amour - Stevie Wonder
9 Put A Little Love In Your Heart - Jackie DeShannon
10 Baby, I Love You - Andy Kim

1969

1 **Honky Tonk Women** - The Rolling Stones
2 Saved By The Bell - Robin Gibb
3 Make Me An Island - Joe Dolan
4 Give Peace A Chance - John Lennon & Plastic Ono Band
5 My Cherie Amour - Stevie Wonder
6 Goodnight Midnight - Clodagh Rodgers
7 Conversations - Cilla Black
8 Early In The Morning - Vanity Fare
9 Bring On Back The Good Times - The Love Affair
10 Wet Dream - Max Romeo

UK Number One album: *Stand Up* - Jethro Tull
US Billboard Number One album: *Blood, Sweat & Tears* -
Blood, Sweat & Tears
US Cashbox Number One single: *Honky Tonk Women* - The
Rolling Stones
Also this week: The riotous Battle of the Bogside begins in
Londonderry at the end of an Apprentice Boys' Parade. (12th)

US Billboard singles for the week ending August the 16th

1 **In The Year 2525 (Exordium And Terminus**) - Zager And
Evans
2 Honky Tonk Women - The Rolling Stones
3 Crystal Blue Persuasion - Tommy James
4 Sweet Caroline - Neil Diamond
5 A Boy Named Sue - Johnny Cash
6 Put A Little Love In Your Heart - Jackie DeShannon
7 Ruby, Don't Take Your Love To Town - Kenny Rogers
8 My Cherie Amour - Stevie Wonder
9 What Does It Take - Jr. Walker & The All Stars
10 Baby, I Love You - Andy Kim

1969

  1 **Honky Tonk Women** - The Rolling Stones
  2 Saved By The Bell - Robin Gibb
  3 In The Year 2525 (Exordium And Terminus) - Zager And Evans
  4 My Cherie Amour - Stevie Wonder
  5 Make Me An Island - Joe Dolan
  6 Give Peace A Chance - John Lennon & Plastic Ono Band
  7 Goodnight Midnight - Clodagh Rodgers
  8 Too Busy Thinking 'Bout My Baby - Marvin Gaye
  9 Conversations - Cilla Black
10 Early In The Morning - Vanity Fare

UK Number One album: *Stand Up* - Jethro Tull
US Billboard Number One album: *At San Quentin* - Johnny Cash
US Cashbox Number One single: *Honky Tonk Women* - The Rolling Stones
Also this week: Soviet tanks re-enter Prague. (21st)

US Billboard singles for the week ending August the 23rd
  1 **Honky Tonk Women** - The Rolling Stones
  2 A Boy Named Sue - Johnny Cash
  3 Crystal Blue Persuasion - Tommy James
  4 Sweet Caroline - Neil Diamond
  5 In The Year 2525 (Exordium And Terminus) - Zager And Evans
  6 Put A Little Love In Your Heart - Jackie DeShannon
  7 Green River - Creedence Clearwater Revival
  8 Polk Salad Annie - Tony Joe White
  9 Get Together - The Youngbloods
10 Laughing - The Guess Who

1969

 1 **In The Year 2525** (**Exordium And Terminus**) - Zager And Evans

 2 Honky Tonk Women - The Rolling Stones

 3 Saved By The Bell - Robin Gibb

 4 My Cherie Amour - Stevie Wonder

 5 Make Me An Island - Joe Dolan

 6 Viva Bobby Joe - The Equals

 7 Too Busy Thinking 'Bout My Baby - Marvin Gaye

 8 Bad Moon Rising - Creedence Clearwater Revival

 9 Don't Forget To Remember - The Bees Gees

10 Early In The Morning - Vanity Fare

UK Number One album: *Elvis In Memphis* - Elvis Presley

US Billboard Number One album: *At San Quentin* - Johnny Cash

US Cashbox Number One single: *Honky Tonk Women* - The Rolling Stones

Also this week: England play their last test for a year. (26th)

US Billboard singles for the week ending August the 30th

 1 **Honky Tonk Women** - The Rolling Stones

 2 A Boy Named Sue - Johnny Cash

 3 Sugar, Sugar - The Archies

 4 Put A Little Love In Your Heart - Jackie DeShannon

 5 Sweet Caroline - Neil Diamond

 6 Get Together - The Youngbloods

 7 Green River - Creedence Clearwater Revival

 8 In The Year 2525 (Exordium And Terminus) - Zager And Evans

 9 Lay Lady Lay - Bob Dylan

10 Crystal Blue Persuasion - Tommy James

1969

 1 **In The Year 2525 (Exordium And Terminus)** - Zager And Evans

 2 Bad Moon Rising - Creedence Clearwater Revival

 3 Honky Tonk Women - The Rolling Stones

 4 My Cherie Amour - Stevie Wonder

 5 Don't Forget To Remember - The Bees Gees

 6 Too Busy Thinking 'Bout My Baby - Marvin Gaye

 7 Viva Bobby Joe - The Equals

 8 Je T'Aime...Moi Non Plus - Jane Birkin And Serge Gainsbourg

 9 Saved By The Bell - Robin Gibb

10 Natural Born Bugie - Humble Pie

UK Number One album: *Stand Up* - Jethro Tull

US Billboard Number One album: *At San Quentin* - Johnny Cash

US Cashbox Number One single: *Honky Tonk Women* - The Rolling Stones

Also this week: Colonel Gaddafi seizes power in Libya. (1st)

US Billboard singles for the week ending September the 6th

 1 **Honky Tonk Women** - The Rolling Stones

 2 A Boy Named Sue - Johnny Cash

 3 Sugar, Sugar - The Archies

 4 Green River - Creedence Clearwater Revival

 5 Get Together - The Youngbloods

 6 Put A Little Love In Your Heart - Jackie DeShannon

 7 Lay Lady Lay - Bob Dylan

 8 Easy To Be Hard - Three Dog Night

 9 Sweet Caroline - Neil Diamond

10 I'll Never Fall In Love Again - Tom Jones

1969

1 **In The Year 2525 (Exordium And Terminus**) - Zager And Evans

2 Bad Moon Rising - Creedence Clearwater Revival

3 Don't Forget To Remember - The Bees Gees

4 Natural Born Bugie - Humble Pie

5 Too Busy Thinking 'Bout My Baby - Marvin Gaye

6 Je T'Aime...Moi Non Plus - Jane Birkin And Serge Gainsbourg

7 Viva Bobby Joe - The Equals

8 My Cherie Amour - Stevie Wonder

9 Honky Tonk Women - The Rolling Stones

10 Saved By The Bell - Robin Gibb

UK Number One album: *Stand Up* - Jethro Tull

US Billboard Number One album: *At San Quentin* - Johnny Cash

US Cashbox Number One single: *Sugar, Sugar* - The Archies

Also this week: Australia's Rod Laver wins the men's singles at the US Open, ensuring an historic tennis grand slam. (8th)

US Billboard singles for the week ending September the 13th

1 **Honky Tonk Women** - The Rolling Stones

2 Sugar, Sugar - The Archies

3 A Boy Named Sue - Johnny Cash

4 Green River - Creedence Clearwater Revival

5 Get Together - The Youngbloods

6 I'll Never Fall In Love Again - Tom Jones

7 Lay Lady Lay - Bob Dylan

8 Easy To Be Hard - Three Dog Night

9 Put A Little Love In Your Heart - Jackie DeShannon

10 I Can't Get Next To You - The Temptations

1969

UK singles chart for the week ending September the 20th
 1 **Bad Moon Rising** - Creedence Clearwater Revival
 2 Don't Forget To Remember - The Bees Gees
 3 In The Year 2525 (Exordium And Terminus) - Zager And Evans
 4 Je T'Aime...Moi Non Plus - Jane Birkin And Serge Gainsbourg
 5 Natural Born Bugie - Humble Pie
 6 Too Busy Thinking 'Bout My Baby - Marvin Gaye
 7 Viva Bobby Joe - The Equals
 8 Good Morning Starshine - Oliver
 9 I'll Never Fall In Love Again - Bobbie Gentry
10 Honky Tonk Women - The Rolling Stones

UK Number One album: *Blind Faith* - Blind Faith
US Billboard Number One album: *Blind Faith* - Blind Faith
US Cashbox Number One single: *Sugar, Sugar* - The Archies
Also this week: Lillian Board wins the women's European 800 metres gold. (18th)

US Billboard singles for the week ending September the 20th
 1 **Sugar**, **Sugar** - The Archies
 2 Honky Tonk Women - The Rolling Stones
 3 Green River - Creedence Clearwater Revival
 4 A Boy Named Sue - Johnny Cash
 5 Easy To Be Hard - Three Dog Night
 6 I'll Never Fall In Love Again - Tom Jones
 7 Get Together - The Youngbloods
 8 Jean - Oliver
 9 Little Woman - Bobby Sherman
10 I Can't Get Next To You - The Temptations

1969

1 **Bad Moon Rising** - Creedence Clearwater Revival
2 Je T'Aime...Moi Non Plus - Jane Birkin And Serge Gainsbourg
3 Don't Forget To Remember - The Bees Gees
4 I'll Never Fall In Love Again - Bobbie Gentry
5 In The Year 2525 (Exordium And Terminus) - Zager And Evans
6 Natural Born Bugie - Humble Pie
7 Good Morning Starshine - Oliver
8 Too Busy Thinking 'Bout My Baby - Marvin Gaye
9 Viva Bobby Joe - The Equals
10 A Boy Named Sue - Johnny Cash

UK Number One album: *Blind Faith* - Blind Faith
US Billboard Number One album: *Blind Faith* - Blind Faith
US Cashbox Number One single: *Sugar, Sugar* - The Archies
Also this week: Two hundred police are required to evict hippie squatters from their commune at 144 Piccadilly. (21st)

US Billboard singles for the week ending September the 27th

1 **Sugar**, **Sugar** - The Archies
2 Green River - Creedence Clearwater Revival
3 Honky Tonk Women - The Rolling Stones
4 Easy To Be Hard - Three Dog Night
5 Little Woman - Bobby Sherman
6 I Can't Get Next To You - The Temptations
7 Jean - Oliver
8 I'll Never Fall In Love Again - Tom Jones
9 Hot Fun In The Summertime - Sly & The Family Stone
10 Oh, What A Night - The Dells

1969

1 **Bad Moon Rising** - Creedence Clearwater Revival
2 I'll Never Fall In Love Again - Bobbie Gentry
3 Je T'Aime...Moi Non Plus - Jane Birkin And Serge Gainsbourg
4 A Boy Named Sue - Johnny Cash
5 Don't Forget To Remember - The Bees Gees
6 Good Morning Starshine - Oliver
7 Throw Down A Line - Cliff And Hank
8 It's Getting Better - Mama Cass
9 Lay Lady Lay - Bob Dylan
10 In The Year 2525 (Exordium And Terminus) - Zager And Evans

UK Number One album: *Abbey Road* - The Beatles
US Billboard Number One album: *Green River* - Creedence Clearwater Revival
US Cashbox Number One single: *Sugar, Sugar* - The Archies
Also this week: Concorde 001 breaks the sound barrier for the first time. (1st)

US Billboard singles for the week ending October the 4th

1 **Sugar**, **Sugar** - The Archies
2 Jean - Oliver
3 Little Woman - Bobby Sherman
4 Easy To Be Hard - Three Dog Night
5 I Can't Get Next To You - The Temptations
6 Honky Tonk Women - The Rolling Stones
7 Green River - Creedence Clearwater Revival
8 Everybody's Talkin' - Nilsson
9 Hot Fun In The Summertime - Sly & The Family Stone
10 Oh, What A Night - The Dells

1969

UK singles chart for the week ending October the 11th
 1 **Je T'Aime...Moi Non Plus** - Jane Birkin And Serge Gainsbourg
 2 I'll Never Fall In Love Again - Bobbie Gentry
 3 Bad Moon Rising - Creedence Clearwater Revival
 4 A Boy Named Sue - Johnny Cash
 5 Lay Lady Lay - Bob Dylan
 6 Good Morning Starshine - Oliver
 7 Don't Forget To Remember - The Bees Gees
 8 Throw Down A Line - Cliff And Hank
 9 It's Getting Better - Mama Cass
10 Nobody's Child - Karen Young

UK Number One album: *Abbey Road* - The Beatles
US Billboard Number One album: *Green River* - Creedence Clearwater Revival
US Cashbox Number One single: *Little Woman* - Bobby Sherman
Also this week: The ground-breaking new comedy Monty Python's Flying Circus is first broadcast on BBC2. (5th)

US Billboard singles for the week ending October the 11th
 1 **Sugar**, **Sugar** - The Archies
 2 Jean - Oliver
 3 Little Woman - Bobby Sherman
 4 I Can't Get Next To You - The Temptations
 5 Hot Fun In The Summertime - Sly & The Family Stone
 6 Everybody's Talkin' - Nilsson
 7 Easy To Be Hard - Three Dog Night
 8 Honky Tonk Women - The Rolling Stones
 9 This Girl Is A Woman - Gary Puckett & The Union Gap
10 Green River - Creedence Clearwater Revival

1969

UK singles chart for the week ending October the 18th

1 **I'll Never Fall In Love Again** - Bobbie Gentry
2 Je T'Aime...Moi Non Plus - Jane Birkin And Serge Gainsbourg
3 I'm Gonna Make You Mine - Lou Christie
4 A Boy Named Sue - Johnny Cash
5 He Ain't Heavy...He's My Brother - The Hollies
6 Nobody's Child - Karen Young
7 Lay Lady Lay - Bob Dylan
8 Space Oddity - David Bowie
9 Oh Well - Fleetwood Mac
10 Good Morning Starshine - Oliver

UK Number One album: *Abbey Road* - The Beatles
US Billboard Number One album: *Green River* - Creedence Clearwater Revival
US Cashbox Number One single: *Suspicious Minds* - Elvis Presley
Also this week: Millions of Americans protest against the continuing Vietnam War. (15th)

US Billboard singles for the week ending October the 18th

1 **I Can't Get Next To You** - The Temptations
2 Hot Fun In The Summertime - Sly & The Family Stone
3 Sugar, Sugar - The Archies
4 Jean - Oliver
5 Little Woman - Bobby Sherman
6 Suspicious Minds - Elvis Presley
7 That's The Way Love Is - Marvin Gaye
8 Wedding Bell Blues - 5th Dimension
9 Easy To Be Hard - Three Dog Night
10 Tracy - The Cuff Links

1969

UK singles chart for the week ending October the 25th
1 **Sugar, Sugar** - The Archies
2 I'll Never Fall In Love Again - Bobbie Gentry
3 I'm Gonna Make You Mine - Lou Christie
4 Je T'Aime...Moi Non Plus - Jane Birkin And Serge Gainsbourg
5 He Ain't Heavy...He's My Brother - The Hollies
6 Space Oddity - David Bowie
7 Oh Well - Fleetwood Mac
8 Nobody's Child - Karen Young
9 Lay Lady Lay - Bob Dylan
10 A Boy Named Sue - Johnny Cash

UK Number One album: *Abbey Road* - The Beatles
US Billboard Number One album: *Green River* - Creedence Clearwater Revival
US Cashbox Number One single: *Suspicious Minds* - Elvis Presley
Also this week: Willy Brandt is elected as West Germany's new Chancellor. (21st)

US Billboard singles for the week ending October the 25th
1 **I Can't Get Next To You** - The Temptations
2 Hot Fun In The Summertime - Sly & The Family Stone
3 Sugar, Sugar - The Archies
4 Jean - Oliver
5 Suspicious Minds - Elvis Presley
6 Little Woman - Bobby Sherman
7 Wedding Bell Blues - 5th Dimension
8 Baby It's You - Smith
9 Tracy - The Cuff Links
10 I'm Gonna Make You Mine - Lou Christie

1969

UK singles chart for the week ending November the 1st
1 **Sugar**, **Sugar** - The Archies
2 I'm Gonna Make You Mine - Lou Christie
3 He Ain't Heavy...He's My Brother - The Hollies
4 Oh Well - Fleetwood Mac
5 Space Oddity - David Bowie
6 I'll Never Fall In Love Again - Bobbie Gentry
7 Nobody's Child - Karen Young
8 Return Of Django/Dollar In The Teeth - The Upsetters
9 Je T'Aime...Moi Non Plus - Jane Birkin And Serge Gainsbourg
10 A Boy Named Sue - Johnny Cash

UK Number One album: _Abbey Road_ - The Beatles
US Billboard Number One album: _Abbey Road_ - The Beatles
US Cashbox Number One single: _Wedding Bell Blues_ - 5th Dimension
Also this week: The Palestine Liberation Organisation and the Lebanese government agree to have a cease-fire. (1st)

US Billboard singles for the week ending November the 1st
1 **Suspicious Minds** - Elvis Presley
2 Wedding Bell Blues - 5th Dimension
3 Sugar, Sugar - The Archies
4 I Can't Get Next To You - The Temptations
5 Baby It's You - Smith
6 Hot Fun In The Summertime - Sly & The Family Stone
7 Little Woman - Bobby Sherman
8 Jean - Oliver
9 Tracy - The Cuff Links
10 Come Together - The Beatles

David Bowie's Space Oddity later achieved two weeks as a UK No.1 in November 1975.

1969

 1 **Sugar**, **Sugar** - The Archies
 2 Oh Well - Fleetwood Mac
 3 I'm Gonna Make You Mine - Lou Christie
 4 He Ain't Heavy...He's My Brother - The Hollies
 5 Return Of Django/Dollar In The Teeth - The Upsetters
 6 Nobody's Child - Karen Young
 7 Space Oddity - David Bowie
 8 Love's Been Good To Me - Frank Sinatra
 9 I'll Never Fall In Love Again - Bobbie Gentry
10 Delta Lady - Joe Cocker

UK Number One album: *Abbey Road* - The Beatles
US Billboard Number One album: *Abbey Road* - The Beatles
US Cashbox Number One single: *Wedding Bell Blues* - 5th Dimension
Also this week: 64 people are killed by a mine explosion in South Africa. (7th)

US Billboard singles for the week ending November the 8th

 1 **Wedding Bell Blues** - 5th Dimension
 2 Suspicious Minds - Elvis Presley
 3 Come Together - The Beatles
 4 I Can't Get Next To You - The Temptations
 5 Baby It's You - Smith
 6 Sugar, Sugar - The Archies
 7 Hot Fun In The Summertime - Sly & The Family Stone
 8 And When I Die - Blood, Sweat & Tears
 9 Something - The Beatles
10 Smile A Little Smile For Me - The Flying Machine

1969

1 **Sugar, Sugar** - The Archies
2 Oh Well - Fleetwood Mac
3 (Call Me) Number One - The Tremeloes
4 He Ain't Heavy...He's My Brother - The Hollies
5 Return Of Django/Dollar In The Teeth - The Upsetters
6 Something/Come Together - The Beatles
7 Wonderful World, Beautiful People - Jimmy Cliff
8 Love's Been Good To Me - Frank Sinatra
9 Nobody's Child - Karen Young
10 I'm Gonna Make You Mine - Lou Christie

UK Number One album: *Abbey Road* - The Beatles
US Billboard Number One album: *Abbey Road* - The Beatles
US Cashbox Number One single: *Wedding Bell Blues* - 5th Dimension
Also this week: Mrs Irene Hanson, aged thirty-three, gives birth to five girls. (13th)

US Billboard singles for the week ending November the 15th

1 **Wedding Bell Blues** - 5th Dimension
2 Come Together - The Beatles
3 Something - The Beatles
4 And When I Die - Blood, Sweat & Tears
5 Baby It's You - Smith
6 I Can't Get Next To You - The Temptations
7 Suspicious Minds - Elvis Presley
8 Smile A Little Smile For Me - The Flying Machine
9 Sugar, Sugar - The Archies
10 Take A Letter Maria - R.B. Greaves

1969

1 **Sugar**, **Sugar** - The Archies
2 (Call Me) Number One - The Tremeloes
3 Oh Well - Fleetwood Mac
4 Something/Come Together - The Beatles
5 Return Of Django/Dollar In The Teeth - The Upsetters
6 Wonderful World, Beautiful People - Jimmy Cliff
7 Sweet Dream - Jethro Tull
8 Nobody's Child - Karen Young
9 Ruby, Don't Take Your Love To Town - Kenny Rogers
10 Yester-Me, Yester-You, Yesterday - Stevie Wonder

UK Number One album: *Abbey Road* - The Beatles
US Billboard Number One album: *Abbey Road* - The Beatles
US Cashbox Number One single: *Come Together* - The Beatles
Also this week: Eighty-seven people are killed when an
aeroplane crashes in the Nigerian jungle. (20th)

US Billboard singles for the week ending November the 22nd

1 **Wedding Bell Blues** - 5th Dimension
2 Take A Letter Maria - R.B. Greaves
3 Something - The Beatles
4 And When I Die - Blood, Sweat & Tears
5 Smile A Little Smile For Me - The Flying Machine
6 Na Na Hey Hey Kiss Him Goodbye - Steam
7 Come Together - The Beatles
8 Yester-Me, Yester-You, Yesterday - Stevie Wonder
9 Suspicious Minds - Elvis Presley
10 I Can't Get Next To You - The Temptations

Something/Come Together is the first Beatles' single to fail to hit the UK Top 3 since 1962

1969

1 **Sugar**, **Sugar** - The Archies
2 (Call Me) Number One - The Tremeloes
3 Yester-Me, Yester-You, Yesterday - Stevie Wonder
4 Oh Well - Fleetwood Mac
5 Ruby, Don't Take Your Love To Town - Kenny Rogers
6 Something/Come Together - The Beatles
7 Wonderful World, Beautiful People - Jimmy Cliff
8 Return Of Django/Dollar In The Teeth - The Upsetters
9 The Liquidator - Harry J All Stars
10 Sweet Dream - Jethro Tull

UK Number One album: *Abbey Road* - The Beatles
US Billboard Number One album: *Abbey Road* - The Beatles
US Cashbox Number One single: *Come Together* - The Beatles
Also this week: The UK government authorises the creation of
new local radio stations. (25th)

US Billboard singles for the week ending November the 29th
1 **Come Together** - The Beatles
1 **Something** - The Beatles
2 And When I Die - Blood, Sweat & Tears
3 Wedding Bell Blues - 5th Dimension
4 Take A Letter Maria - R.B. Greaves
5 Na Na Hey Hey Kiss Him Goodbye - Steam
6 Smile A Little Smile For Me - The Flying Machine
7 Leaving On A Jet Plane - Peter, Paul And Mary
8 Yester-Me, Yester-You, Yesterday - Stevie Wonder
9 Down On The Corner - Creedence Clearwater Revival

Come Together/Something earned the Beatles their 18th US No.1, one more than Elvis.

1969

UK singles chart for the week ending December the 6th
  1 **Sugar**, **Sugar** - The Archies
  2 Yester-Me, Yester-You, Yesterday - Stevie Wonder
  3 Ruby, Don't Take Your Love To Town - Kenny Rogers
  4 (Call Me) Number One - The Tremeloes
  5 Two Little Boys - Rolf Harris
  6 Oh Well - Fleetwood Mac
  7 Melting Pot - Blue Mink
  8 Something/Come Together - The Beatles
  9 Sweet Dream - Jethro Tull
10 Suspicious Minds - Elvis Presley

UK Number One album: *Abbey Road* - The Beatles
US Billboard Number One album: *Abbey Road* - The Beatles
US Cashbox Number One single: *Come Together* - The Beatles
Also this week: Police shoot dead two Black Panthers in Chicago. (5th)

US Billboard singles for the week ending December the 6th
  1 **Na Na Hey Hey Kiss Him Goodbye** - Steam
  2 Leaving On A Jet Plane - Peter, Paul And Mary
  3 Come Together - The Beatles
  3 Something - The Beatles
  4 Take A Letter Maria - R.B. Greaves
  5 Down On The Corner - Creedence Clearwater Revival
  5 Fortunate Son - Creedence Clearwater Revival
  6 And When I Die - Blood, Sweat & Tears
  7 Wedding Bell Blues - 5th Dimension
  8 Yester-Me, Yester-You, Yesterday - Stevie Wonder

1969

UK singles chart for the week ending December the 13th
 1 **Sugar, Sugar** - The Archies
 2 Ruby, Don't Take Your Love To Town - Kenny Rogers
 3 Two Little Boys - Rolf Harris
 4 Yester-Me, Yester-You, Yesterday - Stevie Wonder
 5 Melting Pot - Blue Mink
 6 (Call Me) Number One - The Tremeloes
 7 Winter World Of Love - Engelbert Humperdinck
 8 Suspicious Minds - Elvis Presley
 9 The Onion Song - Marvin Gaye & Tammi Terrell
10 Wonderful World, Beautiful People - Jimmy Cliff

UK Number One album: *Abbey Road* - The Beatles
US Billboard Number One album: *Abbey Road* - The Beatles
US Cashbox Number One single: *And When I Die* - Blood, Sweat & Tears
Also this week: Terrorist bombs in Milan and Rome leave thirteen people dead. (12th)

US Billboard singles for the week ending December the 13th
 1 **Na Na Hey Hey Kiss Him Goodbye** - Steam
 2 Leaving On A Jet Plane - Peter, Paul And Mary
 3 Someday We'll Be Together - Diana Ross And The Supremes
 4 Come Together - The Beatles
 4 Something - The Beatles
 5 Down On The Corner - Creedence Clearwater Revival
 5 Fortunate Son - Creedence Clearwater Revival
 6 Take A Letter Maria - R.B. Greaves
 7 Yester-Me, Yester-You, Yesterday - Stevie Wonder
 8 And When I Die - Blood, Sweat & Tears

1969

UK singles chart for the week ending December the 20th
 1 **Two Little Boys** - Rolf Harris
 2 Ruby, Don't Take Your Love To Town - Kenny Rogers
 3 Sugar, Sugar - The Archies
 4 Yester-Me, Yester-You, Yesterday - Stevie Wonder
 5 Melting Pot - Blue Mink
 6 Suspicious Minds - Elvis Presley
 7 All I Have To Do Is Dream - Bobbie Gentry/Glen Campbell
 8 Winter World Of Love - Engelbert Humperdinck
 9 (Call Me) Number One - The Tremeloes
10 Tracy - The Cuff Links

UK Number One album: *Let It Bleed* - The Rolling Stones
US Billboard Number One album: *Abbey Road* - The Beatles
US Cashbox Number One single: *Leaving On A Jet Plane* -
Peter, Paul And Mary
Also this week: The House of Lords agrees to abolish the death
penalty. The House of Commons had already done so. (18th)

US Billboard singles for the week ending December the 20th
 1 **Leaving On A Jet Plane** - Peter, Paul And Mary
 2 Someday We'll Be Together - Diana Ross And The
Supremes
 3 Down On The Corner - Creedence Clearwater Revival
 3 Fortunate Son - Creedence Clearwater Revival
 4 Na Na Hey Hey Kiss Him Goodbye - Steam
 5 Raindrops Keep Fallin' On My Head - B.J. Thomas
 6 Come Together - The Beatles
 6 Something - The Beatles
 7 Yester-Me, Yester-You, Yesterday - Stevie Wonder
 8 Take A Letter Maria - R.B. Greaves

1969

 1 **Two Little Boys** - Rolf Harris
 2 Ruby, Don't Take Your Love To Town - Kenny Rogers
 3 Sugar, Sugar - The Archies
 4 Suspicious Minds - Elvis Presley
 5 Melting Pot - Blue Mink
 6 Yester-Me, Yester-You, Yesterday - Stevie Wonder
 7 All I Have To Do Is Dream - Bobbie Gentry/Glen Campbell
 8 Winter World Of Love - Engelbert Humperdinck
 9 Tracy - The Cuff Links
10 Without Love - Tom Jones

UK Number One album: *Abbey Road* - The Beatles
US Billboard Number One album: *Led Zeppelin II* - Led Zeppelin
US Cashbox Number One single: *Someday We'll Be Together* - Diana Ross And The Supremes
Also this week: The young Irish Nationalist MP Bernadette Devlin is found guilty of incitement to riot. (22nd)

US Billboard singles for the week ending December the 27th

 1 **Someday We'll Be Together** - Diana Ross And The Supremes
 2 Leaving On A Jet Plane - Peter, Paul And Mary
 3 Raindrops Keep Fallin' On My Head - B.J. Thomas
 4 Down On The Corner - Creedence Clearwater Revival
 4 Fortunate Son - Creedence Clearwater Revival
 5 Na Na Hey Hey Kiss Him Goodbye - Steam
 6 Holly - Neil Diamond
 7 Come Together - The Beatles
 7 Something - The Beatles
 8 I Want You Back -The Jacksons

THE BEST 10 SONGS OF 1969?

He Ain't Heavy, He's My Brother by The Hollies

Long before the emergence of Madchester or before Manchester became a mecca for the indie/ new wave scene, it was the Hollies who originally flew the flag for this city. The group regularly flirted with the upper echelons of the UK singles chart, having been 'top of the pops' in 1965 with 'I'm Alive'. However, arguably their greatest 'sixties recording was this slice of brotherly love, ably assisted by a prominent harmonica, strings, and the group's trademark harmonies.

If I Can Dream by Elvis Presley

The king of rock 'n' roll made a belated attempt to re-gain his throne by abandoning his mediocre acting career and returning to what he always did best: singing and performing. A 'Comeback Special' was filmed and screened to wide acclaim with Elvis showcasing a new tune, 'If I Can Dream'. It wasn't exactly hip-swivelling stuff, but 'If I Can Dream' is a mini-epic which reminded one and all of the majesty of Mr P. Buoyed by this comeback, Elvis enjoyed a brief flurry of big hits.

I Want You (She's So Heavy) by The Beatles

After group relations were frayed by the sessions for the not-yet released 'Let It Be' album, the once fab four managed to patch up their differences and re-enlisted George Martin for the more harmonious 'Abbey Road' project. Determined to go out on a high, John Lennon weighs in with the lengthy and slightly disturbing 'I Want You (She's So Heavy)'. Dominated by guitar and Lennon's unremitting demand of 'I want you', the song ends abruptly when Lennon states: cut the tape 'there'.

Nothing Is Easy by Jethro Tull

Long-haired flautist Ian Anderson carved out his own niche in the world of rock with a number of unique singles and albums. Nothing is indeed easy but Jethro Tull serve up a treat with this item from their 'Stand Up' album. Not only is the flute-playing a joy to behold, but the intro is out of this world. Jethro Tull are largely unheard of by the 21st century audience of X Factor devotees. One can feel nothing but sympathy for those who are oblivious of this quirky recording.

Ramble On by Led Zeppelin

Ace guitarist Jimmy Page alternated between acoustic guitar and electric guitar while Bonzo Bonham's drumming was both sedate and ferocious as the mighty Zeppelin demonstrated their light and shade dynamic in this outstanding piece from their second album. Robert Plant meanwhile re-visits the well-worn theme of the rolling stone, born under a wanderin' star who is unable to settle down and whose itchy feet set out for pastures new. Here was a new band really hitting its awesome stride.

THE BEST 10 SONGS OF 1969? (Continued)

Reflections Of My Life by Marmalade

Marmalade were the toast of the airwaves with their own joyful rendition of the Beatles' 'Ob-La-Di-Ob-La-Da' which reached the top of the pops in the UK in early 1969. At the end of the year, the gang were back again with something completely different. 'Reflections Of My Life' was a sensitive tune and didn't belong in the happy-go-lucky bracket. The track is notable for a backwards guitar whilst also decorated with strings. It is one of the best sad songs in popular music.

Someday We'll Be Together by Diana Ross & The Supremes

The Supremes closed out the decade by occupying familiar territory, the summit of the Billboard Hot 100. It was something of a bitter-sweet triumph as this was the swansong for the leading Supreme, Diana Ross, who had just announced that this single would be her last with the group, as she prepared to launch her own solo career. Whether the song title suggested a group reunion was open to question, but the tragic death of original Supreme, Flo Ballard in 1976, scuppered any such hopes.

Something In The Air by Thunderclap Newman

There was certainly something in the air in 1968, which was something of a year of protests and riots. This theme surfaces in this memorable tune from the short-lived 'Thunderclap Newman'. This revolutionary single was a call to arms which if nothing else climbed to the peak position of the UK chart in mid-summer. This studio band included Jimmy McCulloch, future guitarist with Wings and the song was produced by Pete Townshend. It was his only involvement with a UK chart-topper.

Wonderful World, Beautiful People by Jimmy Cliff

Before Jimmy Cliff found fame with his leading role in the film, 'The Harder They Come', he made a few forays into the UK charts. Notable among them was this single which revealed Cliff's longing for a better world. Cliff even exhorts Prime Minister Wilson and President Nixon in mid-song, though one could argue that his pleas fell on deaf ears. Here was another song that fell into the skinhead reggae category as Jamaican music found an unlikely audience with working-class white men.

You Can't Always Get What You Want by The Rolling Stones

1969 witnessed the death of Rolling Stone, Brian Jones, (who was almost certainly murdered) while Marianne Faithfull nearly joined him a few days later when she overdosed. Undaunted by these traumas, Mick Jagger rode on regardless, as he went down to the demonstration to get his fair share of abuse! A choir was thrown in to this epic for good measure. This was the long closing track to the critically acclaimed 'Let It Bleed' album which had opened with the equally remarkable 'Gimme Shelter'.

THE BEST ALBUM OF 1969?

Led Zeppelin

by **Led Zeppelin**

peaked in the UK charts at No.6

peaked in the US charts at No.10

produced by Jimmy Page

released in January

It was a bizarre coincidence that as the brilliant Cream were bowing out of the rock scene in November 1968, a new act were filling their considerable void. Whilst Cream are hailed as the first supergroup, Led Zeppelin (or the New Yardbirds, as they were initially known) were themselves drawn from previous dalliances in the world of pop. In fact, Jimmy Page and John Paul Jones were prolific session men who had been hired to lend their professional expertise to a plethora of rather unlikely pop songs. Their CV makes for interesting viewing as they offered their assistance to a variety of pop acts. Now at last, Page and Jones were stepping out from the shadows of the recording studio, determined to make their own mark. They hired Robert Plant and John Bonham from the heart of the Black Country of the West Midlands, and it wasn't long before their new appointments were vindicated, as Led Zeppelin cemented their reputation as one of the hottest live acts on the globe. In between live performances, this particular fab four managed bouts of recording which helped give birth to their debut long player. It is famed for being recorded with much haste and little expense, and lambasted for being a little too plagiaristic for some scoffers. However, it is not unnatural for a new group, finding their feet, to draw upon their own musical influences in their first recorded tracks. Whilst the debate rages

THE BEST ALBUM OF 1969? (continued)

on about the originality of their debut album, the musicianship is of the highest order. True, Robert Plant was still in his infant stages as a songwriter and by his own admission had not yet blossomed as a vocalist, but the foursome's interpretation of the blues was without equal from a group of white English lads. Their rendition of Willie Dixon's 'You Shook Me' is an obvious highlight. 'Dazed And Confused' meanwhile is a Page original that was intended for the Yardbirds. Here is its finest version before the group would fail to resist the temptation to play prolonged live attempts of this classic which at times would last the guts of half an hour. I once found myself driving along to the sound of 'Dazed And Confused', wondering if it was wise to be steering my way through such a heavy, sinister-sounding track. Elsewhere, the album-opener 'Good Times, Bad Times' and 'the sonic mayhem of 'Communication Breakdown' were much shorter and thus laden with high energy. John Paul Jones's prowess on keyboards also is in evidence on the vengeful 'Your Time Is Gonna Come'. No sooner had this album made a triumphant invasion of Transatlantic album charts than a follow-up surfaced later in 1969 to reinforce the mighty Zep as the originators of a new genre, heavy metal. If nothing else, their first album is the greatest karaoke offering ever, and no 21st century fledgling rock act dare bypass this important manual which has left all imitators and competitors trailing miles behind.

The album's best song? - *How Many More Times*

SPORT IN 1969

English Division One soccer champions: Leeds United
English FA Cup final : Manchester City 1 Leicester City 0
English League Cup winners: Swindon Town
Scottish Division One soccer champions: Glasgow Celtic
Scottish FA Cup final: Glasgow Celtic 4 Glasgow Rangers 0
Scottish League Cup winners: Glasgow Celtic
Irish League soccer champions: Linfield; Irish Cup winners:
Ards
League Of Ireland soccer champions: Waterford; cup winners:
Shamrock Rovers
European Cup final: AC Milan 4 Ajax Amsterdam 1
European Cup-Winners' Cup final: Slovan Bratislava 3
Barcelona 2
European Fairs' Cup final: Newcastle United beat Ujpest Dozsa
6-2 on aggregate
English county cricket champions: Glamorgan
Five Nations' rugby union champions: Wales (triple crown)
Formula One world drivers' champion: Jackie Stewart
Gaelic football All-Ireland champions: Kerry; hurling
champions: Kilkenny
British Open golf champion: Tony Jacklin
US Masters golf champion: George Archer
US Open golf champion: Orville Moody
USPGA golf champion: Ray Floyd
Rugby league Challenge Cup final: Castleford 11 Salford 6
Wimbledon men's singles tennis champion: Rod Laver
Wimbledon ladies' singles tennis champion: Ann Jones
The Aintree Grand National steeplechase winner: Highland
Wedding
The Epsom Derby winner: Blakeney
The Ryder Cup: Great Britain & Ireland 16 USA 16

DEATHS IN 1969

January 11th: Richmal Crompton Lamburn (British author), aged 78
January 26th: Jan Palach (Czech student protester), aged 21
February 2nd: Willaim Pratt aka Boris Karloff (British actor), aged 81
February 23rd: King Abd el-Aziz Ibn Saud (ex-Saudi Arabian monarch), aged 66
February 26th: Levi Eshkol (Israeli Prime Minister), aged 73
March 11th: John Wyndham Parkes Lucas Beynon Harris (British author), aged 65
March 28th: General Dwight David Eisenhower (ex-US President), aged 78
May 2nd: Franz von Papen (ex-German Chancellor), aged 89
May 12th: Martin Francis Lamble (British musician), aged 19
June 16th: Field Marshal Earl Alexander of Tunis (British soldier), aged 77
June 21st: Maureen 'Little Mo' Connolly (US tennis player), aged 34
June 22nd: Frances Ethel Gumm aka Judy Garland (US actress), aged 47
June 29th: Moise Tshombe (Congolese statesman), aged 49
July 3rd: Brian Jones (British musician), aged 27
July 5th: Walter Gropius (German architect), aged 86
July 18th: Mary Jo Kopechne (US secretary), aged 28
July 25th: Otto Dix (German artist), aged 77
July 28th: Frank Loesser (US composer), aged 59
August 9th: Abigail Anne 'Gibbie' Folger (US heiress), aged 25
August 9th: Wojciech Frykowski (Polish actor), aged 32
August 9th: Thomas Kummer aka Jay Sebring (US hairdresser), aged 35
August 9th: Sharon Tate (US actress), aged 26
August 17th: Philip Blaiberg (South African dentist), aged 60
August 17th: Ludwig Mies van der Rohe (US architect), aged 83
August 31st: Rocco Marchegiano aka Rocky Marciano (US boxer), aged 45
September 3rd: Ho Chi Minh (North Vietnamese statesman), aged 79
October 21st: Jack Kerouac (US author), aged 47
November 10th: Sir David James Gardner Rose (British diplomat), aged 46
November 18th: Joseph P.Kennedy (ex-US diplomat), aged 81
December 3rd: Marshal Kliment Voroshilov (Soviet commander), aged 88

MY BACK PAGES

Appendix 1: THE BEST OF THE REST? TEN MORE
GREAT ALBUMS, 1965-1969
Blonde On Blonde by Bob Dylan (1966)
Axis: Bold As Love by Jimi Hendrix Experience (1967)
Forever Changes by Love (1967)
The Doors by The Doors (1967)
A Saucerful Of Secrets by Pink Floyd (1968)
Ogden's Nut Gone Flake by The Small Faces (1968)
The Notorious Byrd Brothers by The Byrds (1968)
Abbey Road by The Beatles (1969)
Led Zeppelin II by Led Zeppelin (1969)
Let It Bleed by The Rolling Stones (1969)

Appendix 2: TEN GREAT INSTRUMENTALS, 1965-1969
Spanish Flea by Herb Alpert (1965)
Captain Soul by The Byrds (1966)
Let's Go Away For A While by The Beach Boys (1966)
Flying by The Beatles (1967)
Pow R Toc H by Pink Floyd (1967)
Classical Gas by Mason Williams (1968)
Jill's America by Ennio Morricone (1968)
Albatross by Fleetwood Mac (1968)
The Liquidator by Harry J All Stars (1969)
Return Of Django by The Upsetters (1969)

MY BACK PAGES

Appendix 3: EUROVISION SONG CONTEST WINNERS, 1965-1969

1965 - Winner - Luxembourg; hosted by Naples

1966 - Winner - Austria; hosted by Luxembourg

1967 - Winner - United Kingdom; hosted by Vienna

1968 - Winner - Spain; hosted by London

1969 - Joint Winners - France, Netherlands, Spain, and United Kingdom; hosted by Madrid

Appendix 4: OSCAR WINNERS, 1965-1969

1965 Best Picture - My Fair Lady

1965 Best Actor - Rex Harrison (My Fair Lady)

1965 Best Actress - Julie Andrews (Mary Poppins)

1966 Best Picture - The Sound Of Music

1966 Best Actor - Lee Marvin (Cat Ballou)

1966 Best Actress - Julie Christie (Darling)

1967 Best Picture - A Man For All Seasons

1967 Best Actor - Paul Scofield (A Man For All Seasons)

1967 Best Actress - Elizabeth Taylor (Who's Afraid Of Virginia Woolf?)

1968 Best Picture - In The Heat Of The Night

1968 Best Actor - Rod Steiger (In The Heat Of The Night)

1968 Best Actress - Katharine Hepburn (Guess Who's Coming To Dinner)

1969 Best Picture - Oliver!

1969 Best Actor - Cliff Robertson (Charly)

1969 Best Actress - Katharine Hepburn (The Lion In Winter) and Barbra Streisand (Funny Girl)

MY BACK PAGES

Appendix 5: LANDMARK CONCERTS AND FESTIVALS, 1965-1969

August 15 1965 - The Beatles perform to a record-breaking 55,600 at Shea Stadium

May 17 1966 - Bob Dylan is heckled at Manchester Free Trade Hall for his new 'electric' sound

July 31 1966 - Cream make their first official appearance at the Windsor Jazz & Blues Festival

August 29 1966 - The Beatles appear on stage for the last time at Candlestick Park, San Francisco

June 16-18 1967 - The Monterey pop festival takes place on the west coast of the USA

January 13 1968 - Johnny Cash records a live album at Folsom Prison, California

April 29 1968 - Hair: The American Tribal Love-Rock Musical opens on Broadway, New York

June 29 1968 - Pink Floyd and Jethro Tull appear at Hyde Park's first-ever free rock concert

September 6 1968 - The Doors make their debut UK appearance at the Roundhouse, London

November 25/26 1968 - Cream perform their farewell concerts at the Royal Albert Hall

December 11 1968 - The Rolling Stones' Rock' N' Roll Circus is staged

December 26 1968 - Led Zeppelin perform for the first time in the USA at Denver, Colorado

January 30 1969 - The Beatles perform on the rooftop of the Apple Corps office in central London

February 24 1969 - Johnny Cash records a live album at San Quentin prison, California

March 1 1969 - Jim Morrison of the Doors allegedly exposes himself at a gig in Miami

July 5 1969 - The Rolling Stones top the bill at a free concert in Hyde Park

July 31 1969 - Elvis Presley returns to the stage at the International Hotel in Las Vegas

August 15-18 1969 - The Woodstock festival occurs in upstate New York

September 13 1969 - John Lennon and his Plastic Ono Band play at a festival in Toronto

December 6 1969 - The Altamont festival descends into chaos in northern California

MY BACK PAGES

Appendix 6: TRANSATLANTIC NUMBER ONE SINGLES, 1965-1969

1965

I Feel Fine - The Beatles

You've Lost That Lovin' Feelin' - The Righteous Brothers

Ticket To Ride - The Beatles

Mr.Tambourine Man - The Byrds

(I Can't Get No) Satisfaction - The Rolling Stones

I Got You Babe - Sonny & Cher

Help! - The Beatles

Get Off Of My Cloud - The Rolling Stones

1966

We Can Work It Out - The Beatles

These Boots Are Made For Walkin' - Nancy Sinatra

Paint It, Black - The Rolling Stones

Paperback Writer - The Beatles

Strangers In The Night - Frank Sinatra

Reach Out I'll Be There - The Four Tops

Good Vibrations - The Beach Boys

I'm A Believer - The Monkees

1967

Somethin' Stupid - Nancy Sinatra And Frank Sinatra

All You Need Is Love - The Beatles

Hello, Goodbye - The Beatles

1968

Hey Jude - The Beatles

I Heard It Through The Grapevine - Marvin Gaye

1969

Dizzy - Tommy Roe

Get Back - The Beatles with Billy Preston

MY BACK PAGES

Appendix 7: ROLLING STONE MAGAZINE'S ALL-TIME GREATEST SONGS

A famous poll conducted by the American Rolling Stone publication revealed that twenty-two of the so-called Top 50 best-ever songs were drawn from the semi-decade of 1965 through to 1969. Listed below are the top 25 songs from these years from this imaginary chart.

1. Like A Rolling Stone - Bob Dylan (1965)
2. Satisfaction - The Rolling Stones (1965)
5. Respect - Aretha Franklin (1965)
6. Good Vibrations - The Beach Boys (1968)
8. Hey Jude - The Beatles (1968)
11. My Generation - The Who (1965)
13. Yesterday - The Beatles (1965)
17. Purple Haze - The Jimi Hendrix Experience (1967)
23. In My Life - The Beatles (1965)
24. People Get Ready - The Impressions (1965)
25. God Only Knows - The Beach Boys (1966)
26. A Day In The Life - The Beatles (1967)
28. (Sittin') On The Dock Of The Bay - Otis Redding (1968)
29. Help! - The Beatles (1965)
32. Sympathy For The Devil - The Rolling Stones (1968)
33. River Deep - Mountain High - Ike And Tina Turner (1966)
35. Light My Fire - The Doors (1967)
38. Gimme Shelter - The Rolling Stones (1969)
41. The Weight - The Band (1968)
42. Waterloo Sunset - The Kinks (1967)
48. All Along The Watchtower - The Jimi Hendrix Experience (1968)
50. The Tracks Of My Tears - Smokey Robinson And The Miracles (1965)
54. When A Man Loves A Woman - Percy Sledge (1966)
57. A Whiter Shade Of Pale - Procol Harum (1967)
63. For What It's Worth - Buffalo Springfield (1967)

MY BACK PAGES

Appendix 8: THE TOP 20 BEST-SELLING UK SINGLES,

1965-1969 {*The top seven all sold at least one million copies*}

1. Tears - Ken Dodd (1965)
2. The Carnival Is Over - The Seekers (1965)
3. Day Tripper/We Can Work It Out - The Beatles (1965)
4. Release Me - Engelbert Humperdinck (1967)[BEST-SELLER OF 1967]
5. Green Green Grass Of Home - Tom Jones (1966)
6. The Last Waltz - Engelbert Humperdinck (1967)
7. Sugar, Sugar - The Archies (1969)
8. Two Little Boys - Rolf Harris (1969)
9. Hey Jude - The Beatles (1968)***
10. Hello Goodbye - The Beatles (1967)
11. There Goes My Everything - Engelbert Humperdinck (1967)
12. Help! - The Beatles (1965)
13. My Way - Frank Sinatra (1969) [BEST-SELLER OF 1969]****
14. Distant Drums - Jim Reeves (1966) [BEST-SELLER OF 1966]**
15. Get Back - The Beatles with Billy Preston (1969)
16. All You Need Is Love - The Beatles (1967)
17. Strangers In The Night - Frank Sinatra (1966)
18. The Last Time - The Rolling Stones (1965)
19. I'll Never Find Another You (1965) [BEST-SELLER OF 1965]*
20. Eleanor Rigby - The Beatles (1966)

This chart compiles sales in the 1960s and beyond, hence the following:
*I'll Never Find Another You actually sold most copies within the year of 1965.
**Distant Drums actually sold most copies within the twelve months of 1966.
***What A Wonderful World/Cabaret by Louis Armstrong sold most copies in 1968.
****My Way sold more copies within 1969 than Sugar, Sugar or Two Little Boys.

THIS IS THE END